To Stuart-Leekis

Best wishes

John Bean

December 1999

Many Shades of Black

John Bean

By the same author

Ten Miles From Anywhere Hedgerow Publishing 1995
(Available from Hedgerow Publishing, Wickhambrook,
Newmarket CB8 8YA £6.95 P+P incl)

Many Shades of Black

by

John Bean

New Millennium

292 Kennington Road, London SE11 4LD

British Library in publication data.
A catalogue record for this book is
obtainable from The British Library.

Printed and bound by Arm Crown, Northolt, Middx.
Issued by New Millennium*
Set in 12 point Times New Roman Typeface
ISBN 1 85845 256 2
* An imprint of The Professional Authors' & Publishers' Association

DEDICATION

To the memory of Andrew Fountaine, a friend,
and A K Chesterton, a mentor

CONTENTS

LIST OF ILLUSTRATIONS

Front Cover Photos
Top: Sir Oswald Mosley leading his followers away from a left-wing Trafalgar Square meeting, Feb 28th 1960. L to R front row: Michael English, Jeffrey Hamm, Sir Oswald, Bill Webster (NLP St Pancras Nth candidate), Roger Clare (later to join the BNP), and Harry Jones.
Bottom: The author immediately behind the party flag-bearer (Roland Kerr-Ritchie), leading a BNP torchlight march through New Cross in 1962. The drummers and those in white shirts were members of the Spearhead.

The Stranger

The Stranger within my gate,
He may be true or kind,
But he does not talk my talk–
I cannot feel his mind.
I see the face and the eyes and the mouth,
But not the soul behind.

The men of my own stock
They may do ill or well,
But they tell the lies I am wonted to,
They are used to the lies I tell.
And we do not need interpreters
When we go to buy and sell.

The Stranger within my gates,
He may be evil or good,
But I cannot tell what powers control –
What reasons sway his mood;
Nor when the Gods of his far off land
Shall repossess his blood.

The men of my own stock,
Bitter bad they may be,
But, at least, they hear the things I hear,
And see the things I see;
And whatever I think of them and their likes
They think of the likes of me.

This was my father's belief
And this is also mine:
Let the corn be all one sheaf –
And the grapes be all one vine,
Ere our children's teeth are set on edge
By bitter bread and wine.

Rudyard Kipling

CHAPTER 1
EAST OF OXFORD

As we left the pub in Wendover to walk back to RAF Halton camp, John Black and I adjusted our forage caps to the correct angle, and made sure that the white flashes indicating RAF Aircrew were suitably visible. Although neither of us was yet eighteen we had had no difficulty in being served two halves of brown ale apiece.

In fact the barmaid had not noticed that our uniforms were those of the Air Training Corps. It was May 5th 1945. Aircraft activity overhead had been very busy for the past two hours. We had not been walking more than ten minutes when from out of the evening shadows appeared a long line of Army lorries coming from the camp. As they got nearer we could hear raucous singing, and vaguely recognised the tunes of *"Roll Out The Barrel"* and *"Bless 'Em All."*

As the first lorry went past we saw that they were not RAF types, but Pongos (soldiers) in uniforms that had seen better days. By the tailboard of virtually every lorry there was a soldier, in some cases two, pulling a German steel helmet along the road by a piece of string. They were British prisoners of war released by the advancing Allied armies in those closing days of the Second World War, and were being flown back by every available aircraft to any available UK air base.

We cheered them as they went past and felt honoured when these men, who unlike us had seen action, waved back. We even forgave those who, seeing our boyish faces, shouted: "Get some time in, son!" Or: "Does your mother know you've joined?"

As the last lorry faded into the distance, presumably making its way to Wendover or Aylesbury railway station, I felt deeply depressed. My Walter Mitty dream of a growing line of swastikas on the side of my Spitfire had been destroyed. The war against Germany would certainly be over by the time we had finished our training.

John Black was obviously thinking on the same lines. We walked for a few moments in silence. Then he said: "Well, they

1

will still need bomber crews to finish off the Japanese. They don't believe in surrendering and it will probably take another two years." I can remember having my first regrets at having volunteered for RAF Aircrew. If you were shot down over Germany and made the ground more or less in one piece, then you ended up in a prisoner of war camp. If you were shot down over Japan and made the ground alive, you would probably be beheaded or shot.

I kept my thoughts to myself.

As a member of the Air Cadets I had volunteered for RAF Aircrew Reserve at the end of March when I was seventeen and three-quarters, which was the minimum age. At the Holborn Kingsway offices in London I had scraped through the written examinations and talked my way through the oral. The fact that I exaggerated by presenting myself as an orphan probably tipped the balance, in that if I had been killed they would not have to write any letters home. Of some 50 entrants only ten got through to the medical, and to my surprise four were then rejected, mainly on grounds of non-perfect eyesight. At that stage you were put into one of two categories: Wireless Operator/Air Gunner (WOP/AG) or Pilot, Navigator or Bomb Aimer (PNB). I was graded PNB.

We were sent home, which in my case was then near Hayle in Cornwall, to resume part time training with the Air Training Corps, plus periodical long weekend training visits to RAF Halton in Buckinghamshire. This included training on a flight simulator and air gunnery in a dome turret.

The big day came when eight of us were packed into a DeHavilland Rapide for our first flight. We sat around a map board and were given 'calculators', consisting of concentric plastic circles revolving round a central pin and into which you fed air speed, wind speed and, I believe, compass bearing. Some of the cadets soon became efficient with these 'calculators', but I was not one of them. Unfortunately those who had mastered the black art were those who succumbed to air sickness.

When the Flight Sergeant in charge asked us to 'calculate' where we were, as one of the two cadets not being sick in a bag I looked out of the window to see a large town, with a river running to the south, connected by a railway to a smaller town some twenty miles to the east. After a quick look at the map, I said:

"Just east of Oxford, Sergeant."

The following day my grading of PNB became more precise. The RAF decided I would be a navigator. (In later life I have heard people say that by the way I drove a car I would certainly not have made a pilot.)

It was on the training visits to RAF Halton that I met John Black. Black by name, he was a shade of black by nature. I never thought to ask him why he had this dark pigmentation, although I recall thinking on first meeting him: "This is odd, he has this dark skin but his features are just like ours: British." I never met him again after Halton.

A week or so after one's eighteenth birthday, if you were still on the course, you received the official notification of acceptance to Royal Air Force Volunteer Reserve. Mine came on 16th June 1945, addressed to 3039500 AC2. Bean, J.E., with the note that call up for permanent service was deferred.

With the dropping of the atomic bombs on Hiroshima and Nagasaki and the subsequent end of the Japanese war on August 15th 1945 I knew the writing was on the wall. The RAF would not be needing fresh aircrew At least in later years it gave me the chance to pre-empt Spike Milligan and tell people, usually children, of my part in Hitler's downfall. Sheltering in his Berlin bunker he was told that the British and American armies were pouring over the Rhine and the Russians were hammering on the gates of Berlin. Then came the telegram (a month late) with the news that John Bean had joined the RAF; Hitler shot himself.

* * * * *

I was born at Warwick House, Denmark Road, Carshalton, Surrey on June 7th, 1927. My father, Frederick John Bean, was born in Jesmond Dene, Newcastle-upon-Tyne, where his Scottish father, Edward Lawson Bean, had settled. My great grandfather, an engineer who built rail bridges in India, came from Glasgow. The family story is that the name was originally MacBean (part of the Clan Chattan) with the 'Mac', as with many Highland names, being dropped in order to avoid persecution after the defeat of Bonny Prince Charlie at Culloden in 1746.

My paternal grandmother, Catherine Martin, came from Derry, Northern Ireland. The Martin family were originally French Huguenot protestant refugees who came to Ireland in the mid 17th century. But as my grandmother was a devout catholic, someone along the line had converted and it seems that the original voyage from France was wasted.

My grandfather, Edward Bean, was manager of the confectionery business of William Tulloch in the latter years of the nineteenth century and then became manager of the British branch of the leading German confectioner, Stollewerke. This came to an end in the 1914-18 war. He then ran his own confectionery manufacturing business in Bermondsey, South London. He was a personal friend of Lord Leverhulme and knew him as a young man when he started his Sunlight Soap business near Liverpool.

In 1922 Edward Bean bought Bridge House in Wallington (next to Carshalton), partly as an investment. It was a fine Georgian house with the river Wandle running through the garden. The last time I heard of it, the house was being used as council offices, with the garden becoming a small public park. My father had joined the East Surrey regiment during the First World War and spent nearly four years in India. I can recall him saying how fortunate he was not to have been sent to the trenches in France or Flanders, where two of his cousins were killed. Nevertheless, the four years in India seriously affected his health.

Trained as an accountant, my father became the book keeper for grandfather's business on his return to England. In 1922 he met and married my mother, Eliza Hartley, and they took up residence in No.2 Bridge House Cottages. She was

4

grandmother's cook at Bridge House. I was told that the marriage led to some of the Bean family (but not my Irish grandmother) ostracising my parents because my father had "married beneath him." So much for the middle class values of the nouveau riche at that time, rarely found amongst the true gentry. I was not to forget this when my father told me the story when I was nine or ten.

My mother's parents owned and operated a red sailed Thames barge from Charlton, with a boy as the only other crew member. The main business was carrying horse manure from the stables of London's horse drawn cabs up to Ipswich for fertilising Suffolk farmers' fields and returning with second quality grain for horse feed. I have vague recollections of being lifted up on to a giant ship, as the barge would appear to a boy of four or five, and then eating winkles and brown bread and butter for tea.

I was the third child of my parents' marriage. The first, Barbara, died when she was two – it might have been from diphtheria. My eldest surviving sister Madeleine, two and a half years older than I, had the job of trying to stop me throwing my glass feeding bottle on the ground (no plastic bottles then) when I was taken out in my pram. My younger sister, Josephine, survives well to this day, despite being a very small baby and a delicate child. Another baby was still born.

Our mother died in 1929 from tuberculosis. She was only thirty.

All I can remember of my mother (and it is really a case of 'remembering remembering') is sitting on the floor in a bay window area with this woman with a 1920,s page boy bob smiling down at me with other adults, presumably including my father, laughing at whatever I was saying. I was enjoying the attention of my first audience.

Within twelve months of my mother's death my grandfather also died. My uncle Ted (my father's younger brother) told me that the general life style and upkeep of Bridge House exceeded income, which meant that the family were then forced to sell, and at a time when property was at its lowest this century. It realised only £2,500.

My two sisters, aged four and a half and eighteen months, were put in a catholic convent although we were all Church of England Protestants. I was the lucky one. I was sent off to live with my mother's elder sister, Aunt Jenny, and her husband Henry Hedger and their teenage son and daughter. Henry was a farm labourer living in a tied cottage on Ranmore Common, near Dorking. They were halcyon days, when Ranmore Common had a truly rural life pattern and was yet to become part of stockbroker belt territory.

My memory recalls but snatches of that life. Hiding in the heather whilst my cousins tried to find me. Being held on the elder cousin's motorbike as he drove over the tracks with one arm around me. Being held on a toboggan as it flew over the snow in its downward flight towards distant Dorking. Walking all the way to Dorking with Aunt Jenny and, in Woolworths, seeing this fascinating array of lead soldiers, sheep, pigs and other farm animals. I touched them, picked some up carefully and put them down again. Aunt Jenny bought six soldiers and a selection of farm animals for my birthday.

Harvest time at the farm, and the steam engine and giant threshing machine have arrived. The air is full of dust; the sacks beginning to billow, laden with golden corn; two Jack Russells nip in and out of the waiting stacks chasing rats. My elder sister Madeleine had come to stay. We were making mud pies outside in the lane, when over the hill a man comes walking from Dorking.

"Look John, Look! It's Daddy!"

Above all, I remember Liebestraume and the Blue Danube Waltz coming from the wind up gramophone on winter evenings. Perhaps Aunt Jenny and my female cousin (I can't remember her name) had other records. Perhaps not, because I cannot recall any being played.

The cottage was bombed during the war, but fortunately no one was seriously hurt. A German bomber on his way to London

6

had been attacked and jettisoned a stick of bombs over Ranmore Common in order to facilitate his escape.

In 1932 things improved for my father. He obtained a book-keeper/administrator job with a building estate company called Leach at Blackfen, near Sidcup in Kent. He was on big money too! £4 10s a week, compared with the then national average of £2 10s. I was taken from Aunt Jenny and my rural paradise, my two sisters were rescued from the convent, and we all set up home at 7 Wellington Avenue, Blackfen, with Aunt Maggie, an unmarried cousin of my father's, as housekeeper.

Now five, I was sent off to the local infant's school. At playtime on my first day a boy was shot in the eye by an air pistol. I can vividly recall going rigid and being unable to move as the boy lay screaming on the ground. I wished I was back on Ranmore Common.

When I was six or seven I devised a scheme whereby we could get a free supply of nuts from the local greengrocer's stall. I would chase Madeleine past the stall and knock against the outer section containing assorted nuts as I ran past. This managed to dislodge a few, which my younger sister, Josephine, had been instructed to pick up. As she was so small and looked so angelic, usually nothing was said. However, on the day she retrieved a coconut the stall holder decided he had had enough. He marched all three of us back to Aunt Maggie. When my father came home there was much shouting (he rarely used corporal punishment) and I was sent to bed without my tea.

As is the wont of most sisters, mine used to dare me to do various things. One was to drink some of my father's whisky straight out of the bottle. I can remember thinking that it tasted pretty foul but nevertheless managed to swig away at it. The outcome was my being rushed to hospital and put on a stomach pump.

For another dare I jumped out of the upstairs bedroom window. The result of this was another visit to the hospital: to reset a broken arm.

Perhaps understandably Aunt Maggie, who seemed quite elderly, could not stand the pace. When I was about seven she left. We never saw her again.

7

My father then advertised for a housekeeper. Dorrie Pavely, a schoolmaster's daughter from Old Bexley, appeared. She was twenty-four and my father was then forty-eight. We rather liked her, but Madeleine and I thought she was "a bit bossy." Probably our father had told her to be firm with us. I recall she took the three of us to the fun fair which had arrived in Blackfen. I was only used to walking out with elderly aunts, not a lady with fine clothes and a fashionable hat.

"Come on John," she said. "Why are you dragging behind?" Apparently I replied: "I don't want my friends to see me walking with a posh lady."

The inevitable happened. Frederick Bean and Dorrie Pavely were married. She soon became more "bossy" as the poor young woman tried to put some discipline in our lives, particularly mine.

On one occasion I had gone off playing with friends straight from school and did not arrive home until gone seven. My father not being there (he was either working or in the local "Woodman" pub), I was sent to bed with no tea. I shouted down the stairs: "You are not my mother. You are just an old rat!" Understandably, Dorrie seemed quite hurt at this. When my father came home he exploded. This time there was corporal punishment: I was smacked on the legs and made to apologise. My stepmother and I got on reasonably well after that but I knew, and she knew, that she would never be a replacement for my mother. My elder sister felt the same.

Two things of significance happened on my seventh birthday. One was that for a present my friend Jackey Cooper gave me the first bar of white chocolate I had seen. The second was Oswald Mosley's Olympia meeting of the British Union of Fascists. From what I recall, my father had some interest in what Mosley was doing, but the following day after reading the newspapers he seemed rather disappointed. He said Mosley was a fool to surround himself with his Blackshirt thugs.

From what I have read since and from speaking to Mosley men who were there, there was a preconceived plan by over a thousand militant left wing opponents to wreck the meeting. With no police inside the hall, the Blackshirt stewards deliberately overreacted with their treatment of their opponents. This was the turning point that lost Mosley many potential supporters, such as my father.

My friend Jackey Cooper lived opposite. He had two elder brothers, Ronnie and Philip. When war broke out Ronnie joined the Navy and Philip the RAF. Ronnie was killed when his motor torpedo boat was blown out of the water by a German E boat. Philip was killed on a bombing raid over Germany.

To this day I often think of them and the anguish their parents must have gone through.

In those pre-war days I believe my sister Madeleine had a crush on Philip Cooper. She in turn had a great admirer in our cousin Michael, who came to visit us from time to time. In order to gain her admiration he pushed me into the lake at nearby Danson Park and, after leaving me to splash about a bit (I couldn't swim then), he dived in to save me, followed by what he considered to be artificial respiration. Not long after that Michael taught me to swim.

He was another victim of tuberculosis and died during the war years at the age of twenty.

In January 1936 Dorrie gave birth to a son, another Frederick. I was delighted. Sisters were all very well but now I had a brother. I never really thought of him as a half brother. This was followed by another brother, Bob, in 1938 and a sister, Dawn, in 1940. My father had sired his two batches of three.

His salary of £4.10s a week must have been reasonable money in those days, for he became one of only two people in our immediate neighbourhood to own a car. It was a Singer saloon into which we would all squeeze on summer Sundays to go to Allhallows on Sea on the Thames Estuary.

I do not think I was a particularly outstanding scholar at the elementary school, although my father was told by the headmaster that if only I would pay more attention I might stand a chance of passing my scholarship to the grammar school. He

9

was also told: "The brightest of your three children, Mr. Bean, is the youngest, Josephine." Unfortunately, Josephine was absent from school far too often, not just because of illness, but to assist her step-mother in the chores of running the house for an expanding family. She was never given the chance to take her scholarship.

Again, fortune smiled on me. I was sent two evenings a week down to Bexley where Dorrie's father, Frederick Pavely the schoolmaster, would give me private tuition in maths and English, and set homework that had to be done! Although he rarely laughed, he combined kindness with his strictness.

Thanks to him I managed to pass my scholarship – the eleven plus in June 1938. As in later life, I believe I did better with the oral examination than the written. In September I became a pupil at Chislehurst and Sidcup County Grammar School for Boys in its then new building at Crittall's Corner, Foots Cray.

With war clouds on the horizon we spent the last week in August 1939 on holiday in Herne Bay. My father had taken us all down there in his Singer and came to collect us on Saturday, September 2nd. The following morning we sat round the wireless to hear Neville Chamberlain's historic words: "From 11 o'clock this morning we are at war with Germany." Within ten minutes this was followed by the wail of the local siren giving an air raid warning, and we all made our first visit en famille to the Anderson shelter that had been erected in our back garden some three weeks previously. It was, of course, a false alarm.

Within two or three days my father had sent his wife and the five children by train to a remote farm house two miles from North Bovey near Moretonhampstead, Devon, on the edge of Dartmoor.

I can still remember the first meal we had when we arrived early evening. The only edible things in the house were some potatoes and a small tin of pineapple slices. Dorrie prepared some chips then spoke to the nearby farmer, who gave us a bowl full of crusted Devonshire cream which was shared out to go with the half a slice of pineapple we each had. We children had never tasted anything so delicious in our lives.

North Bovey and Dartmoor were a great adventure. The furthest I had been away from home before was on a school trip to Portsmouth. My two sisters and I quickly settled in the school at North Bovey and the local children were soon accustomed to our strange accents. The school had only two classes and we three sat together in the senior class.

This was the period of the 'phoney war' when very little happened in Western Europe. We returned to Blackfen within a month.

Nevertheless, Dartmoor had fascinated me and I longed to return. I persuaded two friends to join me in a plan I hatched to run away from home and walk to Dartmoor. Little consideration had been given to the onset of winter. We sneaked away on a damp early November morning with two old Army greatcoats (probably First World War vintage) to keep us warm at night, and a sackful of tinned food we had stolen over a period of time from our mothers' cupboards. An hour or so after nightfall we had walked as far as Purley, some fifteen miles, and settled down for the night under a railway arch. It was cold, despite the army greatcoats, and after a while my two friends began to cry. They had had enough and wanted to go home. The expedition to Dartmoor no longer seemed such a good idea to me either, but I did not want to admit it. So I readily agreed to their suggestion that we 'give ourselves up' at the nearest police station.

My father, who had been scouring Dartford Heath, came and picked us up. I recall little of what he said, other than that he was surprisingly quiet and seemed rather sad. I do recall that I was glad to see him. In later years my stepmother told me that from behind the curtains he watched me the day after getting on my bike to go to school. He turned to her and said: "Whatever is going to happen to that boy?"

* * * * *

Although I liked cricket I never achieved anything outstanding at school, usually going in at number eight or nine and in the field being delegated to longstop. I had a similar lack of success in football and rugby, although with the oval ball I could run and weave as good as the best as long as I had caught the ball. However, I was quite a good long distance runner, invariably coming home in the first five and often to be greeted by the sportsmaster: "Ah, here comes the scarlet runner. Well done, Bean." I was also in the junior and then the senior advanced gym squad. Being smaller than the average boy before the age of fifteen, when at last I began to grow up, was perhaps an advantage.

My enthusiasm for gymnastics meant that I was usually spared the wrath of the school PT master, a Mr. Dellar. Any breaking of the rules, such as skylarking in the gym, or taking too long to change after coming out of the showers, meant that you would be given a blow across the buttocks with an eighteen inch piece of wall bar. In my case it left a red and blue weal across my backside which made sitting down uncomfortable for a week. My crime was putting my fingers over the holes of the shower head so that it squirted on the boy opposite. Today, Mr. Dellar would find himself in court and probably barred from teaching for life! On reflection I don't think it did me any permanent harm. And it certainly did not give me a taste for flagellation.

It was in the middle of May 1940 and we were changing into our PT kit immediately after lunch. Two boys who lived nearby had been home for 'dinner'. They had heard on the wireless that the Germans had gone round the Maginot line in France and were sweeping all before them, including the British Army. We were all shocked and could not believe it. As patriots we believed that the British Army was invincible. Mr. Dellar, who had joined us in thoughtful mood, said that things would soon stabilise and it would settle down to trench warfare as in the Great War.

Each day brought more disastrous news, culminating in the debacle of Dunkirk. We boys and girls of that time knew that we were living in a historic moment. But we did not know that it was to change our world completely. It now seems that those days of the thirties were two centuries ago. The life we had bears little resemblance to that of today.

Old railway wagons appeared overnight on the school playing fields. Their function was to stop Germans landing by gliders, as were the lengths of wire suspended between polls that were placed all along the Sidcup by pass.

Then in August nearby Biggin Hill and Kenley air bases and Croydon Airport were repeatedly attacked. Boys came to school trading aircraft machine gun bullets – some of them still live, shrapnel and twisted pieces of fuselage. It was all so exciting. And most of us wished we were that much older so that we could get into the action.

It was Saturday afternoon, September 7th, when the air raid sirens again began to howl. Knowing that this was unlikely to be another false alarm, my father ushered us all down into the Anderson Shelter.

We soon heard the drone of many engines overhead and the ack ack guns opening up from nearby. Then they stopped and all was quiet for a while. My father left the shelter, and I followed him. Soon my stepmother and my sisters were outside in the front garden, as were many of our neighbours in their gardens or by the door steps. We were all gazing upwards at the criss-cross of vapour trails of Hurricanes and Spitfires locked in mortal combat with the Luftwaffe. To the North West we could see dark smoke rising and hear the crump crump of exploding bombs as the Heinkels and Dorniers that had passed over us reached London's Docklands.

A cheer went up as a Dornier 'flying pencil' came low over us heading to the south, belching out a trail of black smoke. Then another cheer as a plane spiralled downwards and burst into flames.

" No! No!" I cried. "It's one of ours. It's a Hurricane!"

"Yes, it's a Hurricane," shouted Jackey Cooper from across the road. We boys knew our aircraft.

Everybody became silent and my stepmother began to cry. Nobody had seen a parachute open and we knew that the pilot must have been killed. After an hour or so all became quiet. As it got dark we could see the red glow in the sky from the East End, some nine miles from us at its nearest point. Then it started again. Wave after wave of German bombers throbbed overhead to resume their devastation of London's Docklands.

As we sat in the shelter this time the barrage from our ack ack guns was almost continuous. Unlike in the afternoon, we also began to hear the low whistle of descending bombs as some bombers were turned back and dropped their cargo over London's outer suburbs in Kent and Surrey.

At school on Monday the trade in the flotsam and jetsam of aerial warfare was intensified. Some of the boys in class were missing. Most of these had been sent by their parents to safer parts, but one boy was dead. Together with his mother and brother and sisters he had been killed when a bomb fell in Old Farm Avenue, Sidcup. His father was away in the services.

With the air raids continuing, after a week or so my father again sent us away to safety: this time to Mrs. Strickland's Boarding-house in Ambleside in the Lake District. My stepmother now had six children in tow. Her three stepchildren, her two sons, Fred and Robert, and Dawn, who had been born that February. As the train reached Manchester another air raid was in progress. I am sure she had doubts as to whether we were going to the right place.

My education in Ambleside took on a new dimension. I was able to go to the local Kelsick Grammar School, which normally had an enrolment of some 80 boys and 80 girls. However, the school had also become the home of 300 girls who had been evacuated from Dame Allan's School for Girls in Newcastle upon Tyne. This meant I was one of less than ten boys in a class with nearly 40 girls.

So fascinated was I by all these girls that my orthodox education made little progress. Biology and chemistry lessons were particularly instructive in that that if you sat on the stools in the back row you would be joined by the more forward girls, who would allow you to put your hand on their thighs and even give you a kiss when the teacher's back was turned. I found it was to my advantage that I had this London accent, which seemed to appeal to some of those sweet Geordie girls. I did not let on that my father was a Geordie by birth.

Until then close contact with the opposite sex had been confined to the usual "you show me yours and I'll show you mine" at the age of six or seven. I even got to the stage where I thought I was in love with Audrey from Newcastle (I do remember her surname). She also sang in the choir of Ambleside's main church. I too joined the choir! I was her "buttercup from Sidcup."

It was in Ambleside that I also had a latent homosexual encounter.

A vicar appeared at Mrs. Strickland's Boarding house, staying for a week's holiday fell walking. He offered to take me walking on the Langdale Pikes at the weekend, which I was pleased to accept and my stepmother readily agreed to.

It was an unforgettable experience to climb past Stickle Tarn and then to the top of Great Langdale and gain my first mountain top panoramic view. As we sat there eating our sandwiches, the vicar would punctuate each sentence by putting his hand on my knee. It was alright if one of the Geordie girls did this, but I found this unsettling from a man. When we had finished eating he then said that he would teach me the Siamese national anthem.

"Say after me, 'Oh waar, tenar, Siam'." I was then told to say it quickly. He laughed loudly, with another touch of my knee, at my admission that I was an "arse." I gave a feeble laugh, because I thought it was odd coming from a vicar: it was almost like swearing. I then thought about some of the boys' jokes back at school about certain vicars and their desires for choir boys' backsides.

On the way down I made sure I did not have my back to him.

At dinner in the boarding house he offered to take me out again on Sunday, but I made the excuse that I had a lot of back homework to catch up on, not that I ever did much at that time.

Perhaps I misjudged the poor man, because he was most kindly and generous to us all during his stay.

15

At least he gave me an appetite for hill walking. I readily joined in with some local lads to walk up Ambleside's nearby mini mountain, Loughrigg. On several late September evenings we would be joined by some of the Geordie girls. Those of us who were lucky in persuading our female partner to sit down in the heather might have the thrill of putting a hand inside a girl's blouse.

Another partner I took up Loughrigg was young brother Fred, then approaching five. I believe I had to give him a piggy back towards the final summit. Airing my historical knowledge, I pointed out what was alleged to be the site of a Roman encampment and tried to explain to him who the Romans were. At that moment two hill farmers, armed with a stick apiece and no doubt looking for lost sheep, strode over the brow.

"Let's run John!" cried Fred in some anguish. "Here comes some Romans!"

By the time we had reached the bottom I had managed to placate him and felt that I was safe from a wigging from his mother. The trouble was that Fred looked up to me and invariably did everything I told him. Just six months before, at Blackfen, I had climbed up a four sided ladder cage on wheels which was used for cleaning street lamps and at night and weekends would be parked on waste ground and padlocked. Fred eagerly followed me up. Halfway down I jumped to the ground.

"Can I jump?," Fred asked. I thought I would catch him and said: "Yes." But he was a solid little fellow and he slipped through my arms and fell and broke his arm. I carried him home, to find I was in definite trouble, again.

* * * * *

As Blackfen was not in an official evacuation area, the cost to my father of supporting our stay in Ambleside was putting him in debt. There was also the fact that daylight raids over London and its suburbs had virtually ceased, although night raids continued. Thus we returned to Blackfen by the end of October.

16

When we saw our father he was in uniform. He had just come off duty in the Home Guard.

Of the stories he told us, one I remember distinctly. Out on patrol one night immediately following an air raid, they came across a German airman hanging from a tree by his parachute. One of the Home Guard aimed his rifle and shot him dead. My father said that when he got home he was sick in the sink. Although I was an ultra patriot, fed on a diet of wartime anti-German propaganda, I thought this was wrong at the time: it was un-British. I now know that it was also a war crime.

The New Year of 1941 arrived and we moved from Wellington Avenue to nearby Orchard Rise East. Not long after the move my father was taken to hospital. They said he had stomach ulcers.

As the nightly air raids continued, the original sense of excitement was now mixed with apprehension, because I began to realise that our chances of being hit were increasing with each raid. With my father absent, Dorrie was becoming more and more frightened at what might happen. She asked me if I would stand in the porch when the siren went and tell her when it sounded as if a bomb was coming near. I readily agreed to this, although I was not really sure of what I was supposed to do, as it gave me a recognisable sense of purpose for the first time. I was standing in for my father and looking after my brothers and sisters.

It was a February night, not long after youngest sister Dawn's first birthday, when the siren went. As ack ack guns opened up almost simultaneously with the first drone of German bombers, I took up my post in the porch. For protection from falling shell shrapnel I had once tried putting a saucepan on my head, but it fell over my ears, and in any case according to my sisters, "it looked stupid." Instead, I wore my school cap. At least it kept my head warm.

In the house, Madeleine, Josephine and Dawn were under a Morrison table shelter with Dorrie. Fred and Bob had been put on a mattress under the dining room table for greater protection.

In the distance I could hear the low whistle of falling bombs, followed by the 'crump crump' of the bombs exploding, which was different from the sharper, echoing noise of the ack ack guns. The guns suddenly went silent, although you could still hear the drone of aircraft engines overhead. This meant that RAF night fighters were now in action. I wondered whether the pilots were nibbling on carrots held in one hand so as to improve their night eyesight – that was what we had been told on the wireless to hide the fact we now had radar. Suddenly I heard a series of low whistles coming nearer as a Luftwaffe bomber pilot decided to drop his stick of bombs and run for home base. The first bombs were now exploding, and they were coming nearer. Then I heard and felt this rush of air, but not a whistle, and knew that this was going to be very near.

I ran indoors shouting: "Look out Mum! There's one coming for us!," or words to that effect. But what I do remember distinctly is the fear as I ran through the door, aided on my way by the force of the blast from the exploding bomb, and then being hit on the back of the head by the glass from the fanlight above the door. I believe it came out in one sheet and broke on the back of my head. I could hear glass shattering everywhere and a rumbling noise as the tiles on the roof came sliding down. I dived under the table where my brothers were still asleep, as it was the nearest safe place I could reach. Then, in case anyone should think I was a coward, I spread myself out to protect them, even though the worst had passed. It worked. Dorrie came out from under the Morrison shelter with a torch to find me still spread-eagled over Fred and Bob who were asking me what was happening. She was very impressed and gave me a hug.

When she told my father on her next visit to the hospital he cried.

The house was now temporarily uninhabitable. In consequence we moved to Old Bexley, initially to stay with Dorrie's parents in Salisbury Avenue and then to a flat above the premises of Hugh Newman, one of the country's leading lepidopterists at that time.

As 1941 progressed there would be breaks of first one night, then two or three nights without air raids. To many of us the good news was that we were now slowly increasing the number of raids on Germany. I recall that this led to a heated argument with Dorrie's mother. She said how sorry she felt for German women and children who were now being killed by our bombs as we were by the Luftwaffe's. I told her that we only bombed their factories and railways and just a few houses were hit by mistake. She told me I was a stupid boy who knew little of what was really going on. I hope she forgave me for my insolence of innocence.

With my father still in hospital Dorrie's financial situation steadily worsened. In addition to a paper round in the mornings, I would work most evenings weeding Hugh Newman's residential garden, some two miles away. It meant that I did little homework, but apart from sixpence for myself I was able to give Dorrie eight or nine shillings a week. On reflection I no longer begrudge the two bottles of stout I would get for her from the off-licence most nights of the week.

At harvest time there would be several days off from school working on farms in the Cray Valley. The school did everything to discourage this, but could not prevent it because it had Government approval, due to the lack of farm manpower and the pressing need to maximise home food production. More important as far as Dorrie was concerned, I got paid for it.

* * * * *

The day after my father died that October I was working with other boys on a farm lifting potatoes and carrots. It was cold, it was wet and I cannot recall being so miserable and so alone in my life.

Later I realised that much of that misery was due to self pity at losing a mother and then a father by the time I was fourteen. Sympathy from other boys, and masters, eventually became in short supply and they began to avoid me if I was still looking for it. I

19

found that life became a little easier if I became one of the form comedians, particularly as I could turn a joke against myself.

A month or so after his death, I went with my two full sisters to see our father's grave at Bexleyheath cemetery. It was ironic at that time to see nearby the graves of two young German airmen. One was nineteen and the other twenty.

The custom of wearing a black armband for six months on the death of a close relative has virtually disappeared, but it was the thing to do in the forties. A drawback was that it identified you.

A favourite pastime during the school lunch hour was for a dozen or so of the fourteen year old boys to defend one of the ancient railway trucks scattered on the playing fields against the attack of some forty or fifty younger boys, eleven and twelve-year-old's. It would either be Roundheads versus Cavaliers or British versus Germans. As nobody wanted to be a German, this particular day I was one of the Cavaliers defending our base from a Roundhead attack and using lumps of coke stored nearby for the school boiler as our main defensive weapons. The coke was hurled in the general direction of the "Roundheads" and, as far as I was concerned, not at any specific individual. Unfortunately one of my missiles hit a boy straight on the temple and he fell unconscious with his head bleeding. Luckily, he soon recovered and told the master who had rushed to the scene that: "It was that boy with the black armband."

The outcome was my second visit to the study of the headmaster Dr. McGregor Williams (known as "Dr. Bill") to receive six of the best on the bare backside.

The first visit was some six months earlier as a result of my enthusiasm for chemistry. A friend and I had made some gun powder and packed it into a Tate and Lyle's Golden Syrup tin. We passed two leads through the lid and joined them to a 3 amp fuse laid in the gun powder. We then carefully soldered the lid on. We plugged the 'bomb' into the 13 amp power switch in the cloak room and with several school ties knotted together we hooked the length of ties over the switch and then over a coat hook, and I pulled. The resultant explosion was just enough to crack one window and burn the surface of a bench seat. As the headmaster said, if our proportions of the gun powder ingredients had been more accurate and more finely mixed, the results could have been much more serious.

This, and the fact that at the school mock elections in 1942 I spoke as the main supporter for the Communist Party candidate (in spite of being a 'Cavalier') may have been in Dr. Bill's thoughts when he wrote in my school leaving report: "He was a boy who possessed distinctly individualistic ideas."

My transitory support for Communism was not based on any ideological grounds, other than that I empathised with their hostility to class division. It was really a romantically inspired gesture of support for Russia's stand against the Nazi onslaught. This was my theme when I spoke in support of the school Communist candidate. I drew a map on the blackboard showing how small an area of the total Soviet Union was occupied by Germany. It ignored the fact that nearly half of the unoccupied area was Siberian permafrost.

Outside of school I continued this support for Russia by penning little notices calling for "Second Front Now!" and dropping them inside the newspapers I delivered on my morning round. However, somebody complained to the newsagent and my part in the "Help Russia" propaganda campaign came to an end.

My father's death meant that Dorrie's financial situation was now even worse, although it was soon relieved somewhat by my elder sister Madeleine commencing war work at Kolster Brand's factory at Foots Cray, plus my bits from the paper round, gardening and part time farm labouring.

Dorrie's pre-Welfare State widow's pension was a pittance. Irrespective of rationing, food was often in short supply, particularly for her three step children, although Josephine and I did have the bonus of free school dinners.

On occasions, Dorrie would sell part of our ration allowance to her family in order to be able to purchase the remainder. Josephine and I would then augment our food resources by stealing pears and apples from neighbours' gardens and carrots from a farmer's field.

Our clothing also suffered and, as far as I recall, at one time I did not have anything else other than my school uniform, for which a grant was available. This meant that as I also climbed trees in it, clambered through derelict buildings and down dene holes at Old Bexley, my school clothes were somewhat scruffy, to say the least.

This was a view held by my form master. Having been caught whispering jokes to the boys sitting nearest me in an English class, I was called to the front by the form master to make acquaintance with his "little friend." This was a small cane he kept down the inside of his gown. His nickname for me was "Christopher Bean," after a popular play at that time: "The Late Christopher Bean."

"Well, Christopher the comedian Bean, put out your hand. What would you like, twenty little ones or three big ones?"

I opted for three big ones. I knew from experience that with twenty little ones numbers fifteen onwards got much harder, plus the fact that going for the big ones increased your standing (or "street cred," as they call it now) amongst your fellow pupils. I could take all that, but what I could not take was the humiliation that was to follow.

"Look at you, Bean. You are the scruffiest boy in the school! Go and stand in that corner so everyone can see what a mess you are!"

Wishing the earth would swallow me up may be a cliché, but it can not be bettered in this instance. After some five minutes or so of complete silence from the boys, one of them, who was a fee payer and not a scholarship boy (it could have been Al Hitchens) said: "Excuse me Sir. John Bean's dad is dead and his mother has not got much money to keep him and his sisters and brothers."

The form master looked at me slightly embarrassed. "Go and sit down, boy, and do try and smarten yourself up."

I decided I would not go to school again.

22

For the next three July days I set off from home on my bike allegedly for school. In my satchel were two slices of bread and Beetox (an inferior form of Marmite) and a copy of Alexandre Dumas' *Three Musketeers*. En route to Dartford Heath I would stop on the outskirts of Old Bexley and steal a bottle of milk off somebody's doorstep and then, further on, dig up some carrots from a farmer's field (perhaps it was eating all those raw carrots that gave me the near perfect eyesight demanded at the RAF aircrew medical). With food and drink for the day, I would lie on the Heath in the sun lost in my world of Cardinal Richelieu and 17th Century France.

Then came the weekend. I decided to tell my step mother all about it; not least because I was missing the school dinners.

She washed and ironed my uniform and repaired the tears as best she could. She even bought me a pair of second hand trousers and a shirt I could change into at home.

Armed with a note from her saying that I had been sick, I went back to school on the Monday determined to try and pay more attention and make an effort to get my School Certificate, if not Matriculation.

For my first year at Chislehurst and Sidcup Grammar School my position in class would be around halfway, but better in science and history. The reports, as in later years, would be scattered with comments about absence spoiling my work. The form master's comments for the Autumn 1939 report included: "He must learn to pay more attention when in school. If he does this he should approach in other subjects the standard reached in History and Science."

By the third and fourth year I had deteriorated to being second or third from the bottom of the class, with the Autumn 1940 report having "absent for most of the term" against every subject. In Summer 1941's report the form master had written: "In almost every subject his work has deteriorated and from one cause – lack of concentration. He is careless of homework and slovenly in his written work. He is one of the least attentive boys in the form. If he persists in these ways progress will become impossible and his ability will be wasted."

By the Spring term of 1942 my resolve to pay more attention at school began to pay dividends. I had come first in the class overall and first in Science, History and Geography. However, this improvement had to be viewed in the perspective of having been downgraded. Instead of moving from form IVB to VB I had gone to VP: the 'P' standing for practical. For my remaining four terms until leaving school in summer 1943 I came first again, then fourth, then first, and finally sixth. Exam results were always better in every subject than term results.

I obtained my University of London School Certificate with Credits in English Literature, Science, Economic History, Mathematics and Geography, and Passes in English Grammar and Art.

Fitted out with a smart pair of second-hand brown boots, I obtained my first job as a laboratory assistant in the microanalytical lab of Burroughs and Welcome, the pharmaceutical drug manufacturers of Dartford, at £1 7s 6d a week. The boots were really too small for me, causing me to hobble. I recall that the chief chemist asked: "Are you a cripple boy?"

He should, of course, have asked me whether I was bipedially challenged.

* * * * *

With the lengthening nights as the autumn of 1943 set in, night time air raids were resumed, but in no way were they as frequent or as intensive as in 1940 and 1941. Nevertheless, Dorrie had had enough and wanted to get away. After a few weeks she responded to an advertisement in Dalton's Weekly that had a cottage to rent in Cornwall.

She sold all the remaining furniture, plus a Meissen porcelain tea service that had been left to my father by my grandmother – the sole reminder of her affluent days with grandfather. This raised the train fare to St. Erth, near St. Ives, plus the month's rent in advance that was required.

My elder sister did not go, but stayed as a lodger with her stepmother's parents in old Bexley. I too wanted to stay because

I enjoyed my work in the micro-analytical lab. and knew that I was unlikely to find anything similar in West Cornwall. However, I agreed that it was my duty to go and to find a job to help support the four other brothers and sisters; plus the fact that it was another adventure to a distant place.

There are only two things I can recall from that long journey in early December from Paddington to St. Erth, the penultimate stop of the Cornish Riviera express to Penzance. At Reading a tall auburn haired American soldier came into our compartment. He had a deep Southern drawl and soon got into conversation with us, including the younger children. My half sister Dawn, then three and a half, sat on his knee nearly all the way to Plymouth, where he got out. Perhaps he felt an affinity with her auburn hair. Whenever I read, or see film footage, about the American landings at Omaha and Utah beaches on D Day, I think of him. I wonder if he ever made it back to the United States.

I shall never forget the look of horror on Dorrie's face as the train pulled into Plymouth, not much more than an hour from our destination. It was almost flattened: worse than most areas we had seen in London. I tried to reassure her that this was a major naval base and the Germans would not waste bombs on the little hamlet where we were going.

My memory brings the glow of nostalgia for the two years spent in Lelant Downs, mainly in Flax Cottage halfway up Trencrom, the highest point in Cornwall's westernmost tip. It was a time when boyhood is changing to manhood. When girls are no longer there to be teased but to be charmed. A time of conflict between striving to obtain the best job available to help support the family and the desire to be there, in the action, as the country faced the final struggles of the Second World War. Above all, those two years left an indelible mind picture of the wonderful views that changed with the seasons, from Trencrom Hill of Mount's Bay to the south and St. Ives Bay to the north.

Within a few days of our arrival I had obtained a job. This was as a temporary postman helping out with the Christmas mail. I started from Lelant post office working down the street in the direction of Lelant Downs. Then following the postmaster's instructions I asked the way to the next address outside the village, where I would ask directions for the next, and so on and so on. Making my way through lanes, across fields and across heather and bracken around Trencrom, I eventually arrived at Nancledra. By the time I got back to Flax Cottage the round trip would be about twelve miles.

The people I called on, farmers and their wives, farm labourers, small holders and railway workers, all stopped to pass the time of day. I was as fascinated by their accent – sadly greatly diluted today – as they were by mine. Word must have spread of our impoverished condition for as the days progressed there would be a couple of eggs from one person, some sprouts from another and, two days before Christmas, I was given a rabbit. That was our Christmas dinner.

In January 1944 I obtained a regular job at Hayle power station (long since gone) and my younger sister Josephine began working in the house of a nearby farmer and helping out at harvest time. With the two of us bringing in some money things began to improve.

The only chemical work entailed in my new job was determining the salt content of the boiler feed water and cooling water. The rest of the time was taken up in reading and recording various meters around the power station. On night shift this gave an unexpected bonus when a young woman, a year or so older than me, grabbed me behind a boiler and gave me a lingering kiss. Things developed well over the next week, usually at about 4 am., but suddenly she did not want to know me any more. I found out later that she had got herself a boyfriend, an American soldier. So ended my first experience of being a toyboy.

One of the men at the power station had kindly given me an old bicycle to get to and from work. Unfortunately it did not have a chain. For the first week, until I received my wages and was able to buy a chain, I would free wheel all the way down from Trencrom and, with little traffic about in those days, the momentum would often get me half way across Hayle Causeway. Nevertheless, it was a long walk home.

After a few months I was told that there was a vacancy for a laboratory assistant at the ICI factory in Hayle which extracted bromine from sea-water. This was used to form ethylene dibromide which was then sent by rail tanker to an ICI factory in Cheshire for the manufacture of lead tetraethyl, an anti carbon knock additive for aviation fuel. This job was far more interesting and more satisfying, and what is more, it paid £10 16s a month after stoppages.

The chief chemist was Tom Barley, who had two young ladies as his junior chemists, Estelle Peak and Cicely Cruise. Estelle was engaged to an RAF aircrew sergeant. Cicely, who lived in Penzance, had lovely chestnut hair and high cheek bones, which she said came from one of her ancestors, a Spanish pirate who stayed ashore in Penzance. Although she was four years older than I, we started going out together. She was a kind and generous person and usually paid when we went to the cinema in Penzance. That was the last time I became a toyboy.

It was at the ICI factory that I met my first Mosley men. They were two chemical process workers from the North of England who had been interned (without trial) in the Isle of Man under Regulation 18b for being active members of Mosley's British Union of Fascists. Having previously worked in the chemical industry they were released after two years or so to take up chemical industry war work. I would have to go to them to collect lab. samples, and I remember that they were always friendly and ready to joke. "Don't talk politics with them," said Tom Barley, "or else you could find yourself in trouble."

I didn't, but I wanted to.

Although cramped, life in Flax Cottage (since trebled in size by an extension) was certainly an improvement on the two years after my father's death, despite the fact that there was no electricity or running water, and like most dwellings in the area we made do with an outside chemical toilet. I would dig the sewage into the garden, and in the spring of 1944 Fred and Bob helped me to plant our first seed potatoes. We were all delighted at digging up our first crop, followed by runner beans.

Fred and I are still good vegetable gardeners, although we now use more conventional manure.

Josephine and I, assisted by eight year old Fred would collect our water in pails from a spring on the side of Trencrom about 600 yards from the house.

At the top of Trencrom there is an outstanding example of a Neolithic settlement with a circular mound with stone gateways still extant, plus several standing stones. I would take Fred and Bob up there, being careful to avoid the disused tin mine shafts on the sides, now adequately fenced in. In summer months the top of Trencrom was a great place for us local youngsters to gather, and also more serious courting couples. I can remember trying to give Fred an answer when he asked me: "What are they doing, John?"

It was also in the spring of 1944 that Dorrie, still only 34, got herself a boyfriend. He was a British Army Sergeant who, after a while, would sometimes stay overnight. After D-Day he stopped coming. Many years later Dorrie told me that he had been killed in Normandy.

In West Cornwall we knew that D-Day was imminent long before most people.

For over a year a small boat-yard in Hayle was building small landing craft. Slowly their numbers grew until there must have been fifty craft all lined up on the foreshore of the estuary. They could be seen clearly from the lane outside our home. Then one mid-May morning as I set off to work I realised they had all disappeared overnight.

It was the talk of Hayle. Two days later it was reported that they had been seen tied up at Falmouth and then they had again disappeared by the following morning.

"The invasion is only a week or so away. With the Russians giving Jerry a hammering it will all be over by Christmas," said the gateman at our factory.

Having joined the Army Cadets, and later the Air Training Corps, I was trying to find ways of joining one of the services. During the last term at school we were given a talk on what a

28

good career was available as an officer in the Indian Army. I had kept the address and in 1944 wrote away for details. I heard nothing more and suspect that Dorrie intercepted the post. Perhaps it was just as well, for it would have been a short lived career.

When the Normandy invasion took place on the day before my seventeenth birthday I knew that it was unlikely that I would now be actively engaged. Talking to a merchant seaman on leave at his home nearby I learned that you could join the Merchant Navy at sixteen. What is more, he would take me for an interview in Falmouth and I might be able to join a ship straight away.

A plan was made for me to be ready outside the house one morning at 7 am. or thereabouts with a bag of essentials packed and he would pick me up on his motorbike and off we would go to Falmouth.

Came the day and I sneaked downstairs trying not to awaken the family. And there sat Dorrie in a chair by the door. She had found out that I was up to something and was determined that I would not go. I do not know whether it was the thought of losing my income or concern for my life. To be fair, it was probably a mixture of both.

It was not much more than nine months later when I successfully volunteered for RAF aircrew.

A few weeks after VE Day Dorrie departed for London with her own three children. Again, through the auspices of Daltons Weekly, she had replied to the advertisement of a widower with three boys living in New Cross who wanted a housekeeper.

Josephine and I were surplus to requirements; well, at least until she thought the time was ripe to let the widower, Sidney Blake, know of the existence of her three step children. Jo stayed at the Richardson's farm where she worked and I took up lodgings with the parents of my friend, George Cotterill.

Mrs. Cotterill was a very kindly lady who accepted me as an addition to her family of two teenage boys and an elder sister.

Mr. Cotterill was a porter at St. Erth Station, but also grew anemones in his garden which would be packed in boxes and sent off by train to London.

To this day I always try to have some anemones growing in our garden to remind me of Cornwall.

After a few months Dorrie sent for Jo to help out in the house at New Cross. Sid Blake had still not been informed of the existence of my elder sister and myself. A little later Sid Blake and Dorrie were married and eventually Sid found out that he was a step father to six children. For my part I acquired three step brothers: Ken, Frank and Terry, who were to become life long friends. Meanwhile, the atom bombs had been dropped on Hiroshima and Nagasaki and the war against Japan came to an end. I knew that there was then no chance of flying.

Eventually came the letter from the RAF saying that aircrew were no longer required and I was discharged from the Volunteer Reserve. I was offered a choice of undertaking my National Service in RAF ground crew as a drain layer or sanitary inspector, or transferring to the Royal Navy.

The author, aged six, with sisters Josephine and Madeleine

HMS *Collingwood*, radar training base, October 1946, left, author
(hatless) with friends, Desmond Worth, Stan Clayton, and Hugh Vos

Chapter 2
FOREIGN PLACES, FOREIGN FACES

"Radar! Radar! Wake up! Navigator wants you on the bridge."

I blinked open my eyes to see the bearded face of the middle watch keeper. A face surmounted by a cracked sou' wester on which were encrusted numerous splashes of grey paint, relics of many times 'painting ship'.

As his boots clumped down the mess deck I scrambled from my hammock thinking, in a semi-daze, that by the urgency in his voice the Navigator must have either lost faith once more in his new fangled radar set or, more likely, in his equally new fangled radar mechanic.

Thrusting my arms into my seaman's jersey I momentarily forgot that not twelve hours previously I had been inoculated against a string of tropical diseases. This lapse of memory caused me to utter a hastily muffled yell, which was greeted by an irritable voice groaning: "For Christ's sake shut up Radar. I've got the frigging morning watch!"

I grabbed my gear and finished dressing outside in the companion way.

As I made my way across the well deck towards the bridge I noticed that we had run out of the earlier storm and a thin crescent moon was now gleaming intermittently through the thinning clouds. Suddenly I noticed a dark mass on our port bow. It seemed so immense that it appeared to practically overhang the ship.

As I clambered up to the bridge I could see that this dark mass was a cliff face at least a thousand feet high. No doubt this was the cause of the Navigator's urgent summons.

My suspicions were correct.

"Bean!," thundered the Navigator, "at 20.00 hours you reported to me that your set was in working order again. Yet we are now going through the Azores and not one echo has been reported by the operator for the past three hours. If I had relied entirely on your set we would now be piling up on the main island beach, assuming it has one!"

I mumbled something about loose leads at the back of the cathode ray tube, knowing full well that as the sole authority on radar aboard ship the Navigator would not question my explanation.

I shot into the nearby radar office, tripping over the operator who was being sick in a bucket. After banging the set two or three times and replacing two valves that I knew habitually went wrong, I eagerly informed the Navigator that the set was now functioning correctly and that the islands constituting the Azores group could be seen quite clearly on the screen. His reply, when translated into printable English, was that since the islands were fast receding astern this was no longer of any significance.

HMS *Bulawayo* was my first and last ship during my two and a half years in the Royal Navy. It was February 1948 and the first of three trips I would make to Trinidad under Captain K A Short.

The *Bulawayo* (named after the town in the then Southern Rhodesia) had originally been the German supply ship *Nordmark*, a sister ship to the *Altmark*, which in the famous incident in February 1940 was boarded by sailors from the destroyer *Cossack*, who released nearly 300 British merchant seamen prisoners.

Under its German Captain Grau, *Nordmark* was very active in the Atlantic during 1940-41 refuelling and passing stores to German surface raiders, including the pocket battleships *Scheer* and *Deutschland*, as well as U boats. A full account of the history of the *Nordmark/Bulawayo* is given in *Under Three Flags* by Geoffrey P.Jones, published by Corgi Books, 1975. The author says that by mid-1941 597 prisoners had been passed to the *Nordmark* from various surface raiders after the sinking of allied (mainly British) ships. All the prisoners arrived safely in Europe and it would appear that although their food rations were often abysmal and conditions in the holds cramped, there was not one case of ill treatment of the prisoners by the *Nordmark's* crew.

During my time on HMS *Bulawayo* the initials and names of British merchant sailors could still be seen scratched on the bulkheads in the for'ard holds. Before I joined the ship Captain Short had written to one ex-prisoner who had inscribed his address in Coventry. He arrived on the ship in Portsmouth and confirmed that although conditions were very cramped and the food poor, the German sailors were almost always perfectly correct. He said that an exception was at the time of the sinking of the *Bismarck* in May 1941. With the Royal Navy occupied elsewhere, after 212 days at sea, mainly in the South Atlantic, the *Nordmark* made a dash for home via the English Channel. During this time the lights fused in the prisoners' for'ard holds. Thinking it was an attempted break out, the German guard fired off three rifle shots above the prisoners' heads. For this, Captain Grau had him clamped in irons for seven days.

On hearing this story I first began to question the image that wartime propaganda had given our recent enemy.

In the radar office I had found tucked away at the back of a drawer a curiously shaped valve which had belonged to the rather crude German radar system. It stood about eighteen inches high with a dozen or so odd shaped metal grids inside the glass. It could quite well have been a stage prop for an early "Dr. Frankenstein" film. This sole souvenir of the ship's previous inhabitants fascinated me. Every time it caught my eye I started speculating on what my German opposite number was like; what did he think of the war, and what was he doing now? I wondered if he was an ardent Nazi or just a man serving his country.

Following the redundancy from RAF Aircrew Reserve, I joined the Royal Navy on December 31st 1945. Taking the train up to London from Cornwall, I was directed by the Naval authorities to the deep air raid shelters on Clapham Common – a unique way to spend New Year's Eve. Thirty months later the same air raid shelters were used as temporary accommodation for the first Jamaican immigrants arriving on the *Empire Windrush*.

After basic training, during which time I met the late Randolph Turpin, the very likeable future champion boxer from Leamington Spa, I started a fifteen months radar technology course at HMS *Collingwood*, Fareham, passing out as a Leading Radar Mechanic. I then joined the *Bulawayo* in Portsmouth harbour where she was having a refit.

The Admiralty aimed to use the *Bulawayo* for similar duties to those designated her by her previous owners, that is as a general fleet supply ship with emphasis on fuel oil. In this capacity we did one or two runs in the Channel with units of the Home Fleet, such as refuelling the destroyer *Dunkirk* at a speed of eighteen knots. A similar operation was carried out with the cruiser *Superb*.

On returning from Christmas leave 1947 we learnt that the *Bulawayo* was to make two or three trips to Trinidad for cargoes of crude oil from the Trinidad oil field. With a capacity of 13,000 tons of oil (quite large at that time) the Government considered her more useful as a tanker, which were in short supply in the immediate post-war years.

* * * * *

Music, songs and noises are renowned for summoning up a vision of a past incident in life, but for me it is a smell that brings back memories of the panoramic beauty of Trinidad. I last encountered this smell walking past a fruit barrow in Oxford Street whilst nearby workmen were resurfacing the road with hot asphalt. This composite smell of fresh fruit and bitumen is the smell of Trinidad.

At Point à Pierre, where the *Bulawayo* tied up to take on her cargo, were the oil refineries of Trinidad Leaseholds. Nearby is the town of San Fernando where most of the oil workers live and which, incidentally, is the home town of Trevor McDonald, Britain's favourite news reader. He would probably be about eight or nine years old when I was there.

San Fernando originally started life as a Spanish settlement nestling between two hills, but has now sprawled up and over them on each side. I am told it is still liberally sprinkled with palms, the yellow candled pouyi trees, and trees of less spectacular foliage whose comparative drabness is offset by nature endowing them with creepers that blossom into dazzling violet, mauve and crimson hues. In 1948 the general effect was to minimise the eyesore of the slum huts of galvanised iron, packing cases and other discarded materials. These were almost exclusively inhabited by those Trinidadians of African descent. More than one third of the Trinidadian population at that time were descendants of indentured labourers from India. The remainder were mainly descendants of African slaves, with a fair proportion of French Creoles, British and Spanish colonists, and quite a few who are a combination of the lot. But it was always the African descendant who ended up as the inhabitant of the shanty hut.

The Chinese had a virtual monopoly in general stores and the wholesale trade of domestic articles. The Indians controlled all taxicabs, public transport and the cinemas; and the Portuguese the rum industry. In the face of these closed shops the black Trinidadians had nothing left but to labour in the sugar-cane fields; a position that has changed little today.

There were two significant political developments in 1948. One was that the British Government signed the General Agreement on Tariffs and Trades (the GATT Agreement) whereby Britain had to buy sugar from Cuba in hard earned dollars. This led to a cut-back in Trinidad and Jamaican sugar production and a rise in unemployment. The second development was the passing of the Labour Government's British Nationality Act which made Commonwealth and Colonial people also citizens of the United Kingdom and with a legal right to come here. One development was the main cause for West Indian emigration, and the other gave the key for entry into Britain.

Four years later the USA virtually excluded all further West Indian immigration so what had been an immigration trickle into Britain became a stream.

On our 'runs ashore' in Trinidad what impressed many of us at that time was the then loyalty to Britain, yes, 'the mother country', expressed by so many Trinidadians, and not least those of African origin. Not for nothing do you find today so many middle-aged 'Winstons'. With jobs becoming scarcer they considered it their right to come to Britain. In fact during the three visits several asked us if we would help them to stowaway on the *Bulawayo*. Needless to say we did not.

After taking on our oil cargo at Point a Pierre it was the custom for the *Bulawayo* to up anchor and sail across the Gulf of Paria, which separates Trinidad from the Venezuelan mainland, to Port of Spain, Trinidad's capital, where we would stay for a couple of days "showing the flag." Each watch would have a turn to go ashore.

Down by the docks one could find seamen from all over the globe. Bronzed Dutchmen who had just come in after braving the Atlantic in a two masted schooner; British merchant sailors from Tyneside and Poplar, from Glasgow and Liverpool; German sea captains from Hamburg who were just beginning to pick up their old trade where they left off in 1939. Through the open door of a cafe, which flattered itself with the name of "The Miami Club," came the sound of calypso music the first time that any of us had heard it. Through the haze of tobacco smoke we could see some Negros locked in the ecstasy of their music. Around small tables sat merchant sailors and American Servicemen, many of them lucky enough to have the company of the resident 'hostesses', each of whom was assuring her beau that she was the original 'Minnie from Trinidad'.

The American servicemen were there because of the shrewd deal struck by Roosevelt in 1940 when he gave us fifty old age destroyers for a ninety nine years lease of West Indies bases stretching from Bermuda to Trinidad. In Trinidad the base covered fifty square miles.

Our first meeting with the Americans occurred when we attended our first calypso meeting. As is now the established custom, the audience shout out a subject and the calypso singer composes a song about it as he goes along.

Among the audience was a considerable number of the *Bulawayo*'s crew and even more American soldiers and sailors. One of the American sailors shouted out to the calypso singer: "Hey Mac, give us a song about the Dollar Loan to the Limeys!" (which was very topical at that time).

38

The singer started to sing: "Oh, Britain is dependent on America ...," but that was as far as he got.

The next moment Anglo-American relations had taken a decided turn for the worse. Chairs and tables were being cracked over American and British skulls, including mine, in true Hollywood style. It was all over in ten minutes though, and the rest of the evening was spent in drinking the health of Uncle Sam and John Bull. By the time the American and British Naval Police arrived it was smiles all round.

On the way back to the ship a 'two badger' (a sailor who had served twelve years) told us that the incident reminded him of a time when he was in the Azores in 1943. He was then on a destroyer which had been searching for a U-boat. The Azores, being Portuguese, was neutral; warships from the belligerent powers could use its harbour for short periods if they were suffering from some defect or problem that could endanger the life of the crew in adverse weather. The U-boat captain thought of some problem and was allowed to come in. Fed up with waiting for the U-boat to come out, after some 36 hours the destroyer captain also thought of a problem. He came in and tied up near to the U-boat.

Some of the destroyer's crew were allowed ashore, including our two badger. They entered a cafe to try the local drink, to find that most of the customers were from the U-boat. Chairs and tables were soon being demolished over British and German heads when, according to our two badger, in came some American sailors who apparently found it a laughing matter. The British and Germans then joined forces and threw the Americans out and then resumed their private battle, until they in turn were ejected by the local police.

The outcome was that the U-boat was ordered to leave the harbour and the British destroyer not allowed to leave until some twelve hours later. We were told that neither saw each other again.

The only time I was 'ejected' (it was really a tactful withdrawal) from a Trinidad establishment was during a visit to the Queen's Park hotel on the edge of the picturesque Savannah racecourse in Port of Spain.

The Queen's Park hotel, then Trinidad's finest, was exceedingly difficult to gain admittance to when dressed in matelot's rig. Three of us had been seeing the sights, and the bottoms of a few rum glasses, in company with the ship's Chief Petty Officer Carpenter (the Chief Chippy). He always showed when he had had too much to drink by starting a conversation with two imaginary parrots, one green and one red (port and starboard) whom, he was convinced, sat on his shoulders and talked about him behind his back whenever he bent his head forward to take a drink.

To the uninitiated, the Chief's uniform, with its peaked cap and gold badge, gave him the appearance of an officer. Under this misapprehension the Chief Chippy led us past the eagle eyed doorkeeper into the Queen's Park. But our hour of glory was short lived, for we had no sooner downed one glass apiece when we spotted two authentic *Bulawayo* officers and had to beat a hasty retreat before things became embarrassing for the Chief, and for the officers for that matter.

By now the Chief was talking to his parrots, so we decided to go off and make our first visit to a Trinidad steel drum percussion band. Now widespread in the West Indies and in immigrant communities in Britain, the steel band started in Trinidad and was still a novelty in 1948.

The players, in vivid floral shirts, squatted round a variety of discarded metal drums into the top of which were fixed varying lengths of steel strips. By plucking at these strips with a small piece of leather, the players produced a wide selection of rhythmic tunes in the traditional 2/4 and 4/4 African time. Their ingenuity at producing a tune out of any two objects that can be banged, rubbed, rattled or scraped against each other is surely unsurpassed. I know that when I took up one of the players' offer to have a go at his instrument, which I thought looked quite simple to play, the noise I extracted brought nothing but howls of laughter from all present.

By the time we had made our third trip to Trinidad we had

come to accept the shanty towns of Port of Spain and San Fernando. We also began to accept the view of a number of Indian, Portuguese and Spanish origin Trinidadians that to a certain extent many of the inhabitants of the shanty towns were there of their own choosing. It is all a question of values. Many of them considered it is better to spend their hard earned cash on a gaily coloured new shirt or a bottle of rum rather than waste it on rent for shelter in such an equable climate. Any Sunday morning we could see proof of this as a black family trooped out from their brightly painted ramshackle huts to go to church dressed up in their best clothes, that were clean and well pressed.

* * * * *

As the ship's engines throbbed into activity, pulsing life into the silent ship for our return trip to England with our third oil cargo, I wondered if I would ever see Trinidad again. For on my return I was to report to Chatham barracks for demobilisation, and I knew that if I resumed my pre-service occupation in industrial chemistry this would hardly be likely to take me to the West Indies.

Dusk falls quickly and early in the tropics, and as the ship's bows swung round pointing for England the lights of Port of Spain were already beginning to flicker on. The vivid colours of the buildings were losing their contrast and running into each other as individuality disappeared under the purple cloak of twilight. The peaks that stand guard over the capital, clad in their exotic tropical foliage with yellow candle trees as their jewels, seemed even more majestic in the gathering dusk and made me realise that they are the only thing that is stable in Trinidad.

These three peaks have seen a greater variety of people come and go in 500 years than even England's white cliffs have in 2,000 years.

Perhaps they saw Sir Walter Raleigh come sailing into the bay below one day towards the end of the sixteenth century, when he was reputed to have caulked his boats at the famous pitch lake. Then came the Spanish conquistadors with their complex character of bravery, cruelty, religious passion and pride: whilst the native Arawak race either fled or died off – though local gossip in 1948, unsubstantiated by the text books, contended that a few descendants still lived their primitive life up in the inland mountains.

In 1797 Britain came and conquered.

Between them, in a deplorable act for which we will forever pay the consequences, England and Spain brought Africa to the New World. Hundreds of thousands of Negro slaves were herded across the Atlantic under inhuman conditions, many of them Trinidad bound to work in the sugar and then the cocoa plantations. (Not so well known is that, after the Highlanders' defeat at Culloden in 1746, several thousand Scots were also sent as slaves to the West Indies: hence the Scots names.) When the Negro slaves were freed, this freedom often meant freedom to do only sufficient work to keep alive. Hence the arrival of the indentured workers from India in the nineteenth century.

* * * * *

As the S.S. *Corfu* nosed her way down Southampton Water in the gathering dusk of a January evening, my feelings as I watched the friendly lights of Southampton winking in the receding distance were very mixed.

When one is twenty-three and off to the other side of the world for three years, leaving a newly wedded wife behind, the feeling of isolation strikes very sharply; particularly as you first notice that strip of water appear between ship and quayside and you are tempted to dive in and strike for the shore before it is too late. But with a 'stiff upper lip' you console yourself with the thought that this is the chance to establish your career and the opportunity to meet new people, customs and outlooks.

Twelve months after release from the Navy in June 1948 (as the *Empire Windrush* was making its way to Britain from Jamaica) the wanderlust had bitten so deeply that I had eagerly

42

accepted the opportunity to go to India for a firm of paint manufacturers. However, during the period of training in the UK for my new post, that is from June 1949 to the end of the year, I found myself married.

Unless you are one of those people who miss all the adventure of life by planning carefully for every move, you find that marriage is like that. One day no thought could be furthest from your mind; two months later you find you have a wife.

Apart from our love for each other, my wife and I shared another common bond, which was to make the early parting that much more difficult. She knew no true parents; only a foster mother, albeit a kind and loving one.

On Friday the 13th of January 1950 I sailed for newly independent India, ostensibly for three years. But within six months I was to be back in England and starting my association with Mosley's movement in my quest for the political truth.

I recall that my companions at the dining table on the *Corfu* were three Portsmouth dockyard technicians going out to the then British Naval dockyard in Singapore. There are some people who would say that their conversation and table etiquette were not quite 'refined', but I found them good company: men who were proud of their job and who were typical of what was once the backbone of our island race.

On that voyage there was one person, to me an elderly gentleman, who stood high in the respect of his fellow passengers. "Old bring'em back alive," we called him.

During his lifetime he had travelled practically all over the world collecting wild animals, ranging from elephants to black mambas, for various zoos (it would not be approved of today). Here he was at the age of sixty-one off to Malaya, taking Communist bandits in his stride no doubt, to capture some rare bird species. I can still recall this 'ambassador of Britain' sitting pipe in hand, his clear blue eyes gazing into the horizon, whilst he recounted some tale of adventure in his habitual modest manner.

Amongst the passengers were several Indians, mainly students returning home after studying in Britain. I became

43

friendly with several and we had many interesting and animated discussions. Being fairly liberal -minded at that time I considered them to a certain extent to be typical of what I would find in India. Once ashore in that vast sub-continent, the feeling of mutual friendship that existed whilst arguing in the European surroundings of the ship, slowly diminished. It was a great disappointment to find instead of goodwill, the honeymoon atmosphere, prophesied by liberal-minded journalists, an abundance of criticisms, open abuse and sometimes precocious advice on how Britain should run her affairs.

Before starting the fifteen-hundred-mile rail journey to Calcutta, my new place of employment, I had the opportunity to spend a couple of days looking round Bombay, a tumultuous, exciting and in many places a beautiful city. With four friends from the ship, eager to stretch our legs after the voyage, we decided on a sight-seeing tour on our first night in the East.

As we strolled along Hornby Road, a fine thoroughfare with many imposing buildings, the street lamps cast their pools of light on an unending stream of kaleidoscopic humanity: prosperous, olive-skinned Parsees immaculately dressed out for an evening stroll; Hindu women, with their vivid coloured saris gracefully draped around them, walking with an elegance that is the envy of many a European woman.

A beggar went by leaning heavily on his stick as he searched for a comfortable corner for the night, his lean, bare legs appearing abnormally bandy due to the dhotti which was wound between them and round his waist. A group of young men, probably students, dressed in light fawn or cream coloured European style clothes, talked excitedly amongst themselves quite oblivious of the cry for alms from the old beggar.

Accompanying this scene is an incessant background of noise: the multi-toned 'peep peep' of motor horns rising above the constant babble of myriad tongues; the clip clop of horses' hooves as the gharri carts go past, carrying passengers to other parts of this great city of contrasts; and the scamper of small feet as urchin children come running up with outstretched palms crying: "Backsheesh! Backsheesh, Sahib!"

44

In contrast to the splendour of those fine main streets, each side turning, each alleyway, gave a glimpse of another world; a world of teeming squalor. By this time we had acquired a trio of self appointed 'guides', who now seemed eager to lead us into these slums or chawls. As we were making our way back to the ship along a dimly lit road, bounded on one side by the dockyard wall, the leader of the trio suddenly stopped his friendly chatter. He was very dark for an Indian, with an ugly scar on his chin. In the dim light I could no longer see his expression as he informed me that he had just completed two years imprisonment for killing an Englishman. Wishing to get rid of him and his fellow Cook's Tour agents with the least possible commotion, I uttered a non-committal "Oh yes" to give him the impression that it was nothing new for us to stroll in ill lit back streets with a self confessed murderer.

"We don't need you any longer now. Here you are, share this amongst you."

In a fit of generosity we offered them five shillings (it was 1950), not having any Indian money on us as yet.

Prodding me in the leg with a knife he had quickly drawn from inside his shirt, Scarface laughed and said: "We want an English pound note each for our work, then we go away."

It was then that we made two important observations, one being that by now we had a following of six or seven villainous looking Indians. The other was that the dockyard gate had now come into view at the end of the road with two policemen standing there on guard. Discretion being the better part of valour we decided to run for it. As a good runner I led the way and we all made it in safety.

In case some readers might think that this early minor incident prejudiced me against India, I would add that a similar incident with a dockyard thug in Calais has not changed me from being a Francophile.

* * * * *

45

The vastness of India and its dense population must still be the foremost impression that the traveller gets when making the rail journey from Bombay to Calcutta for the first time. After passing through the Western Ghats, the mountainous range that runs down the Western coast of the Indian peninsula, we entered the vast, dusty plain of the central provinces, broken here and there by small groups of hills. Whenever I looked out of the train window there was always some human figure in view. Sometimes it would be a farmer tilling his land with a wooden plough and oxen as his ancestors have done for countless generations. Or there would be an old woman bent under a load of sticks; or two little children smiling and waving as the train went by, as children do all over the world.

At every station we stopped at or just passed through, the platform would be crowded with people, some squatting, some standing and some laying down. Like every place in India where the people of this complex and ancient culture gather together, no one looked the same. There were old, young, babes in arms; well dressed Hindus, Hindus dressed in rags; and Sikhs, each with a different coloured turban. Two or three Indians wearing Ghandi caps would be walking up and down the platform selling drinking water to the passengers, with their cry of "Pani Wallah! Pani Wallah!" Others would be selling chippattis – strange to me at that time – which in various forms seemed to be India's staple diet. "Chippatti Wallah! Chippatti Wallah!"

A couple of elderly Punjabi Sikhs, deep in conversation, could be seen pacing the platform with slow measured tread, hands behind their backs, like a couple of business men waiting for the 8.30 am. City train in a London suburb.

At Allahabad station it was just after midnight when the train pulled in. The platform was one mass of sprawling, sleeping figures, in the midst of which a tall, bearded Sikh sat dozing cross-legged with his worldly goods piled around him and a curved sword resting on his lap. This was a warning, no doubt, to any would be sneak thieves. He was still sitting there like some forgotten sphinx when the train pulled out half an hour later.

When we had left Bombay's Victoria Station on the Tuesday evening my companions in the compartment were two fellow Britons. One was a Scotsman returning from home leave to a jute mill near Calcutta; the other a young Londoner going to the Assam tea plantations to start a career as a planter. About three in the morning we were awakened by a loud hammering on the carriage door. This no doubt was the fourth passenger for the compartment we had been told to expect.

He turned out to be a Gurkha Captain attached to the Indian Army – one of the tough little men from Nepal. He had fought alongside the British 14th Army in Burma against the Japanese. Irrespective of his small stature, he had a great personality and one felt completely at ease with him. There was no sense of that indefinable barrier that then existed between you when in conversation with Indians of the same educational level. At that time I put it down to the fact that, as Nepal had never been under the British Raj, the attitude of the ex-servant conscious of his new freedom, discerned at that time in Indians to British visitors, did not pertain to the Gurkha.

We arrived at Howrah Station Calcutta an hour early after two days and nights travelling. Consequently I had to find my own way to my employer's offices in Farley Road. Having spent some time on the platform looking for one of the firm's representatives who was supposed to meet me, I found that all the best taxis had been taken. I had to content myself with a rather battered old Ford of pre-war vintage.

What this taxi lacked in comfort its driver made up for in speed. We shot over the Howrah bridge that crosses the river Hooghly. The driver, as with all Calcutta car drivers, had his finger permanently on the horn. Split eardrums, then and now, are no doubt an occupational hazard of Calcutta's taxi drivers.

After meeting the managing director and other executives at my employer's offices, I was driven off to the factory, situated by the Hooghly, a tributary of the Ganges, thirty miles upstream from Calcutta.

My drive through Calcutta and its endless suburbs of teeming squalor soon showed that it was entirely different to Bombay, regardless of the many large British built buildings, monuments and broad roads. Bombay had a touch of the West about it and I am told it still has. Calcutta was true India.

It was in the streets of Calcutta on 16th August 1947 (little more than two years prior to my visit) that the first blows were struck between Hindu and Moslem that set off a chain reaction all over India of massacre, rape, arson and the uprooting of millions of refugees. The outcome was the birth of the twins, India and Pakistan.

I was to hear the story from many sources: from Moslem, Hindu and European, each with their own slant on those tragic events. One thing seems clear, however. The riots were originally planned and organised by a hard core of religious fanatics of both sides such as the R.S.S. (Nation Service Society) of the young Hindus, who preached Hindu supremacy above all creeds and especially the Moslem 'foreigners', and the Moslem League fighting for a Moslem state.

The morning of 16th August had apparently started with lorry loads of Moslem and Hindu 'goondas' patrolling the streets. The 'goondas' were gangsters and rough necks who haunted the Calcutta docks and could be hired for riots and strike breaking. They were armed with brickbats, stones and soda water bottles, which they shook up and hurled into the crowds so that they exploded like grenades when striking the ground, sending slivers of glass tearing through human flesh.

Rival gangs started firing Hindu and Moslem shops. Cars and rickshaws were turned over and burnt. The sacred cows that wander the streets were being slaughtered by the Moslems to antagonise the Hindus still further. The goondas had done their work and by mid day all Calcutta was at its neighbour's throat.

The streets rang with the rival cries of "Pakistan Zindabad!" (long live Pakistan) from Moslem throats and "Jai Hind!" (Victory to India) from Hindus. Sikh taxi drivers drove down the streets with outstretched swords lopping off the heads of passing Moslems. It was not until the military came on the streets with tanks five days later and began machine gunning the mobs that the police ventured to come out and restore order.

The official Indian Government figure was given as less than 10,000 dead but Calcutta people said that it was more like a hundred thousand bodies that the vultures hovered over when peace came at last to the city.

Whatever the final death toll, it was only a fraction of the loss that all India and Pakistan suffered as the flames of religious hatred fanned out from Calcutta until they finally reached the Punjab. Here, the cruelties the Sikhs and Moslems inflicted upon each other are beyond description.

Amritsar in the East Punjab is the holy city of the Sikhs and also an important rail junction through which the trains carrying Moslem refugees to Pakistan had to pass. The Sikhs would sit on the station platform with their heavy curved swords on their laps patiently awaiting the arrival of each refugee train, so that they could methodically slaughter its passengers. At Lahore, across the border in West Punjab, Moslems waited to administer a similar fate to Hindu and Sikh refugees fleeing south to India.

If Britain's Labour Government and its emissary, Lord Louis Mountbatten, had not been so eager for Britain to scuttle from India at top speed, then this terrible loss of life need never have happened. Anyone who visited India around that period knew that we had to grant independence. Had we not done so, then our position would have been made untenable by native opposition and the post-war United Nations bodies under Rooseveltian American influence. But surely it would have been more in keeping with our record of administration in India, that was both efficient and incorruptible (as even its most strongest critics admit), to have stayed firm until a peaceful plan of transition to independence was evolved?

* * * * *

Contrary to a popular belief, the life of British civilians working in India around the time of Independence was far removed from indolent ease punctuated by frequent gin swilling parties. I found we worked harder and longer than we did at home, but also played harder.

The paint factory at Naihati employed approximately five hundred Indians, ranging from the chief chemist to the man who swept up the yard, and eight Europeans including myself. Work started at the factory at seven and finished at five, except for Saturdays when we finished at mid day. Our hours were exactly the same as the Indian labourers. They had to be, for without our presence at that time little work would have been done. Apart from the works manager and other senior executives at the head office, Indians could be found with appropriate qualifications to do our work as work's control technicians and engineers perfectly satisfactorily, except for one important detail: they would not be able to get more than a token of work from the men. Today, more than fifty years after the end of the Raj, this situation no longer exists, of course.

At the time I thought that after emancipation from the British Raj Indian workers would be only too willing to work for Indian officials, but the fact was that to get a satisfactory output of work it was then still necessary to have Europeans in charge. This low output of the Indians' work should be remembered when the low wages they were being paid are compared unfavourably with European standards.

The machinery used at Naihati in 1950 for manufacturing the paint products was just as modern as that used in the average British factory, but on estimate I should say at least three times as many men had to be employed as in an English factory of the same size. A classic example of this difference in working power was that in India a common or garden shovel was very often operated by two men. One man grasped the handle whilst the other aided him in his work by means of a piece of string tied just above the blade.

The reason why the Indian should have worked harder for a European is rather puzzling. It was certainly not through fear of any physical punishment, as I must admit sometimes occurred during the days of British rule. The use of force, physical or otherwise, would have been inviting serious trouble, trouble such

50

as the three British engineers suffered at Dum Dum just outside Calcutta two months before I arrived in India: they were thrown alive into an open furnace for making themselves unpopular. The fact is, I feel, that the Indian still respected the authority of the European even though he may have disliked him.

In the compound where we lived I shared a bungalow with a young Yorkshireman who had been at the factory for four years. We had a bearer each who kept our rooms tidy and also acted as a valet, and a cook whom we shared. Like all the servants in the compound they were Moslems, and while appreciating the fact that they naturally wanted to create a good impression with us so as to earn the maximum amount of "backsheesh," they were well liked by us all and certainly stood head and shoulders above Bengali Hindus of the same social class in regard to honesty, cleanliness and their more friendly nature.

My bearer, an elderly man of grave appearance, was a man of strict religious habits, unlike my companion's bearer, who had a perpetual grin on his face ready to break into a laugh at the slightest opportunity. The Moslem religion frowns upon the drinking of alcoholic liquor and whenever my companions and I pulled out a bottle to drink in the evenings my old bearer would look at me sadly, slowly shaking his head. It was a standing ritual with us on these occasions to offer him a glass and see him throw up his hands in horror and hurry off as if pursued by the devil in person. On reflection I can see that our insensitivity could be criticised.

In the evenings and at weekends when the weather was not too oppressive, we occupied most of our time in playing tennis or swimming in the small pool that the firm had had built in the compound. As Calcutta was thirty miles distant, trips into town were not very frequent. In spite of this somewhat isolated existence, many enjoyable social evenings were had in the company of other Britons employed at adjacent factories and jute mills. At Naihati there were four or five of these jute mills near us, the technicians and engineers being practically one hundred per cent Scotsmen; in fact we were the only

Sassenachs for miles around. The Scots must have taken pity on us, however, for they allowed us to become honorary members of their club, but needless to say we were carefully watched for any signs of un-Scottish activities.

Once a month a general get-together would be organised by the club for the members and their wives – the more senior men at these factories were allowed to bring their wives out from the U.K. Peter Baume, whom I shared the bungalow with, took me along to one of these affairs shortly after my arrival at the factory, but did not warn me that everybody was expected to contribute to the evening's entertainment. As the evening wore on this entertainment meant the singing of nostalgic Scottish songs about "the heather and the heelands" punctuated by an impromptu reel from one of the more inebriated members. Therefore it was with a glowing sense of local patriotism that, when asked to perform, I gave a "spirited" version of "We knocked 'em in the Old Kent Road," which to the everlasting honour of Scotland was well received. The next morning, however, my triumph was rudely shattered when I overheard one of the Scotsmen talking to Peter Baume outside the bungalow. "Och," he said, "The new laddie certainly knows some songs, but what a reet horrible voice he has."

After I had been less than three months in India, my wife's letters began to get more and more depressing and it was then that I began to realise more fully the responsibilities of marriage.

Owing to the acute shortage of accommodation in the compound, my employers were unable to bring my wife out, so this left me to make the hardest decision of my life so far: whether to return to my wife, as I suppose was my duty in the circumstances, or stay with my job with all its potential opportunities, plus the all important fact that by not doing so I was letting my employers down badly. After wrestling with this problem for a fortnight I decided, rightly or wrongly, that my duty was with my wife and accordingly handed in my resignation.

The day of my resignation was marked by a serious fire at the factory which occurred in the varnish manufacturing department.

Peter Baume, Jess Cooper the engineer, and myself, were strolling back into the factory after our afternoon tea break, when we spotted a black column of smoke rising from the direction of the varnish kitchen. We raced to the spot to find everyone running away in panic except for a few "Sirdars" (foremen) who had managed to free three varnish workers who had been trapped in the fire. With the aid of the "Sirdars" and a few more Indians who regained confidence to come back to help us, we managed to rig up hoses and play them on the fire. Barrels of white spirit and xylole were by this time dangerously near the fire, in fact two of them had already exploded with considerable violence, adding to the discomfort of we fire fighters. However, Jess Cooper had organised the fire fighting in rapid time, mainly by his example of being the first into the blazing varnish kitchen with a hose.

After we had got the fire under control and handed over our work to the local fire brigade, who had arrived with a loud clanging of bells and the excited shouts of many voices, it was found that the three Hindu varnish workers who had been caught in the fire were badly burned around the stomach and groin. Apparently these three had been thinning a pot of varnish with spirit, which had left a trail along the floor and had ignited from a nearby open fire, the fire thus running along the trail of spirit, between their legs and up into the varnish pots. As the men were wearing the customary Hindu dhotti, a length of cloth twined round the waist and thighs and secured under the groin, it was some time before they could get their blazing garments off, thus causing their serious burns.

As the unfortunate men were being carried to the sick bay for treatment by the firm's resident doctor, they were practically knocked off their stretchers by their fellow workers crowding round in eagerness to view the gore. In trying to protect the injured men, one old "Sirdar" became so exasperated that he cuffed one persistent gawker around the ear. For his pains he was beaten up in what I was told was a typically cowardly Bengali fashion by a mob of the factory workers waiting to meet him outside the main gates on his way home. It so happened that my two companions and I were near the main gate talking to the manager at the time. We could hear the commotion and the old man yelling outside, so Cooper threw open the gate, picked the old chap up bodily and carried him inside. Judging by the wounds on his head that his fellow Hindus had given him from blows with their wooden sandals, he was rescued just in time.

Two of the injured men died from their burns after a few days and were given a ceremonial Hindu funeral.

The Hindus burn their dead on an open funeral pyre, the locality where these funerals take place being known as a burning ghat. As one of these ghats on the banks of the Hooghly was situated comparatively close to the compound, with the aid of a pair of binoculars I was able to get a view of this fascinating ceremony. The traditional pyre is made of sandalwood logs well anointed with several pints of melted butter to facilitate burning, but in this case the dead men's relatives had to suffice with any wood that was available plus a few gallons of white spirit from the factory to aid the blaze. As the heat from the fire tightened the muscles and sinews in the corpse I was astounded to see the corpse beginning to sit up, a most uncanny experience if you are viewing the procedure for the first time. Due to the increased smoke from the fire and the large number of mourners moving around the pyre, it was hard to discern at that distance what happened next, but I was told that it is then the duty of the dead man's eldest son to knock the corpse into a prone position again, as it is supposed that it is the devil causing the dead man to sit up and, by beating him, the devil spirit will be driven from his body. When the pyre had finally burnt itself out the ashes were scattered over the waters of the nearby Hooghly, a tributary of the sacred river Ganges.

From the balcony above the entrance hall of Howrah station, I could look straight across the river into the heart of Calcutta, the largest city in Asia. I only stood there for five minutes that evening as I waited for the train that was to take me to Bombay en-route for home, but the memory and the associations of that view will remain permanently fixed in my mind: the hot, night sky reflecting the glare of a million lights from the city below; lights that ranged from the vivid greens and brilliant reds of the illuminated advertisements to the flickering oil lamps in the bazaars. Cars, buses, taxis and lorries, ancient and modern, jostled each other as they tore across the bridge with the inevitable blare of horns. I looked towards Chowringhee, the Oxford Street of Calcutta, where in the afternoon I had seen Pandit Nehru drive up to address a large crowd in the nearby Maidan, Calcutta's famous park. This was India; the changing face of India. From the mere glimpse I had seen, it was my impression that, although the iron foundries were going up, more coal mines being opened and the Universities turning out hundreds of young scientists, engineers, doctors and lawyers, the heart of the nation, the millions of peasants and the inhabitants of the chawls, still thought, loved and in most cases lived, in the manner of their ancestors of a thousand years ago.

* * * * *

The three trips to the West Indies and then the three months working in India in 1950 was a very formative period for my mind. On reflection the combined experiences signposted the political path I was to follow. In the West Indies I found something predominantly likeable about the character of those of African descent. Perhaps it was its simplicity: a certain childishness of quick to love and quick to hate; a liking for noise, flamboyant colours, constant physical activity, but without much purpose to some Western eyes. The whole expressed in their effervescent, simple but highly rhythmic music.

Then there were those who were descendants of indentured workers from India, such as I had met in Trinidad. In those days they still kept themselves much to themselves, ran most of the small trading operations, and tended to look down upon the black West Indians. It was my impression that they begrudged the European his position of dominance far more than the Negro seemed to do. The main impression was that because, in the

55

main, the Asian had kept strong racial ties, he had roots and a distinct culture which was lacking among those of Negro descent.

Slavery, the indelible blot upon the character of the European (and the Arab) had severed the Negro from his own African cultural roots. Fifty years on from my time in Trinidad and from the arrival of the very first West Indian immigrants, we witness in Britain the tragedy of complete rootlessness of young blacks born here and who in consequence are even further distanced from the roots of their African racial homeland. To those who say that the answer to this problem is to develop a multi-cultural society, history tells us that there is not one example of different cultures living side by side for any length of time. One either completely dominates the other or they mutually reject each other, with resultant spiritual and physical conflict.

The Indian experience gave several surprises. There were the number of Indians who said: "We wish the British Raj was back," and praised the British for their incorruptibility. Also, in spite of that British presence for nearly two hundred years, the average Indian did not differentiate between a Briton, Frenchman, Swiss or German: we were all Europeans, all white men to them. Perhaps more important, I was soon conscious of the fact that I was in the presence of a deep seated culture, but only as an observer and that for reasons I could not then define I would always be an observer, never to be enjoined within that culture. In contrast to the outward looking cultural ethic of the European (and particularly the North European), ever looking to cross previously defined frontiers, whether in space exploration or genetic research, that of India generally is inward looking: each concentrating on his own soul; personified by the navel contemplation of Buddha. Nevertheless, I am still drawn after all these years to return to that Indian culture one more time (and I will soon), if only to see whether it has kept itself partially free of the influences of Western culture.

What I also found interesting was the Hindu caste system, still almost as strong today as it was fifty years ago. The word is of Sanskrit origin and just means 'colour'. It was devised by the Aryan invaders from the Caucasus mountains who founded the Indus valley civilisation of around 1500 BC in order to retain their identity among the numerically superior, darker Negritto type Dravidian Indian peoples. It is not without significance that today the lowest caste, the untouchable's, are still the darkest and that the highest, the Brahmins, are almost European in appearance, as also are many Sikhs.

I had become aware of the racial differences that had created the varied cultures of mankind. This made me a racialist, but certainly not a 'race hater'. Twenty years of radical right activity were to make me realise that there can be, unfortunately, a rather narrow dividing line.

CHAPTER 3
BLACKSHIRT APPRENTICE

"There will be no reason for us to live in fear of Soviet Russia then, for in our new found unity we shall have the Germans ..." The speaker's ensuing words are lost in the thunder of applause that greets this eagerly awaited point. "The Germans! Who, with one hand tied behind their back, threw the Russian hordes 600 miles back into Asia and had them down and were choking the life out of them, until we and the Americans stepped in and drew them off the prostrate figure of Soviet Russia!"

Near hysteria breaks loose among the audience as the speaker practically shrieks his climax. I too am clapping vigorously, but my wife beside me just sits quietly with a cynical smile of disbelief on her face. Two rows from the front a figure in a khaki drill shirt and with an appearance not unlike the Asiatic Mongolian's the speaker had just been referring to, yells a slogan at the audience. "Two! Four! Six! Eight! Who do we appreciate?" The audience roars back: "M-O-S-L-E-Y Mosley!"

During my first few weeks back in England, several times I asked myself: "It's the same England I have returned to, surely its habits cannot have changed in so short a time?" Slowly I began to realise the obvious. England had not really changed that much. I was the one who had changed.

Having partly felt the effect of India's culture made me look more for our North European culture, of which the British element was a part. All around me I could see that it was becoming more and more dominated by the rootless culture stemming from America, particularly in popular music, the cinema, and in its growing effect on the rising power of television, then solely in BBC hands.

In London I could also see the first West Indian immigrants. They bore little resemblance to the jolly people I had met in Trinidad and seemed to harbour more than their fair share of ne'er do wells. My experience told me that here we had the

59

makings of a culture clash: racial clash did not then readily spring to mind.

As a reaction to the stories I had heard in the Navy about the generally civilised behaviour of German sailors during the war, which greatly contrasted with wartime propaganda, whilst on leave I had obtained a copy of *The Greater Britain* by Oswald Mosley from New Cross public library. I was quite impressed with much of what he had to say, but did nothing about it for two years.

Joining the Mosley movement in the Summer of 1950 now gives me less regret than certain other actions I mistakenly took in the next fifteen years. This meeting of Mosley's Union Movement at Kensington Town Hall in the autumn of 1950 was as typical of his post-war meetings as any, except that at this stage violent opposition had more or less ceased.

The audience would consist of the same faithful three or four hundred supporters with perhaps an additional fifty or so new members, inquisitive persons, wives and girlfriends who had been dragged along to keep the peace. The corps of faithful supporters would turn up at every London Mosley meeting from Kensington to Walthamstow. From 1947 to the end of 1949 every meeting would end in a fight as Communists and the Jewish 43 Group tried to break up the proceedings.

Towards the end of 1949, however, the Communist Party must have received instructions from Moscow that Fascism in Britain no longer constituted a major threat to 'democracy', for the organised opposition practically ceased overnight.

The 43 Group was a group of militant Jews who had banded together in 1943 with the express purpose of rooting out and destroying any Fascist or anti-Semitic elements that reared their heads following the release of Mosley and his supporters from 18b internment – without charge or trial. Often in conjunction with the Communist Party, they were soon attacking meetings organised by Jeffrey Hamm's League of ex-Servicemen and then Mosley's Union Movement, when it was formed in 1948. In reality, they acted as recruiting agents for Mosley and in the early post war years possibly gained him at least another hundred members from amongst those with some strong grudge against Jews, or those looking for a scrap to relieve the monotony of the Welfare State.

Pitched battles were fought at the famous stamping ground in Ridley Road East London, where no holds were barred by Jew or Gentile. Their fanatical hatred of each other was carried to absurdity when the Mosleyites decided to hold a march in Brighton. Two lorry loads of supporters left East London to aid the six or seven Brighton members who were staging the march. At the same time two coach loads of 43ers were also leaving London for Brighton. That Sunday morning about a hundred and fifty Mosleyites and Jews could be seen chasing each other down the Brighton road at 60 m.p.h. hurling threats of death to each other, and occasionally halting for liquid refreshment to give them strength for the afternoon battle.

It was raining in Brighton that afternoon, so most of the inhabitants wisely stayed in and had a nap after their Sunday lunch. Outside however, in the wet and practically deserted streets, twenty stalwart Sussex bobbies were doing their best to keep Mosley marchers and Jewish ambushers apart, but with little success. A good time seemed to be had by all, many bloody noses being given and received, although Queensbury rules were broken with great frequency. But seeing that eighty per cent of the participants were from London, I still can't see why they could not have fought it out on Hampstead Heath and saved the petrol.

When the Communists and the 43 Group so abruptly ceased their organised attacks on the Union Movement, this was a greater blow to the Mosleyites than all the bans that were imposed on their marches and the distribution of their literature through normal trade channels. Their main source of publicity was now greatly curtailed. For it was only when a fight broke out at a meeting that they received any mention in the press. Isolated groups of two or three Communists occasionally started a rumpus at a meeting. Union Movement would have to be content with these minor incidents for their publicity, until, however, they decided to take the fight to the opposition.

* * * * *

My association with the Mosley movement could be put down to youth. Youth is the age of intolerance, where there are no shades of grey, let alone black. I felt that the political creed I adopted would have to fit one hundred per cent the views that I had gradually acquired. The word 'compromise' had no meaning for me.

Socialism, with its obsession with equality (equality of opportunity is an entirely different thing) and its desire to destroy the traditions of the past, regardless of whether those traditions are healthy or bad for the nation, was and still is incompatible with my way of thinking.

Although the Conservative rank and file, as distinct from its leaders, at that time seemed more concerned with National and European values, the Party as a whole gave the impression of wandering aimlessly along, picking up discarded bits of Attlee brand Socialism as its main commitment to a post-war policy. To me they appeared a party of old men, where youth and modern viewpoints were suppressed, especially if you did not wear the old school tie: a viewpoint which was verified on joining the Conservative Party two years later.

Liberalism as a political party had reached its post-war nadir. But liberalism as a way of thinking was flourishing afresh in the political beds of the Conservative and Labour Parties. I wrote at that time: "Liberalism is the creed of hypocrisy adopted by the *nouveau riche* of the Industrial Revolution for paying high lip service but low wages to the labouring classes. Theirs was the creed of *laissez faire*, whereby finance and big business is freed from all restrictions to become the master and not the servant of the nation. The philosophy that stems from Puritanism: Puritanism that has always hated the people of life, the people of action, the men that achieve."

Looking at my definition of liberalism again after nearly fifty years, perhaps it was a little immature. Nevertheless, strip liberalism of its transitory and fluctuating window dressing and it wasn't a bad definition of its basic thought! I joined Mosley's Union Movement for three main reasons. I was becoming disgusted by the continual Germanophobia of the press that I welcomed the pro-German aspects of Mosley's policy, which I found out later was just as much a mania to the Mosleyites. Secondly, I considered, and still do to a lesser extent, that the policy of British participation in a United Europe (a Europe of Nations – not a federal Europe) would go a long way towards answering the political and economic troubles of that time. Thirdly, Mosley as a man who had gone to prison for his political beliefs, struck me then as the very antithesis of the average politician, who would turn a political double somersault to gain a little extra power or more moronic votes at the next general election.

In August 1950 I started going to a meeting pitch on a bomb site near Lewisham clock tower, where Union Movement would hold regular Saturday evening meetings. This Lewisham branch of the Movement was the nearest to me, living at Peckham, and it is quite probable that if I had gone to some other branch first I would never have stayed two years in the Union Movement.

On reflection the principal active members at Lewisham were distinguished from some other Union Movement members that I met later by the fact that they all seemed to wash and shave regularly; they could read and discuss their own policy; and they did not seem to suffer from sexual aberrations. The branch leader, Carl Harley, was an efficient young man of about my own age and very active for the Movement. A cordial friendship soon existed between us, and still does fifty years on.

The Cook family were to be seen regularly at all Union Movement functions. There was old man Cook, permanently sucking his pipe and democratically raising points of order. His son Syd, a well built young man in his early thirties, always took the trouble to look up his facts before he mounted a street corner platform, which was itself unusual. Olive, the daughter, supported her father devotedly and was one of the Movement's best sellers of the paper, *Union*. Cook senior was never a fascist in the true sense of the word, for although he could be very argumentative, his manner was the very essence of democracy.

Pat Dunigan, another leading member of Lewisham branch and at one time a member of Mosley's personal bodyguard, was a heftily built chap with the strength and courage of a lion, though unlike many such men, he did not spend his time demonstrating this strength on his weaker bretheren. He would not make any claims to be above average political intelligence but could probably convert a person to his way of thinking easier and quicker than some of Mosley's so called skilled orators with all the facts behind them. Dunigan had been wounded fighting a rearguard action at Dunkirk, but even when we were being taunted by the opposition with the then perpetual cry of, "What did you do in the war?," like all true servicemen who had seen blood spilt in anger, he remained silent whilst they continued screaming how they spent "five years fighting the fascists."

It was not long before my attendance at U.M. meetings became active participation. Apart from speaking, a member's task at a street corner meeting could be quite varied and was roughly the same for any minority extremist movement. One or two of the heavier built or more pugnaciously expressioned members stood close to the platform, letting it be known by their attitude that any attempt at violence on the speaker would be duly attended to. The new boys were usually given the task of leaflet distribution amongst the audience. This could be most boring and frustrating, for the average bystander either stood there with his hands in his pockets looking fixedly at the speaker when offered a leaflet, or grabbed it from your hand and, after quickly scanning it, proceeded to tear it up, dropping the pieces at your feet with a derisive "Huh." Hardly encouraging to say the least.

From leaflet distribution the next step was selling the party news sheet; in Mosley's case the *Union*, which was practically unsaleable.

A task which I particularly enjoyed was helping to draw a crowd by acting the part of an opposition heckler. I was usually quite good at this, which on reflection was possibly because even then I was aware of the fallacies, half truths, and prejudices which U.M.'s policy was built on.

* * * * *

Mosley's propaganda policy was based on the assumption that any news is good news. Consequently the greatest blow the opposition struck Mosley's post-war cause, was their cessation of organised attacks on public meetings and marches.

It mattered not one iota to the Mosleyites that whenever they received press publicity over some street skirmish in the East End, the thinking public were assured just that much more of their hooligan and mob-like character. For the most part the only recruits such publicity gained were political morons looking for excitement, or those people who suffer from a brand of anti-Semitism that is not even "blessed" with a political foundation but is sheerly social anti-Semitism often based on jealously. We meet these types in all walks of life: "Can't stand Jews," they say, "Two of them live in my road, and they are both two-car families. Disgusting isn't it?"

The new quest for publicity took many varied turns. The favourite and well tried method of holding a march through some particularly hostile area was at one time the most successful in regard to its publicity yield (and was later copied by the National Front).

If things had been a bit quiet on the Mosley front for two or three months, no members having been jailed, and not a black eye to be seen amongst them, then a suitable area would be picked that was either notorious as a Red stronghold, or had a large Jewish population, or preferably, as was then the case of certain areas of Stepney and Hackney, was a combination of the two. The majority of such marches were held in London, for the simple reason that ninety per cent of Mosley's active supporters were scattered around London and could be easily mustered in any particular area when so desired.

The Movement's newspaper *Union* would announce: "The flags of Europe will be carried through the streets of Hackney by local branch members next Sunday, headed by the symbol of European socialism, the flash and circle banner. The march will proceed to the meeting pitch at Stamford Hill, where

65

members of the local population will be gathering to hear the policy of Oswald Mosley." To a number of Mosley's devoted followers scattered over London, this would read, "We are marching through opposition strongholds next Sunday, finishing at Stamford Hill where the Yids should be waiting to greet us; so look out for trouble."

As I made my way to the customary meeting place for these East End marches, Hoxton Square near Shoreditch Church, I would try to keep my mind off the next hour's embarrassment. But as long as I was a member I felt compelled to turn out for these occasions in case it was thought that my absence was due to cowardice.

On arrival at the Square I would see the same thirty or forty familiar faces; these people were the backbone of such marches, whether they were in Brixton or Brighton, Hackney or Hammersmith. Next to arrive would be the van containing the drum corps and the flags and banners. Up to this point the local populace would be leaning out of their windows hazarding guesses as to what the gathering, with its entourage of Metropolitan Policemen, was likely to be. On the arrival of the van, however, with its slogans and flash and circle emblems on each side, their curiosity would be satisfied and the usual ironic cheers, boos and "raspberries" would break out, interspersed with some manifestations of support.

After the van, the next arrivals would be odd people who turned out once in a while for such affairs, one or two lads who had nothing better to do that evening and had come along in the hope of excitement, and the usual handful of enthusiastic new members turning out for their first or second march. In twelve months these young enthusiasts would have left the Movement sadly disillusioned, to be replaced by five or six others, and so on in ever decreasing numbers. If the opposition were to attack at all, it was very seldom that they attacked in force before the marchers had moved off, but there would invariably be two or three recognised opponents, Communists or 43ers, to lead the jeers, boos and other derisive gestures that greeted our departure. The attack would come later.

I would often be called upon to carry one of the flags or banners. This had its advantage in that I could hide my embarrassment of the theatrical and false bravado atmosphere by letting the folds of the flag hang before my face, and ostrich-like cut me off from the gaze of the crowd.

The drum corps, which would lead the column, varied from four to ten side drums, plus the big drum and cymbals, dependent of course on how many players turned up. Alf Flockhart who stage-managed these shows and led any brawling to be done in the East End, acted as the drum major. These members of the drum corps were in the main boys between sixteen and eighteen years of age, except for the big drummer, an old Mosley follower of pre-war vintage; consequently for a political demonstration this high proportion of practically schoolboys was hardly likely to impress the crowd with its political maturity.

Flockhart was said to have homosexual tastes. In consequence his drum corps was often referred to as the 'bum corps', whether its members were homosexually inclined or not. Flag and banner bearers would number anything from five to thirty-five, while the following marchers would rarely exceed fifty. At one time the Mosleyites had a passion for hawking the flags of European Countries round the London backstreets. This was to symbolise their policy of European unity. By the time half a dozen flash and circle banners had been added to this collection it left about ten marchers to follow the trappings, which looked ridiculous.

It is not my intention to mock those of us who are so unfortunate as to have defective or crippled limbs, but Union Movement seemed to attract such people out of all proportion to their numbers.

On a march these people were made even more conspicuous due to the fact that unlike the Communists and Socialists who shuffle along in a mob, the Mosleyites would space themselves out and try to keep some semblance of military bearing. In fact, the general appearance of Mosley's supporters on the march was not a band of six foot broad shouldered thugs, as the general public seem to visualise, but a rather drab looking crowd of vacant faced nondescript men and women - although not without courage.

The real "hard man" types you would find walking along the pavement each side of the marchers, ostensibly keeping an eye open for ambushers, but whenever brawling did break out these self appointed bodyguards seemed to show less courage than some of the more inconspicuous members marching in the column.

On one occasion a march was being held from Manor House tube station to West Green Corner Tottenham, ending with the usual meeting, we hoped. The proposed route naturally covered a very hostile area, especially picked for the purpose, and the local 43 group boys had intimated that they would bring down a gang of Jews from nearby Stamford Hill to enliven the proceedings. I thought I had better make an appearance, not that I was particularly eager to get my eye blacked by some fifteen stone, hostile Jew, but sheerly to avoid the necessity of having to explain my lack of enthusiasm for such affairs and having it misinterpreted.

As I was unfamiliar with the area, I had arranged to meet several other members at Union Movement Headquarters in Vauxhall Bridge Road. Here we were able to get a lift to Manor House in the U.M. van carrying the drums and banners, which, by the way, was in the charge of the East London Organiser, Alf Flockhart.

Flockhart decided to go via Stamford Hill to see if the opposition were massing there. Sure enough as we passed Stamford Hill Odeon, forty or fifty Jews could be seen gathered on the opposite side of the road. On sighting us they made a spontaneous rush for the van. Then to my extreme disquiet, the traffic lights changed from green to red. But instead of rushing the van and tipping it over as we expected, they just halted in their tracks, shouting "Come out and fight, you Fascist bastards." In actual fact there were no more than ten of us packed in the tailboard end of the van, most of the space being occupied by the drums and banners; this must have given the impression to our pursuers that there were about thirty of us in there. As the van restarted, the irate Jews again made a big show of bravado; two of them taking off their jackets and dramatically throwing them to the ground, then running after the van, which they knew they could no longer catch. The remainder amused themselves by throwing clods of earth and stones at the disappearing van.

As it happened, since the march was so well protected by police, there was little trouble apart from a bit of pushing and shoving at the meeting pitch and some crude name calling of the "Ya! Boo! Fish face!" variety.

The Mosleyites had been expecting a fight all day, so after this anti-climax they eagerly welcomed Flockhart's suggestion that we should pile into a couple of vans to go up to Stamford Hill and join battle in the gathering dusk.

They were there waiting for us right enough, and the earlier volley of stones and clods of earth was replaced by a shower of lumps of concrete, bricks and fireworks. Then a rather amazing thing happened. Flockhart with his animal-like courage drove the van I was in into a dead end alley with a howling mob of now about eighty pursuing us. We were instructed to keep inside the van while Flockhart and his partner Harry Jones grabbed the skid chains and strolled towards the mob nonchalantly swinging them in their hands. The mob just turned and ran. At the time we liked to think that this was because they were afraid of us, that may well have been the case, but it is possible that they were told by their leaders to leave us alone and not give us the chance of publicity that they knew we were seeking.

When marches began to fail in regard to their publicity value, since the opposition would no longer play ball, the Mosleyites had to look for new stunts that would get a press write up. The phoney Communist-run "Peace" Campaign of the early fifties presented an excellent opportunity to crash the press once again, for what newspaper could resist a story of a free for all at a "Peace" meeting?

The plan of campaign was quite simple. Twenty or thirty U.M. members would go along to the particular meeting that was to be "done," and for the first half hour or so behave as if they were in full agreement with the platform, thus setting the stewards at their ease. Then spasmodic heckling would break out, gradually intensifying in hostility until the stewards would request that the hecklers be silent. This was the opportunity for starting an argument which usually ended up with the steward getting a punch on the nose for his trouble. The fight would then be on, and all that remained was to leave a visiting card in the form of a few shouts for Mosley and beat a hasty retreat before the police arrived.

The "Anti-Peace" Campaign yielded its best results, from the publicity point of view, in South London, getting off to a flying start with a general fracas in Lambeth Town hall which received a lengthy report in the "*South London Press*" and a couple of paragraphs in the national dailies.

One particular "raid" on a meeting held in a schoolroom in Norwood proved quite comical. As this was a small meeting, the "Peace" Campaigners only numbered about twenty and were soon in a minority when thirty Mosleyites trooped in half an hour after the start. Without a blow being struck we managed to install our own members on the platform, Syd Cook of Lewisham being voted Chairman of the proceedings for the rest of the evening. The resolutions on peace that were passed that evening would have given King Street quite a few shocks.

The climax to these "Peace" raids came with the attack on a meeting held at the Civic Hall, Croydon, on a Sunday evening in the spring of 1951. East London members were going down in a plain van to pay a visit, while two or three of us South London members were to make our own way there.

I arrived at about a quarter past seven, just after the meeting had started. Due to the fact that I had gone in by a side door which opened into the hall near the platform, I was seated in the front row. After carefully looking around the hall I could see no sign of any U.M. members until Syd Cook of Lewisham came in about ten minutes after my arrival. Sitting down in a vacant chair next to me, he pulled a cigarette from his case. After fumbling in his pocket he leant towards me saying, "Could

I trouble you for a light?," then whispering out of the corner of his mouth, "Are the boys here yet?" "Certainly," I replied, adding under my breath, "Seen nothing of them yet."

The hall had a capacity of two thousand, though not more than four hundred people were present that night. Even so, four hundred could be quite an opposition.

We waited impatiently for the best part of forty five minutes for the others to arrive. Then, at the end of a long diatribe by one of the speakers on how Russia "liberated" Europe (in the interests of peace we assume), I heard the stamping of boots as a crowd of latecomers came in. The "boys" (and some "girls") had arrived.

The noise they made on entry, coupled with the fact that they immediately started vigorous heckling, left little doubt in the minds of the Communists and fellow travellers as to their purpose. In fact it took only about five minutes for the fight to commence.

As I had been in the hall for nearly an hour by this time, listening to speaker after speaker uttering thinly veiled Communist propaganda, I was in a state of high tension and eager to get the business over. The speaker at that moment was Platts-Mills, the ex-Socialist M.P., who had been kicked out of the Labour Party for his pro-Communist activities. He was giving the usual sob story about the innocent little children who had been killed by the bombs of the wicked Germans. I leapt to my feet and shouted at him: "I suppose our bombs were especially made so that they only hit German factories, eh?" A steward rushed over to me, yelling, "Sit down you bloody Fascist," and giving me such a hefty shove in the chest that I had little option but to sit down. Syd Cook, sitting beside me, immediately jumped up and closed with the steward, whilst an even heftier one came tearing over to deal with me. I stood my ground – primarily due to the fact that a row of chairs was blocking my exit – and we started exchanging blows, although to the best of my knowledge the exchange was rather one sided. Suddenly his fist hit me on the side of the ear and knocked me back into the seat once more. Acting as a human yo yo was getting rather monotonous, so I swung myself over the back of the chair into the next row; but I found I was just as unpopular there as in the front row.

While all this was going on, the rest of the Mosley mob had gone into action at the back of the hall. Being heavily outnumbered, they were being driven down towards the exit near where we were scrapping.

The actual fight must have only lasted ten minutes or so, during which I noticed that all the brave talkers amongst the Mosley roughnecks had left a few of us to do most of the fighting whilst they bravely kicked out all the windows in the glass doors. When it came to courage, the person who walked off with this honour was in my opinion the Jewish steward who had tackled me in the first place. He took up a position by the exit, trying to stop us as we went out, consequently everybody took a swing at him as they made their exit. The last I saw of him he was covered in blood but still standing there on guard.

We had all managed to escape before the arrival of the police. On looking around, our only serious casualty was Carl Harley, the Lewisham branch leader, who had received a nasty cut on the inside of his lip. He was taken to the local hospital where he had six stitches put in the gash, which could hardly have been caused by a fist.

There were two hospital casualties on the other side, one of them our friend the "door keeper."

The publicity seekers were satisfied. Next morning the British public read in their newspapers that Mosley's supporters were still living up to their reputation as trouble makers.

The "Daily Express" reported thus:

JU JITSU GIRL IN 'PEACE' BATTLE

More than 70 men and women fought and struggled for 15 minutes at a "peace" meeting in Croydon last night. The meeting had been on an hour when 20 young men and four well-dressed girls entered the Civic Hall. They began heckling, and a steward went up to one man. There was a scuffle. In a moment a punching, kicking, scratching mob was swaying to and fro. One man ripped a fire extinguisher from the wall and floored his opponent with it. As he did so, a young girl threw him with a ju jitsu tackle. The man was trampled. A blonde in a red swagger coat exchanged blows with a man almost twice her size. Windows were broken and blazing paper was thrown about before the police arrived. The building was surrounded. Three men were taken to hospital with severe cuts. Mr J. Platts Mills, former Independent Socialist M.P. for Finsbury, was a speaker at the meeting. He said: "The shouts of the interrupters showed they were pro-Nazis."

* * * * *

At the close of the anti-peace meeting season, Union Movement decided that, since the Communists would still not resume their earlier organised attacks on Mosley marches and meetings, they would start attacking theirs. All this, of course, in the quest for publicity, and to keep the "boys" occupied.

Before the big attack in Kingsland Road Dalston, there had been several small Communist open air meetings; four or five man affairs, which had been well and truly broken up by visiting Mosley squads.

It was at one of these assaults, in a side street near Kings Cross Station, that I realised how much the British sense of fair play was lacking not only amongst the Communists but also amongst some of the followers of Mosley. At this particular meeting there were five Communists, two acting as alternate speakers, one selling literature, and the other two flanking the platform. After the usual preliminaries, twenty or thirty Mosleyites began attacking the speaker and breaking up his platform. Two of the Reds took to their heels and ran; the remaining three stood there and fought it out. Although the three

73

were outnumbered ten to one, I was disgusted to see my fellow "comrades" kicking them as they lay on the ground. Afterwards, when one or two of us expressed our revulsion at this incident, we were told, "You can't be soft with the Reds you know. Anyway, they expect the boot and they do it to us when they catch us."

At the General Election of October 1951 the Communists were contesting the East London seats of Stepney and Stoke Newington. The Saturday afternoon prior to the Thursday of polling day they were holding a march from Stepney Green, through Shoreditch, Dalston and Hackney, to Stoke Newington. The Union Movement, getting wind of this, decided to launch an attack on the march as it passed through what they considered their territory, that is, around the Dalston area.

Although the actual attack was somewhat bungled, the plan and organisation was on this occasion first class. This was chiefly due to its organiser Peter Lesley-Jones (later to become a Bevanite), an ex-paratrooper Captain with a good war record. Besides being the leader of the "Special Propaganda Section", a small corps of eighteen picked men, including me, he was acting East London Organiser whilst Alf Flockhart was in jail.

At the Dalston end of Kingsland Road on Saturday afternoon a street market was held, such as one will find in any London working class area. It was decided that this would be an ideal place to ambush the march, as it would be quite simple to hide fifty or sixty ambushers amongst the crowded stalls. Also, most important was the fact that anyone seen pushing a perambulator along with an old wireless set on it would not be conspicuous amongst the usual crowd of second hand dealers.

It was decided that owing to our lack of numbers the attack would more likely be successful if it could be launched during some moment of confusion. So the idea of a really large smoke bomb was thought of. A good ten pounds of the mixture was made up by a U.M. member who had access to and knowledge of the chemicals required (no, it was not me), and placed in the bottom of the pram, on top of which was placed the wireless cabinet equipped with a switch for detonating the material when required.

The bomb party was picked and briefed, also five squad leaders, who were to be in charge of about ten men each. The assembly point was inside Liverpool Street Station where it was hoped that fifty or sixty people scattered around would hardly be noticed at two o'clock on a Saturday afternoon.

When I arrived at the rendezvous I decided that I would pop into "Dirty Dick's," which is opposite Liverpool Street Station, and have a couple of beers to give me "Dutch courage."

Inside, I found several other Mosleyites doing likewise. In the Station, we had commandeered a telephone booth, enabling us to get a full report from our spy at the Stepney meeting point of how many marchers there were and when they were due to set off.

Owing to a delay in the start of the march, we were kept hanging about inside the Station for three quarters of an hour waiting to move off. Consequently we were beginning to attract attention from the Station staff and one or two suspicious looking plain clothes people, whom some of the old hands recognised as Scotland Yard Special Branch men.

Just before three o'clock we were informed that the Communist column, numbering six or seven hundred, had finally set off. This was our cue to do likewise; so we moved leisurely out of the Station in twos and threes to catch a bus up the Kingsland Road.

As we passed Shoreditch Church the surrounding streets were full of police, including the familiar portly figure of Police Superintendent Charlie Satherthwaite. It was obvious that the police had been tipped off that something was in the wind, but they were not sure where it would happen.

I was in the cover party for the bomb, which was being wheeled up and down nearby side streets by two very nervous members waiting for zero hour. In the market there was only one bobby in sight.

One of our runners had just come up to tell us that the Reds were about ten minutes march from us, when a *Daily Worker* van drove up and stopped nearby. Everybody had been told to remain as inconspicuous as possible until the march arrived and the bomb had been detonated. However a particularly obnoxious character by the name of Jock Holliwell, who fancied himself as an East End gauleiter, ran across the road, screaming and shouting, and banged on the side of the van with his fists. The sole bobby, who had now been joined by a companion, arrested him. Five minutes later two bus loads of police arrived. This action of Holliwell's warned the police just in time where the trouble was going to be, and earned him two months in jail.

As the procession, headed by a hired bag pipe band, approached, the fellow in charge of the bomb (still a friend of mine) calmly wheeled the pram and its contents into the roadway, stopped, and flicked on the switch. Before anybody could realise what was happening the bomb had gone off, covering the road and the marchers, who had now reached us, in thick black acrid smoke.

The police flanking the procession, who had now been reinforced at this spot by Holliwell's premature actions, linked arms, but in the ensuing confusion were unable to prevent all the ambushers getting through to attack the marchers and grab a few banners. From the pavement, under cover of the smoke, flour bags, stones and even a dead cat were thrown at the now very confused Communists.

As the smoke cleared, the pipers could be seen marching in all directions, the police busily pulling ambushers and ambushed apart, while from the main body of the column, marchers could be seen hastily quitting the ranks, apparently having had enough. Nobody had been physically hurt by the "bomb".

Although twelve U.M. members, including Lesley-Jones, were arrested, three of them being jailed and the rest costing the Movement (Mosley's private purse) sixty pounds in fines, the general opinion was that it was worth it, due to the publicity that was received in the Sunday papers. Some of these reports were somewhat exaggerated as usual with stories of armed gangs lobbing smoke bombs out of side streets, fights with bottles and coshes (if there were, I did not see any) and an understandable report of how a bomb was thrown into a street trader's pram, burning it to ashes.

This attack on the Communists in Dalston was the climax of yet another publicity campaign. The campaign which the Mosley hierarchy thought would give them nationwide publicity as the only political force actively opposed to Communism, in fact confirmed the general public's view that they were a party of lay-abouts lacking any political argument.

* * * * *

In addition to my increasing attendance at Union Movement meetings, I also attended evening classes twice a week at the Borough Polytechnic (now the University of the South Bank) in a City & Guilds course in Paint & Resin Technology. I eventually passed the finals. My wife was not only long suffering but, on reflection, must have been imbued with outstanding patience, seeing as she was an apolitical person.

With the millennium celebrations now upon us, my mind is often cast back to the 1951 Festival of Britain. I recall it with some sense of guilt. Bored with listening to the 'wireless' by herself whilst I was out being educated either in the mysteries of phthalic anhydride or in street corner politics, my wife sometimes went to the cinema – again by herself. It was whilst she was at Peckham Odeon that she was persuaded to enter the local heat for a search for "Miss Festival of Britain." She won the heat, but I was not there. She went on to win the finals for South East London and then eventually the whole of South London, but I was still not there. In the final London competition to choose London's entry for Miss Festival of Britain, she was defeated by a girl from North London. Her mother was there to give her support but I wasn't. I believe Union Movement had an important meeting in Brixton or somewhere that night.

CHAPTER 4
'INDIGNANT LOCAL PATRIOTS'

Without Mosley's financial backing, and his charisma, which kept the loyalty of a hard-core of followers over several decades, his post-war Union Movement would have faded long before the in Notting Hill race riots 1958. Among that hard-core were men and women of intelligence and no little courage. This included Raven Thompson, long time editor of *"Union"*; Jeffrey Hamm, Mosley's loyal post-war right hand man; F. B. Price-Heywood; and Robert Row. But with several other notable exceptions Mosley's followers post-war contained a higher percentage of degenerates and the socially dysfunctional than they did pre-war in the British Union of Fascists.

It is not the purpose here to discuss in any detail the rights or wrongs of Mosley's pre and post-war policies. Who can, with true confidence? He is the enigma of twentieth century British politics. Even his most virulent opponents recognise that he could have been Prime Minister if his insentient nature had not led him into the fatal mistake of adopting the blackshirt uniform, and allowing his followers to set the pace of his new-found anti-semitism. Others (including myself) were later to make the same mistake, but we did not measure up to Mosley in intellect or economic and political vision.

With Mosley spending most of his time either in Ireland or at his Paris home from 1951 onwards, his speeches to the faithful were now infrequent, until Notting Hill. However, his money did still keep the headquarters going at 302 Vauxhall Bridge Road, the weekly paper *Union* and the wages of its editor, Raven Thomson, as well as those of Jeffrey Hamm.

Practically three-quarters of Union's four pages would be written by Raven Thomson himself under various guises such as "The Editor," "A.R.T.," "Raven Thomson," or just unsigned. Mosley would have a full page article about once a month, whilst other contributors, including F. B. Price-Heywood, Robert Row, Jeffrey Hamm and Victor Burgess, would submit occasional articles for publication.

Price-Heywood was elected as an Independent Councillor for Grasmere in the Lake District during the 1953 Municipal Elections, much to the chagrin of the *Manchester Guardian*. Jeffrey Hamm and Victor Burgess were National Speakers for the Movement. Hamm, of course, having won considerable fame as the leader of the Union Movement forces in the Ridley Road battles of 1948-9, whereupon Mosley, possibly sensing a rival in the East End, dispatched him off to Manchester to organise non-existent forces up there.

Burgess, although suffering from an inflated ego, was a likeable rogue and was at one time West London Organiser for the Movement, and also co-founder with Peter Lesley-Jones of the Special Propaganda Service. Burgess left the Movement at the same time as myself.

Possibly due to its persistent choice of uninspiring headlines, the Mosley paper *Union* was very difficult to sell on street corners. A typical Raven Thomson headline was that for the issue of 7th March 1953: *Blah, Bunk and Blether*. Apparently it referred to the remarks made by Eden and Butler on leaving for a discussion with the American Government.

The most damaging headline to the Mosleyite cause would be one in praise of some neo-Nazi activity, such as the one that finally induced me to resign from Union Movement following six months of inactivity. This read: *Monstrous Injustice, Germans Refused Habeas Corpus*.

The general public were of the opinion that next to Jew-baiting the policy of Mosley's supporters was based on adulation of Germany and Nazi Germany in particular. Consequently, when they purchased literature with this headline protest over the now forgotten Dr. Naumann's arrest by the British authorities during January 1953, they were that much more convinced that what they had been told was true. My objection to this headline, and other pro-German headlines, was not because I agreed with Naumann being imprisoned without any specific charge being made against him, even if he was a neo-Nazi, but because of the appearance it gave to the public of blatant pro-Nazism, which to a certain extent, of course, was true. Up to a year before my departure from the Mosley orbit, although a number of members were pro-Nazi themselves, it was not part of the official policy. But then both Mosley and Raven Thomson began to come out in the open again in support of certain aspects of the Nazi past.

Great publicity was given in Union to minor street meetings and their accompanying brawls and skirmishes. Anyone reading an account of one of these meetings who was never likely to visit the district concerned, would receive a greatly exaggerated impression of their size and importance.

It was the repetition of the same terminology week after week that rendered these articles so boring to the regular reader. For example, when Thomson was describing an incident where a few Mosleyites started heckling and attacking a Communist meeting, the Mosleyites were invariably referred to in pompous tones as "indignant local patriots." Another regular Thomson phrase was: "The audience good naturedly dispersed, discussing Union Movement policy, taking with them a considerable quantity of literature." This was the stock in trade ending for an account of a street corner meeting that had not degenerated into the usual mud slinging match between speaker and audience.

During the October General Election of 1951 the "indignant local patriots" were working overtime, especially in the Fulham constituency of Labour Minister Dr. Edith Summerskill. Dr. Edith received two visits from the Mosleyites at her election meetings, due to the fact that instead of ignoring them she allowed herself to lose her temper with them. This drew the attention of the press to their presence, and in consequence gave them the much desired 'oxygen of publicity' and a rousing action story for *Union's* election issue.

After some vigorous heckling, not only with the platform but with some rather puzzled Tory counter hecklers at the back of the hall, we were shown in our true colours when Dr. Edith was asked if she thought Mosley's imprisonment without trial in 1940 was just. On replying in the affirmative she was greeted with yells of derision followed by shouts of "Hail Mosley" and the giving of the fascist salute.

81

The poor lady looked aghast and shouted: "My God! They are giving the fascist salute in droves back there!" All this naturally led to violent arguments at the rear of the hall with Labour stewards and supporters, and a certain amount of pushing and shoving and "I'll see you outside" talk.

Clement Attlee himself was visited during the same week, and here again considerable publicity was gained when Mr Attlee and his audience were showered with embarrassing leaflets showing him giving the Communist salute in Madrid during the Spanish Civil War.

Needless to say, Union Movement never contested Parliamentary Elections themselves at that time, knowing full well that if they did they would only get a handful of votes and lose their deposit for a certainty. They did, however, occasionally contest Borough and County Council Elections where they considered themselves strong, that is, where they could be pretty sure of getting more than a hundred votes.

In the London County Council elections of 1949 and 1952 they entered candidates for the Kensington division. At the first election their three candidates, led by Victor Burgess, polled just over six hundred votes apiece. In 1952, however, the three candidates, again led by Burgess, received only an average of 470 votes, although Burgess still received 560 himself.

The Mosleyites, although having only about a dozen members at the most in the Brixton area, decided to contest the 1952 L.C.C. Election there on the immigration issue.

Many local people, who no doubt before the war had been staunch believers in their coloured brothers being their equal, now found strong objections to the ever increasing number of West Indians pouring into post-war London, and Brixton in particular. Brixton people were, as in other immigrant areas, feeling very bitter over the way this 'coloured invasion' aggravated the acute housing situation in particular. After being on a housing list for four or five years and unable to afford to buy a house, they saw empty homes being bought up by coloured people who had obtained high interest rate loans from one of several finance companies run by their own people for this specific purpose. The new coloured landlords soon reimbursed themselves by packing their co-racial's in six or seven to a room. There are also cases of coloured people obtaining new Council flats after being in this country only twelve months, whilst couples born and bred in Britain had to wait up to ten years or even more before they were accommodated.

This question of the aggravated housing condition, offered an opportunity for any candidate willing to advocate curtailment of this coloured influx. So Union Movement jumped in, and, as usual, made a complete hash of things.

As I considered the race question to be the most important factor in post-war world politics, I immediately offered my assistance to Mike Ryan, the Brixton organiser. Ryan was also standing as a candidate in the election and had planned to hold open air meetings every night for the fortnight preceding polling day.

The election slogan, devised by Mike Ryan, was "Keep Brixton White," and on nearly every wall could be seen the slogan or its abbreviated form K.B.W., which *Picture Post* interpreted as "Keep Britain White."

The election policy was originally to be based on the lines that Union Movement, whilst advocating that no more coloured people should be allowed to come here as permanent settlers, believed that students and technicians should be encouraged to come over and study and return with their added knowledge to aid their own people. Also they would agitate for the Government to finance new industries and public works schemes, particularly in the West Indies where unemployment was high. But apart from Dunigan, one of the three candidates, who in his limited way did his best to stick to the original policy, Ryan and most of the other speakers turned their meetings into a "hate the Nigger" campaign. These meetings invariably ended with a crowd of West Indians packed round the platform screaming and shouting and calling the speaker "White trash," whilst he returned the compliment with "Black scum."

At the count, Dunigan received 758 votes, which gave rise to a few shocked gasps from the Labour and Conservative candidates, who were of the opinion that the Mosleyites would be lucky to get a hundred votes apiece. Lewis, the other U.M. candidate, received 523, while a very disappointed Ryan was bottom of the poll with 373. These figures averaged out at approximately three per cent of the poll. Any political movement that was not already so discredited as Mosley's at that time could have received twenty per cent of the poll on such an issue as this, if they had handled the matter with some tact and logical argument.

Before it was disbanded, the Special Propaganda Section played a big part in these election campaigns, distributing election addresses, providing speakers for the street corner meetings, and generally making themselves useful or a nuisance, depending on which way you looked at it. Normally their activities included paper selling campaigns which were conducted not only in London but as far afield as Bournemouth and Southampton. They also organised many publicity stunts such as the Kingsland Road smoke-bomb attack on the Communists, and conducted a vigorous whitewashing campaign on the walls of East London, based on the pipe dream slogan "Slump or Mosley."

This Special Propaganda Section was also intended to train potential Mosleyite speakers and leaders, but like so many plans, campaigns and ideas in Union Movement, it eventually fizzled out, killed by the joint jealousies of the Headquarters hierarchy and the East End mobsters.

In January 1952 S.P.S. organised and led a publicity stunt for Mosley, unique in the fact that its propaganda effect was seen and understood by five thousand people directly, plus national press publicity, all without any violence whatsoever. This was at the meeting of the United Europe Movement, of which Sir Winston Churchill was President, in the Albert Hall on the twenty-fourth of that month.

Some of the potential vigour of the meeting was already lost when it was learnt that such staunch advocates of European Unity as Paul Reynaud of France and Henri Spaak of Belgium would not be attending, no doubt as a protest against Britain's continual foot dragging in affairs of European co-operation. Even the star of television at that time, the man of Strasbourg and one of the best men inside the Tory Party, Britain's jovial Bob Boothby, had "another engagement" that night. This meeting, which could have done a great deal for the cause of European unity, eventually had to settle for lesser known continental speakers. Britain's contribution to the proceedings included Lady Violet Bonham Carter and Arthur Greenwood, both somewhat past their prime as first class speakers, and Randolph Churchill, whose sardonic wit helped to pep up the meeting from the British point of view.

The purpose of the Union Movement demonstration was to let the "European" minded of the British public know that the principle of European unity had Mosley's backing. To do this Lesley-Jones, who was again organising the show, had managed to book a block of twelve seats and several groups of two or three seats scattered around the hall. Those of us in the main party were to display a carefully rolled banner on which was painted in eighteen inch letters: "MOSLEY FOR EUROPE." It was quite comical to see Lesley-Jones doing his best to walk naturally through the doors of the Albert Hall with this banner, which was fifteen foot long when unfurled, thrust up his overcoat. But in the crowd nobody seemed to notice anything unusual.

As our forces were scattered all over the hall, including some members well armed with leaflets right up in the top gallery, we had arranged to demonstrate at nine o'clock exactly, regardless of who was speaking. It so happened that nine o'clock came round during a speech by Count Raczynski the former Polish Ambassador in London. The Count looked both puzzled and amazed to see leaflets raining down on the auditorium, young men jumping up and chanting "More action and less talk for European unity," and the banner unfurled in front of his face informing him "Mosley for Europe." The audience, instead of showing their appreciation of the fact that they had none other than the "Leader," Oswald Mosley himself, as an ally in their cause, greeted us with boos and cries of "Gestapo!" and "Down with Fascism."

* * * * *

Whenever an industrial strike occurred it could be guaranteed that Raven Thomson would automatically side with the strikers regardless of whether it was Communist inspired, or a strike for a genuine grievance.

Thomson's reason for such action was, I suppose, to show his East End readers that he was a 'champion of the workers'.

One strike that Thomson in my opinion did rightly back was that of the bus workers on the South Coast between Poole and Southampton, who wanted to form their own Busmen's Union and break away from the National Union of Railwaymen.

Thomson ran a front page story full of information on the strike that he had received from the Bournemouth U.M. branch leader Charlie Elliott, himself a bus driver. With this story so well displayed in Union, S.P.S. went down to Southampton and sold over two hundred and fifty copies outside the bus garage there. Those of us who were selling were elated. For me, this was the only time I had found the thing saleable.

It was in this area, in Salisbury, that S.P.S. carried out one of its last actions before it died its natural death. This was the commencement of Saturday evening fortnightly meetings in Salisbury market place.

These meetings gradually developed both in size and hostility of the audience until lorry loads of police were needed to protect the speaker and his handful of supporters, drawn from a sixty-mile radius. The opposition, skilfully handled by an ex-International Brigade member, and composed of all the local active left-winger's, was beginning to become the complete master of the situation with their "Anti-Fascist Front," so some of the "boys" from London were sent down. Needless to say, bloody noses and general rowdyism became the rule, and the proceedings invariably ended with the platform being swamped under a hail of cabbages, bad tomatoes and other refuse left over from the afternoon's market. All praise must be given to the local police in this instance for preventing a full scale battle and yet allowing the platform their right of freedom of speech.

The People was so perturbed about this state of affairs in Salisbury that it ran a banner headline across the front page, stating: *"Mosley Plans a Comeback."* The article went on to describe Salisbury as a "second Nuremberg" and added that "Mosley waited across the water in Ireland until the economic and political situation was such that he could return to lead a country ripe for revolutionary action." Knowing from experience Union Movement's inability to hold what thinking members they had got, let alone attract the country en-masse, Mosley's wait in Ireland for the country to accept his leadership was destined to be a long one.

The main Salisbury rumpus and its subsequent publicity in *The People* came in the middle of September 1952, a fortnight before the Mosleyites' Annual Conference, thus setting the delegates in a confident mood with the thought of the recent *People* headlines still fresh in their minds.

On looking back I am sure that a Union Movement Annual Conference was one of the biggest farces it has been my lot to witness.

The Conference, which was held in an L.C.C. schoolroom either off Vauxhall Bridge Road or, as in 1953, in the East End where "delegates" were more readily obtained, was advertised in *Union* for six or seven weeks prior to the Conference day. The impression given by the advertisement was that each branch would send one or two delegates to represent them, whereas in actual fact anybody who was a member was persuaded, bribed, or blackmailed to come along to make a presentable show of numbers.

On entering the Conference Hall through a door marked "Junior Boys," one was greeted by the Movement's Treasurer, Maurice Pacey, seated at a desk officiously stamping up membership cards; a paid up membership card being the price of admittance. At an adjacent table stood a girl surrounded by Mosley literature which was on sale. Regardless of the fact that most people present had read practically all this literature at one time or another, it was the recognised thing to buy at least half a dozen pamphlets or booklets before leaving the Conference, thus maintaining sales.

About three quarters of an hour after the Conference was supposed to have started, the small groups of people standing around, some discussing policy, some discussing the latest rough house, and some exchanging Nazi souvenirs such as cap badges, daggers, etc., began to break up and move towards their seats. Then Raven Thomson in his capacity as General Secretary took his place on the platform in company with the Treasurer who talked about everything except the Movement's finances and one of the National Speakers, such as Jeffrey Hamm or, when he was a member, Victor Burgess, whose purpose was to break the monotony of Thomson speaking for two hours.

The first ritual then to be observed was for four or five drummers to march round the room loudly beating their drums. This roused the interest of several small boys playing football outside who clambered onto walls to peer in and view the proceedings. The drummers were followed by two people carrying a Union Jack and a flash and circle banner. The purpose of all this performance still escapes me, but I shall never forget that feeling of embarrassment which reached its peak when one drummer turning a corner trod on the heel of the youth in front, causing him to practically fall into Raven Thomson's lap, to the accompaniment of self-conscious giggles from the ladies at the back of the hall.

After an introductory speech of five or ten minutes by the Secretary, which served to open the Conference proper, it was then announced that the "Leader" had recorded a speech for us on a tape recorder. At this signal a man jumped up, his chest fair bursting with pride at this honour, and set the machine in motion. After ten or twelve minutes of adjustments of volume, tone control and the position of the loudspeaker, Mosley's voice, which had been ranging from a deep base to a high soprano, gradually became distinguishable and the general theme of his speech could be followed.

The speech informed us that Mosley had not deserted us and hinted that from his residence in Ireland he was in close contact with like thinkers on the European mainland. Then, after his annual reassurance that the political and economic situation was coming to a head and in consequence victory was just around the corner, the recorded speech finished to loud cheers and 'Mosley' chants from the "delegates."

Following a few pep talks from the platform and a long review of the current situation by Raven Thomson, the Conference was thrown open to questions and suggestions from the audience. However, seeing that no record was kept of this normally important stage of any conference and that any particularly searching question was answered with the usual platitudes, the whole affair was quite pointless.

After tea and buns, the Conference ended with a film show, depicting plumbing and sanitation under the Peron regime.

In April 1952, just after I had organised, in co-operation with a pre-war Mosley supporter, a Camberwell branch of Union Movement, we moved from our one room flat in Peckham to a maisonette in Mortlake, Surrey. This improvement in our living conditions was the outcome of the publicity in the London evening papers gained by my wife as a result of the Miss Festival of Britain competition.

In nearby Putney a very enthusiastic young Mosleyite, Barry Aitken, who had once achieved fame by throwing a brick through the Russian Embassy windows, was anxious to form a Putney branch. After calling on several contacts, we managed to rope in a dozen members and I became Treasurer of the new branch.

Putney branch, in company with the branches of Fulham, Chelsea and Westminster, formed the Fifth London Area of Union Movement. The area organiser was Oliver Grose, a tactless and humourless young man who thought he could emulate the feat of Lesley Jones and his S.P.S. I eventually became Treasurer for the Fifth London Area as a whole, and was therefore qualified to say that membership for the whole area, including non-active members, never exceeded forty-five, up to mid 1953.

It was in Putney High Street on a corner of a side turning near the bridge, that the British public first had the doubtful pleasure of hearing me address them on Mosley's policy. So did my three months old daughter, who was wheeled up and down in her pram by her mother.

It was the practice for a new speaker to open up a meeting and try to draw a crowd for the main speaker by talking until he ran dry, or until he got so tied up in knots that he had to be dragged off the platform. In my case this usually lasted ten minutes, though once at Richmond, where I had the honour to get up in the middle of the meeting and address a ready formed audience, I lasted twenty-five minutes. This was due to the fact that I was being heckled quite vigorously and could hardly get down without giving some reply to the questions and remarks, even if they were mainly abusive.

This meeting at Richmond in the late autumn of 1952 was one of the last Union Movement activities that I attended before I began to have second thoughts about Mosley and his political movement that I had so impetuously rushed into.

As I have already mentioned, when I first joined the Mosley movement, adulation of Adolf Hitler was only to be heard in the private conversations of some members and rarely on the public platform or in *Union*. Consequently, I assumed, like several other new members, that as we gathered strength, although we should have a realistic and understanding policy towards Germany, the heartland of Europe, this proportion of Nazi hero worshippers would eventually become a very small minority. But as more neo-Nazi groups emerged in Germany, the defence of the crimes, brutalities and mistakes of Hitler and his Nazi gang gradually took pride of place both on the public platform and in the party newspaper. By the end of February 1953 this Nazi apologia had reached such a peak over the Naumann business that my mind was finally made up. I quit the Mosley movement.

* * * * *

Although by the time Mosley had reached his early thirties he seemed booked for a Labour Prime Minister's seat, his subsequent

90

political life became one series of ill-timed and ill-fated moves - nor was luck on his side. In 1930, impatient for power, he thought he could defy the power of the Labour Party machine: a power that partly rested on its acceptance by the establishment. Flushed by the reception delegates had given him at the Party Conference of that year for his referendum on the unemployment problem, Mosley thought that by staging a showdown he would sway the majority of the Government bench over to his side. When it came to the crucial moment, he found he had only six supporters.

On his resignation from the Labour Party, Mosley formed his new party, but found that to make progress the party's title needed a credo, an 'ism. The vogue for new political movements with a nationalist outlook in Europe at that time was to call themselves Fascist. Fascism, unlike Communism and Nazism, as Mussolini its founder stated, was not for export as a fixed political creed. Consequently, in any country where there existed a movement based on nationalist beliefs, active opposition to Communism and support for the authority of the state, such a movement would be called Fascist. However, there would be quite marked differences between it and a similarly named movement in another country. Witness the difference between Salazar's Portugal, Franco's Spain, Peron's Argentina and Mussolini's Italy.

With this knowledge that Fascism as a political creed could be varied at will, and came in many shades of black, Mosley nailed its banner to his mast, though had he sailed under any other he would still have pursued the same course. It is significant that he chose Mussolini's Fascism and not Hitler's National Socialism, for, like Mussolini, Spengler and even Nietzsche, he was of the opinion that culture was more important than race.

During his long sojourn in the political wilderness he must have bitterly regretted his action of leaving the Labour Party to don the cloak of Fascism, and to find himself as far as the public was concerned forever entangled in its folds.

Chapter 5
Loyal To A Lost Empire

In the late summer of 1953, acting on the suggestions of my sisters and the two eldest stepbrothers, I joined the Barnes, SW. London, Branch of the Conservative Party, together with a dissatisfied Union Movement member who had been a fervent supporter of Mosley pre-war. This was a new world of politics, where my fellow members' minds seemed dominated by minutes of the previous meetings, points of order relating to local drainage and other trivia, and a lack of interest in looking at policies now that the country was "back in the safe hands of the Conservatives" under Churchill. We gave it two months and then left.

I have been told that I should not have been so impatient but should have stayed with the Tories. This assumes that I would be able to forget, or suppress, all my radical viewpoints, and accept the reactionary right dogma of the Tories, particularly in relation to trade unionism and general matters affecting the working man. I had joined the Conservative Party because it was more of a home for patriots and nationalists than the Labour Party, but in certain circumstances I would have been more at home in the Labour Party.

It was in December of that year that I came across two references to Andrew Fountaine, a British landowner and wartime naval Commander. The first was in a book by Douglas Reed which heaped praise on this "outstanding, anti-Communist Young Conservative." The second was a comment by "Cross Bencher" in the *Sunday Express*, which pointed out that Andrew Fountaine had contested the Chorley, Lancashire, seat for the Conservatives in 1950 and reduced a Labour majority of several thousand to 361 votes. He had then been sacked from the Party by Lord Woolton, apparently for being too right wing. "Cross Bencher" also said that Fountaine had now formed a National Front Movement. Its platform was:

1. All out opposition to UNO, NATO, Strasbourg and other international tie-ups.
2. All out support for Empire development.
3. All out resistance to Bolshevism.
4. A halt to further coloured immigration.

My curiosity was roused. I wrote to Andrew Fountaine and received a reply from Guy Chesham, then one of his leading supporters in the London area, who asked me to visit him at his flat in Elgin Mansions. He also sent me the objectives of Fountaine's National Front Movement and issue No1 of its political newspaper, *Outrider*. This contained several quotations from a Francis Parker Yockey, plus extracts from his book *Imperium*.

Yockey was a pro-Nazi American who, incredibly, was employed in the US legal team at the Nuremberg War Crimes Trial and eventually sacked. His line was that war crime trials were only favouring the advance of international communism and were "a reversion to barbarism." He had made a deep study of history and was strongly influenced by the ideas of the early twentieth century German philosopher Oswald Spengler. In 1947 he made contact with Mosley, who was unaware of his Nazi past but was attracted by Yockey's intelligence. Mosley found him a disruptive presence in his newly formed Union Movement and he was expelled. Yockey then formed the European Liberation Front in 1949 and issued a manifesto called *The Proclamation of London*. But apart from being beaten up at a meeting in Hyde Park, nothing much happened. Yockey committed suicide in June 1960 whilst being held in strange circumstances in a San Francisco jail.

On my visit to Guy Chesham and his wife in their tastefully furnished flat it soon became apparent that he was the Yockey disciple and had in fact compiled the issue of *Outrider* that I had been sent, and which was the only issue ever published. Its content, particularly over the vision of a "new Europe", contrasted strongly with the Fountaine views expressed in the National Front document. Chesham held an executive position in business and he was always at pains to point out to me that it was essential to look after our economic affairs and that the unemployed were of no use whatsoever to a movement. The outcome was that nothing transpired in the way of activity other than a few meetings in Chorley, Lancashire, where Fountaine had originally stood as a Conservative candidate.

The reason for Andrew Fountaine's lack of political activity was the difficult time he was going through in his marriage. His then wife was the daughter of the Chief Constable of Norfolk. As a former Conservative Central Office worker, she greatly objected to his desertion of the Tory Party. He still had time to come down to London and meet Chesham, who told me that he would then accompany him in the evening to various West End haunts where Fountaine would pick up women.

Throughout his life Andrew Fountaine had always enjoyed the ladies: even after his love marriage with his charming second wife, Rosemary. He was the original Randy Andy long before this sobriquet was given to another naval officer, Prince Andrew.

Typical of Andrew Fountaine's priority of penis over politics was given in a letter to me by a political associate in Norwich writing in November 1955 and describing a meeting he had with Fountaine in that city:

"Unfortunately our discussion was cut short when AF decided to go off with some old doll he'd been ogling all the evening! Before doing so, however, he haggled in the bar, with his deep booming voice, as to the terms of the contract, so to speak!... It does, however, underline all A.K. Chesterton told you about his lack of tact. Guy (Chesham), of course, made the same point."

By April 1954 my meeting with Fountaine had still not materialised. Impatient to see something happen, I suggested to Chesham that at least we should continue to publish *Outrider* (which I thought was a very appropriate title at that time), even if only bi-monthly, and I would be prepared to edit it. In a letter to me, this was turned down on the grounds that " ... it might clash with the new policy, which is, of course, Infiltration as opposed to the old factional 'Movement' line."

This was where I came in. My impetuous nature saw no future in infiltration, based on my brief experience with Barnes Conservatives.

I decided I would put my political life on ice and concentrate on my career. Within three months I had obtained a new job as the Works Manager of a small paint manufacturing firm in Hull. The fact that it only employed some thirty people in the factory was neither here nor there. I was a Works Manager at the age of twenty-seven. As I walked through the factory gate I said to myself: "I bet my father would be proud of me now."

After a month I managed to find a house to rent and my wife, two-year-old daughter and one-year-old son came to join me in Hull. I enjoyed the job and liked the special breed of Yorkshire people to be found in Hull.

* * * * *

In less than a year the political bug was again beginning to bite. I resumed written contact with Andrew Fountaine. He informed me that he had had to disband his National Front, due to the pressures of work in running the estate at Narford. If I still wanted to keep the 'Resurgent' flame alight he would donate a second-hand duplicating machine on which I could produce a publication to mail to the former National Front members and other contacts I had picked up - many were ex-Mosleyites. Issue number one of *National Unity* was published in April 1955. It led off with:

" 'The capital ... was incessantly filled with subjects and strangers from every part of the world, who all introduced and enjoyed the favourite superstitions of their native country.' Thus Gibbons in his *Decline and Fall of the Roman Empire* described Rome in the third century A.D. as it entered its period of decline. This description could be as aptly applied to the capital of that second great Empire; the British Empire."

The article was entitled "Infiltration of the West." Significantly, it ended with: "We do not contend that biologically any one race is superior to another. The fact is we are all different! The

African, the Asiatic, and the European all have something to contribute to this world."

I have never really changed this viewpoint, although I sincerely regret that some of my actions in a subsequent period might appear to have made it a sham.

After a few issues of *National Unity* a mass readership (!) of nearly sixty subscribers was established. Now fired up like a loose cannon, two ephemeral political parties were formed. Pausing for breath one evening I decided to do nothing for a week, apart from the all essential bread winning, and think over my course of political action. Experience had already shown me that a political movement of one hundred per cent unanimous opinion is a movement of one. Therefore, rather than continue with a minuscule nationalist movement from a geographically isolated base, it made more sense to work with an established nationalist movement, even if it was not really radical right, which was not irrevocably tarred with the brush of anti-semitism and Fascism as Mosley's movement was, irrespective of his post-war denial of anti-semitism. That movement was the League of Empire Loyalists. What is more, they had a central London office.

In May 1955 I made contact with A.K. Chesterton. This did not particularly please Andrew Fountaine, who thought that Chesterton had let him down by not supporting his National Front Movement.

He added: "Because of his close association with Mosley pre-war, Chesterton is politically discredited. He is temperamental and would never suborn his personal conceit to the duties of a loyal party member. He is, of course, capable of excellent journalistic efforts."

Chesterton for his part was not over enamoured with Fountaine and found him "too irrational and lacking in tact."

A.K. Chesterton, who was a cousin of G.K.Chesterton, was born in South Africa. He falsified his age and joined the South African Light Infantry in 1916 and before his seventeenth birthday he had been in the thick of three battles in German East Africa. Later he was able to transfer to the 7th Battalion, Royal Fusiliers where he served on the Western Front in France for the rest of the war as an officer. In 1918 he was awarded the Military Cross for conspicuous gallantry whilst leading a series of attacks against enemy machine gun posts. In 1924 he came to England as a journalist in Stratford on Avon and became editor of the *Shakespeare Review*, and a recognised authority on Shakespeare. Although a socialist, in 1933 he joined Mosley in the British Union of Fascists, and became one of his leading propagandists and organisers. His harrowing experiences on the Western Front, as with the author Henry Williamson, played no small part in his attraction to Mosley and what appeared to them to be the heroes' creed of Fascism. The recurring visions of the daily horror of seeing brave young men die in their thousands turned Chesterton into an alcoholic. It was thanks to the generosity of Mosley that he was cured in a special clinic in Germany.

He quarrelled with Mosley's politics and left the BUF in 1938.

When the Second World War started Chesterton rejoined the army, volunteered for tropical service and went through all the hardships of the great push up from Kenya against the Italian forces, across the desert of the Agaden and into the remotest parts of Somalia. In 1943 his health broke down and he was invalided out of the army with malaria and colitis, returning to journalism. In 1944 he became deputy editor and chief leader writer of *Truth*. In April 1953 he became literary advisor and personal journalist to Lord Beaverbrook, and special writer on the Daily Express Group.

In the same year he founded *Candour*, "The British Views Letter", which was to "serve as a link between Britons all over the world in protest against the surrender of their world heritage." Of the early financial support, £1,000 came from R.K. Jeffery, a British millionaire living in Chile, who was later to give many more thousands which enabled both *Candour* and the League of Empire Loyalists to operate on a firmer footing than any other Right Wing or Fascist movement since Mosley's pre-war heyday.

However, establishment journalists and politicians would call Chesterton a 'Fascist' at their financial peril. He won fourteen libel cases and gained further contributions to the funds in consequence. His defence would centre on his outstanding record of service in two world wars plus the book he co-authored with J. Leftwich, who was Jewish, *The Tragedy of Anti-Semitism* (London 1948), which showed that he was genuinely appalled at the horrors of the concentration camps. But this did not stop him from coded references to Jews with the "New York international money power."

The League of Empire Loyalists' image of non-fascist respectability was further helped by the names of the members of its General Council, who had no real power and very rarely met. In its early days these included: Field Marshal Lord Ironside, The Earl of Buchan, Elizabeth Lady Freeman, Maj. Gen. Richard Hilton, Lt. Gen. Sir Balfour Hutchison, and Air Commodore G.S.Oddie, among others.

Having had my first meeting with Chesterton in London that October I returned to Hull to think things over. I was impressed with his courtesy, his intellect and his belief in himself and what he was doing, but particularly in himself. On the other hand this was 1955, not 1935, and the empire which he was asking us to be loyal to was fast disappearing. I wrote once more to Andrew Fountaine asking him if I could not take over as organiser of his erstwhile National Front, or support a new British Nationalist Party founded by a Captain Neville Medforth in Hull, and whom I was in close touch with. In either choice it would require a minimum initial £500 support.

What I did not realise at the time was that Fountaine's first marriage was coming to an end and divorce proceedings were under way. The immediate effect of this was a massive drain on his available cash. In consequence, the appeal for funds was turned down as was my request for a meeting, which had now been postponed for two years. In fact, I was not to meet him until late 1957. He had this to say on A.K. Chesterton:

"The tragedy of AK is that he is a brilliant journalist, but his political thinking is vertical and sterile and he is OLD.

"The only way to get the movement you want started is to base it round a political parliamentary candidate: other than myself I know of none in the offing."

The die was cast. I wrote to A.K.Chesterton accepting his offer of becoming the Northern Organiser for the League of Empire Loyalists.

In his reply he gave me this piece of advice: "Choose your people with care. Give the crooks and the maniacs a wide berth. Quality in this movement is immeasurably more important than quantity."

In the immediate years to follow it was a pity that I did not make full note of Chesterton's caution.

* * * * *

By the time I joined the LEL it was already gaining considerable media coverage through its basically non-violent stunts in calling Anthony Eden to task for "scuttling the Empire" and exposing the anti-British and anti-European actions of the United Nations. Leading the league forays were its charming and highly intelligent Organising Secretary, Leslie Greene, M. A., and Chesterton's right hand man, Austen Brooks.

A major campaign was organised, particularly in London and the West Midlands, in April 1956, against the visit of the Soviet leaders Kruschev and Bulganin. The following agency account was typical:

"As the Russian visitors were nearing their destination today, the side door of No.10 Downing Street was opened to admit a 10-foot silver painted spoon and a cross shaped wreath, symbols of protest against the visit by the League of Empire Loyalists.

"Attached to the spoon was a notice: 'This spoon is presented to the Prime Minister by the League of Empire Loyalists, who fear that it will not prove long enough at Thursday's dinner party.'

"The wreath bore a card: 'In honourable and pitiful memory of the millions of victims of the Soviet regime.' Spoon and wreath had been carried to Downing Street by Mr Austen Brooks, ginger bearded deputy chairman (and wartime naval officer) of the League, and two members from the League office in a basement opposite Big Ben."

Leslie Greene and another member had greeted Kruschev and Bulganin with messages delivered over a portable amplifier when the Russians arrived at Victoria Station. Before being arrested Leslie Greene managed to get over: "Anthony Eden has just shaken hands with murder. Bulganin and Kruschev are in this country to our shame."

She and the other member were fined £20 each, which was a large fine at that time for a protest not involving violence or a potentially violent incident. In Birmingham, Coventry and Leicester LEL posters appeared widely opposing the visit and loudspeaker vans toured the Midland cities with similar messages.

I had taken time off from work and gone from Hull to Coventry to participate. It was here that I was called upon to speak at my first indoor public meeting. The audience consisted of five hundred Ukrainians living in the city. The meeting was organised by the Ukrainian National Committee in Coventry and I was a guest speaker for the League of Empire Loyalists. There was no heckling or any response from the five hundred passive faces and I began to assume that they knew little English. Suddenly, I made a breakthrough, however, and the Ukrainians began to cheer.

The *Coventry Evening Telegraph* of 23.4.56 reported:

"The meeting was addressed in English by Mr John Bean of the League of Empire Loyalists, and in Ukrainian by Mr F. Kovalenko."

"While the speeches were being made, the large crowd, many wearing black arm bands with their national colours of blue and yellow super imposed, remained silent and there were no interruptions.

"The first sign of emotion came when Mr Bean, speaking on behalf of the Empire Loyalists, said that if Britain was made more aware of atrocities behind the Iron Curtain and "B and K" made another visit, 'they would get the welcome they deserved. They would be thrown back in the Thames!' "

For its construction, the speech was probably on a par with that I made in support of the Communist candidate in the school mock election fourteen years earlier.

It was in Coventry on that occasion that I met the LEL Midlands Organiser for the first time. His name was Colin Jordan.

In June I made another visit to the Midlands. Its purpose was to present the Prime Minister with the League's 'Order of the Scuttle'. If the reader thinks that the following report from Chesterton's newsletter *Candour* of 29.6.56 is rather lengthy and much ado about nothing, I republish it because it is a classic example of the League's modus operandi: a way of catching the public eye without resorting to violence or the provoking of violence. It is certainly not republished through vanity: I feel quite embarrassed at reading it again.

"As Sir Anthony Eden rose to speak at Warwick yesterday, a young man pushed his way through the crowd, held up a black painted scuttle, and said: 'Sir Anthony, in view of the development of your Empire policies, I have great pleasure in presenting you with this scuttle on behalf of the League of Empire Loyalists.'"

That paragraph began the *Sunday Dispatch's* report of another League coup which has received world wide attention.

People entering the grounds of Warwick Castle, where Sir Anthony's constituency Conservative Association had organised a garden fete, were confronted by a banner which demanded: "Keep Right! End Edenism! Conserve our Empire, Sovereignty, Race, Heritage." The banner was borne by two members of a party under the leadership of Mr. Colin Jordan, the League's Midlands organiser. Other members of the party distributed League leaflets, and sold copies of *Candour* containing criticism of the Edenite policies.

The Organising Secretary of the League, Miss L.M.C. Greene, toured the vicinity of the Castle in a loudspeaker van, broadcasting a call to the assembling Conservatives to call the Prime Minister to account for his internationalist policies, and to demand that the Government should follow patriotic, national and imperial policies.

Meanwhile, Mr. Bean (who is the League's Northern organiser) had discovered that stewards would not admit people carrying parcels. With Mr. Stanley Edwards and Mr. Austen Brooks, he set out on a tour of inspection of the Castle walls, until they found a spot away from the crowds where the wall was low enough for the scuttle to be tossed over. Brooks remained outside with the scuttle, while Bean and Edwards entered the grounds. Once inside, they made their way to the appointed spot, where Bean wrapped his handkerchief round his cigarette lighter, tossed it high into the air and caught it as it fell. Brooks, on the other side of the wall, could not see Bean, but he could see this prearranged signal, and as soon as the road outside the wall was clear he tossed over the scuttle.

Having collected the scuttle, which was wrapped in brown paper, Bean made his way with it to the place where the Prime Minister was to speak, and settled down to wait within easy reach of the Prime Minister's table. Sir Anthony's arrival, however, was the signal for the crowd to surge forward, so that, when the chairman began his introductory remarks Bean found a number of people between him and his target. He began to make his way forward, unwrapping his parcel as he went.

"Excuse me," he said to those in front of him. "May I come past? I have a presentation to make."

The crowd obligingly made way. As Bean moved steadily forward, an adulatory remark by the chairman brought applause from the crowd, in which Bean, resting his parcel on the grass, joined. Sir Anthony smiled benignly upon him. A moment later the Prime Minister's smile vanished as Bean discarded the wrapping of the parcel, stepped forward and, in full view of the audience, presented him with the scuttle.

Perhaps the ultimate in the League's undergraduate type pranks was reached at the De Montfort Hall, Leicester, in March 1957, when Harold Macmillan had embarked on his first big public speech after becoming Prime Minister. A dramatic call to stop the meeting came from a distinguished-looking man near the front. Again I quote from *Candour*:

"Looking down, the Prime Minister saw the distinguished looking gentleman stoop down to examine a young woman who lay, apparently unconscious, at his feet. Then he continued his speech.

"A moment later he stopped again, as the distinguished looking gentleman rose to announce his diagnosis.

" 'This patient,' said the 'doctor', 'is in a fit because of the Government's policies of betrayal of this country'.

"There was an angry roar from the 'hard core' supporters of the Government in the hall. As it died away, the 'patient' leapt to her feet.

" 'I confirm that diagnosis,' she declared. 'Join the League of Empire Loyalists and fight to keep Britain great.'

"Uproar followed as the 'patient', Miss Rosine de Bounevialle, secretary of the League's Petersfield and District Branch was escorted from the hall by stewards."

The 'doctor' was Phil Burbidge, a retired Merchant Navy officer, with an extremely likeable personality. When I moved back to London he and I went on many LEL escapades together.

Up until early 1957 Colin Jordan was not only the League's Midlands Organiser but also a member of its National Committee. Yet he managed to hide from Chesterton, or Chesterton pretended not to know about it, that he was also the brains behind the Birmingham Nationalist Club of 1955, which later became the White Defence Force. Leading members of this coterie included Peter Ling, Dick Tynan and Don Tenant. The latter also had one foot in the Mosley camp.

Ling and Tynan had something I had not come across before. Both were intelligent; Ling particularly so. Both were extremely courageous and would physically take on five times their number of political opponents, which I saw them do at a White Defence Force meeting in Birmingham. I eventually found out that Ling had served a twelve-year prison sentence for shooting somebody in an armed robbery and Tynan, who was Irish with the appropriate gift of the gab, had served time for smuggling cattle over the border between Ulster and Eire.

We can assume that Chesterton was unaware of their backgrounds when he reported in *Candour* how the Loyalists routed a Fenner Brockway Movement for Colonial Freedom Meeting at London's Conway Hall. The report stated that the League demonstration was made by London and Midland Groups. Amongst the names of members thanked, such as Major B. Wilmot Allistone, Leslie Greene, Austen Brooks, et al, appeared those of Dick Tynan and Peter Ling.

As an Organiser, Colin Jordan being a school teacher with an M.A. in history, was quite acceptable to Chesterton's way of thinking.

Tynan's Irish charm (or perhaps 'guile' was more apt in his case) was manifest at the White Defence Force meeting referred to, and which I had been invited to following my Midlands visit on League activities. Communist sympathisers had stormed into the back of the hall and fierce fist fighting ensued in which Tynan, Ling and also Jordan were prominent. The intruders were driven out of the door and most moved away. One, who stayed his ground, was hit in the face by Tynan with such force that he landed on the other side of the road. The meeting resumed and after a quarter of an hour a police sergeant entered accompanying Tynan's victim. He was covered in blood and his jaw was sagging, probably because it was broken. Keeping his right hand in his pocket to hide his bleeding and rapidly swelling knuckles, Tynan turned to the unfortunate fellow and said in his Irish brogue:

"Good gracious! You poor fellow! Whoever did that?"

With difficulty, the victim muttered: "You did, and I want you arrested for assault."

"Officer, I have never seen this poor soul in my life," came Tynan's shocked reply.

The Police Sergeant pointed out that as it was a private meeting, and he had not been there, the victim would have to bring a civil prosecution. Understandably the erstwhile militant opposer of the White Defence Force left the hall one pace behind the Sergeant.

After the meeting I expressed my reservations to Colin Jordan at Tynan's violence. He gave his schoolmasterish chortle and said: "But we need our Dick Tynans. Without the inspiration he and Ling gave to the others the meeting would have been wrecked."

When I enquired what they did for relaxation, Jordan said that when he had visited the house that Tynan and Ling jointly rented in Coventry, the bannisters were completely missing. Apparently they were broken when Tynan and Ling and two other followers had a game of "Jews and Nazis" on the stairs. Colin Jordan found this amusing. I should have been warned. Instead, I recall thinking that when an effective British nationalist party was formed, "we will need to use people like Tynan and Ling for our defence, but they will have to be kept under control."

I decided I would not "grass" to Chesterton what was going on in the Midlands, I would let him find out for himself. But I had no intention of joining Jordan's White Defence Force which later became the White Defence League.

It was not long before Chesterton did begin to find out about Jordan's and Ling's non-LEL activities. Both went down to Croydon and had a long discussion with A.K., who then sent me carbon copies of the subsequent letters he wrote to them both. Again, my youthful conceit would not let me see that if a wily old fox like Chesterton could be fooled by them, then I had little chance. In his letter to Jordan of 7.11.55 he wrote:

" ... There is a foul creature, who goes under the name of Wolf Cleveland, with whose phantom organisation there has been traced a direct link with Jewish Money. Some months ago a man about-town with a foreign name and title tried to interest us in this bogus concern by telling us it was laying in a supply of guns. Our response was to report the man and his information to the Special Branch at Scotland Yard.

" ... The man responsible for the defamation called repeatedly at Grand Buildings (LEL office) and tried to get Leslie to admit ... to an association between our movement and Mr G. of Croydon, of whom our Organising Secretary at that time had never heard."

Mr G., also referred to as Mr Wagner, because of his love for Wagnerian music, was a Peter Green. Chesterton continued:

" Since that time Mr G. has been investigated and he spoke with the utmost abandon of collecting guns and acquiring a van which, among other things, would run by accident into groups of coloured people in Brixton and elsewhere. That sort of thing did not worry me very much until I heard that Mr G. and Peter Ling were working together. Realising that we had all of us become very vulnerable to attack because of this association between Peter and Mr G., I asked Ling to come down and see me, and I am quite sure that I have managed to make him see the great dangers inherent in the situation, even if I have not managed to convince him that it is sheer political suicide to work with lunatics, whether their lunacy be genuine or feigned."

In the copy of A.K.'s letter to Ling it was apparent that either he was flattering Ling's ego or, more likely, had been beguiled by the intelligent air of rationality that Ling could portray when required. For how else can one explain this passage?

"Having discovered your essential reasonableness, I will henceforward contradict anybody who describes you to me as a fanatic. A zealot, yes, but fanatics are impervious to reason." Chesterton's letter to Ling concluded with a qualified wish for future co-operation:

" ... I sincerely hope that we shall have the honour of the co-operation of our Midland members under the leadership of Dick (Tynan) and yourself. You will not mind my saying this, but it would not help to have somebody (Mr G.) wearing an Afrika Korps helmet and swastika!"

In a letter to me some six months later, Colin Jordan gave an account of his Midland Group's contribution to the Conway Hall meeting of the Movement for Colonial Freedom already referred to:

"Eight of us (largely non-League) went down in two cars from the Midlands to lend a hand. Things really warmed up during the later stages of the meeting with interruptions coming fast and furious from our people all over the hall and nigs getting hysterical and shouting "Hitler, Hitler," "Fascist," and "We're Mau Mau and proud of it," etc. Finally, after I had been busy calling Brockway and Leslie Hale 'renegades' and 'subversives' etc, etc, they pounced on me to sling me out and the balloon went up with our boys from the Midlands racing across the hall to the rescue; Dick clouting to good effect. Dick and myself handed over to the Police and escorted out by them. And little Peter Green in his excitement clouting anything moving that he didn't definitely recognise as on our side and biffing a cop, who rather decently ignored the matter."

It is pretty certain that A.K. Chesterton was unaware that the LEL was being given the support of the notorious Nazi eccentric, Mr G.

* * * * *

In July 1956 I decided to accept Chesterton's offer to return to London and work part-time for the LEL, with the brief of trying to popularise its policy. To obtain a living wage I would try and find another part time post using my experience as a paint chemist. As recompense for what was in effect giving up my career at a potential take off point, A.K. offered to loan me the deposit for a house. One was eventually found in Thornton Heath, only a short bus ride from the *Candour* office in South

Croydon where Chesterton was based. Financially, my wife and I certainly paid for my idealism. My salary as a Works Manager in the Hull paint factory had approached £1,000 p.a. Chesterton paid me £5 per week and I gained another £10 for morning work in the small laboratory of a wood preservative manufacturer, founded by two Jewish brothers, the Goberts, and operating from a former surface air raid shelter in Deptford. The company, Protim, is now one of the leading wood preservative companies nationwide. The Goberts treated me well but I did not mention the nature of my afternoon job in case they interpreted Chesterton's occasional references to "Jewish money power" as anti-semitism, which some would say it was. I would not like to have seen them offended.

We found someone to look after our two pre-school age children so that my wife could work full-time and enable us to pay the mortgage and also repay Chesterton's loan simultaneously.

The increased number of coloured faces in London after my two years away was very noticeable. What had been a steady trickle of West Indian immigrants in 1954 was now a steady stream. That year the Home Office gave their first figures and they estimated that the rate was now 30,000 a year. Generally speaking, it was not particularly a racial problem. In certain areas, such as Brixton, where West Indians were now strong in number, it had become a culture clash between the indigenous Londoner's way of life and that of the noisier, more vivacious West Indian.

The main area of conflict at that time was in housing. This is borne out by the fact that in 1945 the London County Council had 50,000 families on the housing list, mainly as a result of the destruction done by the Blitz. In spite of the immediate post-war building programme, the effect of immigration meant that by 1959 the list had grown to 170,000.

That in fact it was more of a culture clash at that time is reflected in a rather amusing incident I saw in Hull just prior to my departure. Like Liverpool, Southampton, London Docklands and most other British city ports, Hull had had a small coloured population from the early part of the nineteenth century and their descendants had, until recent years, mainly married among themselves. Two such descendants, men in their late forties, wearing flat caps and talking with full East Riding accents, were supping on their pints in a pub in the Land of Green Ginger - I think it was the Earl de Grey. I was in the pub with a couple of political acquaintances when in walked two coloured men dressed in the popular attire of West Indians in the fifties, which included peg bottom trousers and wide brimmed hats: obviously newly arrived immigrants. The response of the two "Hull men of colour" was to look in amazement, gulp on their pints of Hull Brewery ale and say in a loud voice:

"Look at them niggers coomin' in 'ere. They'll be causin' bluddy trouble soon!"

My base for my part time employment with the League of Empire Loyalists was not at their office in Palace Chambers but at Chesterton's *Candour* office in South Croydon, a few hundred yards from his flat. A.K. said that this improved liaison between us, particularly for quick response League demonstrations, but I suspect it was also because he could keep an eye on what I was doing.

Most of the League's stunts were planned, in some considerable detail, at evening soirées in A.K.'s flat. Up to a dozen people would be present. Some would only appear two or three times a year, but the balance was always so that there appeared to be more women than men present. Chesterton liked feminine company, but this does not mean that I put him in the same category as Mosley or Andrew Fountaine in this respect. The regulars would include Austen Brooks, Leslie Greene, Nettie Bonnar, A.K.'s secretary, Aiden Mackay, one of several devout Catholics who supported the League, Rosine de Bounevialle, and often Phil Burbidge, my partner in the art of popping out of boxes and infiltrating Government and Commonwealth Conferences.

Always present was Doris Chesterton, who married A.K. in 1933. A school headmistress, she was a devoted Socialist and had been so in the thirties when A.K. was a Mosley lieutenant. It says much for their marriage that they were still so close up until the very end when Chesterton died in 1973. At the soirées Doris Chesterton would see that the sherry glasses were always filled - or beer for some of the men. When the conversation became non-political she would contribute with wit and clarity. A.K., being an alcoholic, did not drink of course. Nor did he then smoke. His smoking, and possibly drinking, had done the damage in the thirties and he suffered from emphysema, which was the cause of his death.

I was appointed to the Executive Committee and was also the Secretary of the London Branch. As part of my desire to 'popularise' the League, I organised a number of street corner meetings in Earls Court, Lewisham and Bethnal Green. I don't think they achieved much because my memory of these meetings is a blank. Chesterton also allowed me to continue publishing my duplicated news sheet. The *National Unity* title was dropped and it became *The Loyalist* 'Issued monthly in support of the League of Empire Loyalists'. Unlike *Candour*, it gave considerable coverage to the problems of immigration, which was now not only aggravating the housing shortage but posing a threat to indigenous workers' jobs in the Midlands. Great play was made in Issue No.1 of public opinion polls conducted at that time by the *Daily Sketch* and the *News Chronicle*. The former said that 98 per cent of their readers who voted said that coloured immigration should be restricted and 80 per cent said that it should be stopped completely! The *News Chronicle* poll gave a similar number of people wanting restrictions but, being a liberal paper, less than 20 per cent wanted a total ban.

A.K. was also giving me a free rein on my 'left wing' stance. The following is an extract from another article in Issue No.1 of *The Loyalist*:

"The League of Empire Loyalists is not a movement of class. We are a movement of patriotic Britons irrespective of class. Therefore we have to reach also the ordinary British working man. We have to show him that the Empire is not just a question of prestige or flag waving, but is an economic necessity. It can guarantee a source of raw materials to keep the factories going

111

removed from the whims and fancies of foreign control. The Empire lands can also constitute a market for the finished goods of our factories, assuming that is that we give priority to Empire preference in trade and withdraw from such international trade agreements as GATT.

"If we are to succeed in our struggle we must also capture the best of our youth. But in doing so we must remember that youth abhors being thought 'old fashioned' or 'out of date'. The internationalists, knowing this, are installing into the minds of our youth the concept that national sovereignty is 'old fashioned' or 'out of date'. This we have to counter."

Meanwhile, around the same time, Chesterton was writing in *Candour* of further evidence of the 'world plot' to undermine British influence. His example on this occasion was the American support that enabled Kwame NKrumah to become premier of Ghana.

" 'American' support for 'independence' campaigns in Africa will be defended in accordance with the now classic formula of countering such Communist expansion and infiltration as that in the Sudan - a formula which springs a trap for fools.

"Washington (New York's executive instrument) and Moscow are not enemies. They are twin power agencies promoting the same basic policy. They form what might be called the Yalta Coalition, which derived from the conspiracy implicit in the special pleading (for Bolshevik Russia) of the sixth of President Wilson's Fourteen Points ...

"Yet there are simpletons fully persuaded that the destinies of peoples are determined by mouthing demagogues such as NKrumah and who raise supercilious eyebrows at the very suggestion that there is an international plot running like a malignant growth throughout the modern world. How many White settlers in Kenya or the Rhodesias who know that 'American' (the quotation marks were Chesterton code for 'Jewish Bankers') money is being sent into those territories to foster native trade union agitation are also aware that Dollar Imperialism and Communist Imperialism are dual aspects of the same policy?"

I thought then that although the 'world plot' theory of international finance and communism working in tandem was rather far fetched, as least it had the propaganda advantage of unifying your enemies. Looking at it now after the events of the last half of the twentieth century, not least the collapse of the Soviet Empire, it appears even more unlikely.

My move to London also meant that I was now a regular participant in the League's idiosyncratic demonstrations. In the Autumn of 1956 these were particularly concerned with Britain's 'scuttle from Suez' and the part played by American pressure in forcing the departure of the British and French forces when they were on the point of victory.

The League campaign started in August. *Candour* reported:

"After bluffing his way with a portable amplifier into the entrance hall of Lancaster House on the final day of the Suez Conference, Mr John Bean broadcast a message to the delegates on behalf of the League of Empire Loyalists. The full message was to have been:

" 'Delegates to the Suez Conference! Your numbers are incomplete. Where is Peru? Where is San Salvador? Where is the mighty voice of Tristan de Cunha? Without their authority, how can you help Eden to sell out British and French interests in Suez?

" 'Eden has already sold out British interests in Abadan and French interests in Indo-China to international bankers and Communists.'

"Before Mr Bean could complete the League's message, police converged upon him and provided him with a friendly escort from the premises."

There were more demonstrations after the scuttle from Suez and the Soviet suppression of the Hungarian uprising. The main League turnout was for a mass rally of Young Conservatives at the Royal Festival Hall, addressed by Prime Minister Eden.

Rosine de Bouneville had infiltrated backstage and managed to walk straight onto the platform whilst Eden was speaking.

"The League of Empire Loyalists declares that you are acting not in British interests, but in United Nations internationalist interests," she told the Prime Minister.

As I had little difficulty in passing for a 'Young' Conservative, in those days, I had managed to get up in a box overlooking the stage where I barricaded myself in with the chairs. It took some time for the stewards to reach me and then finally eject me by pushing me down the main stairs. This gave time beforehand to get out several League slogans on Suez, plus:" Bulganin and Kruschev, Butchers of the Hungarians, were Eden's honoured guests. Join the League of Empire Loyalists and fight for British honour!"

This was one of many demonstrations I went on in company with the intrepid Rosine. For the publicity gained, our most outstanding 'battle honour' was the pandemonium the two of us caused at the final day of the October 1957 Tory Party Conference in Brighton.

Lord Hailsham had brought the morning session to an end by presenting the chair woman (the chair, if you wish) with a bell. As he held it above his head and rang it he declared that it tolled for the Labour Party.

At the side of the hall, behind a long curtain, was a technicians' platform, which contained no tinkling hand bell but a truly majestic clapper affair with a voice resonant enough to awaken the dead.

No sooner had Harold Macmillan started his speech at the mass rally in the afternoon session than Rosine ensured that the great bell behind the curtain began to boom. Macmillan, disconcerted, stopped speaking. Half the audience stood up, looking towards the curtained platform. Then from the side of the platform my voice came through a portable amplifier.

"The Empire Loyalists toll the bell for the Conservative Party. We toll the bell for the Party that has betrayed our imperial heritage. For the party that scuttled twice from Suez. For the party that scuttled from Malaya, Ghana, the Sudan."

I cannot recall getting much else over. By this time stewards were frantically beating the curtains with chairs and had managed to haul Rosine the bell-ringer out by her leg. Perhaps understandably, the stewards were very annoyed and Rosine as well as myself was punched and kicked and then thrown down the stairs. We had bluffed our way in around ten o'clock that morning and hid under the stage until 3 pm. I cannot speak for Rosine, but I had a stronger bladder in those days.

For world wide publicity, I suppose the honours went to the reception for the Commonwealth Prime Ministers held at St.James's Palace in July 1957 that my old colleague Phil Burbidge and I managed to gatecrash. We achieved this by hiring a black official looking Daimler to arrive in, and then button-holing an official delegate about to make his entry and walking in with him in deep conversation whilst he showed his pass. The doorkeepers assumed that Phil and I were part of his staff.

Phil went to one reception room and I to another, where we made our usual LEL speeches. I believe we called for Empire and Commonwealth unity in opposition to the 'Common Market sell out'.

* * * * *

In February 1957 there was a by-election in North Lewisham. Leslie Greene was chosen as the Empire Loyalists' candidate. If her election meetings, and particularly those where she appeared with the mainstream party candidates, had been televised, then her superior intelligence and honest demeanour would have probably made her the victor.

Most national press journalists covering the by-election were impressed by her performance.

Randolph Churchill wrote in the *Evening Standard* these obviously sincere passages:

"I spent yesterday afternoon and evening in North Lewisham and talked with the three candidates and their agents. Incomparably the best candidate and the one who would make the best Member of Parliament is thirty-one-year-old Miss Leslie Greene, the Independent Loyalist ... I don't like women taking part in politics, and I don't like what the late Mr Damon Runyon called 'gabby dolls'. Miss Leslie Greene is a very talkative lady, but if I had a vote in North Lewisham on Thursday, she would get it. Her warmth, her knowledge, her simple minded faith in Britain, her easy dominion over language, her generally adult minded attitude to life and politics captivated me."

Members and new supporters turned up from all over the country to help her. From retirement in Suffolk came a man from the Mosley past, Jock Houston, who was put up at my house. He had been a leading populist orator for the BUF before the war. He gave me many tips on open air oratory, and also on the conquest of women of all political viewpoints and none, which was another sphere of his pre-war activities. Needless to say, his name did not appear in *Candour* in the lengthy list of people who were thanked for their help.

Among the new young people who turned up to help in the by-election was a twenty-year-old John Tyndall. He was put in my charge.

I was in my element at North Lewisham. This is what I preferred doing to popping out of boxes at Tory Party meetings. However, the experience soon confirmed my growing belief that the League's policies, no matter how patriotic and firm on the need to stop immigration (just becoming a problem in Lewisham), were perceived as being out of touch by the bulk of the electorate. In spite of an intense campaign, with considerable doorstop canvassing, this was confirmed in the result.

The Labour candidate won with 18,516, followed by the Conservative with 17,406, and Leslie Greene with 1,487.

I received my 'mention in despatches' in A.K.'s description in *Candour* of how the campaign was fought:

"John Bean, secretary of the London Branch of the League, joined Phil (Burbidge) every afternoon and worked on canvassing until the time came for him to take charge of open air meetings and to tour the streets in a loud-speaker van. John excelled in this kind of work, having a keen sense of humour, which our opponents found devastating."

A.K. was no stranger to excessive hyperbole. My sense of humour did not exactly 'devastate' our more militant opponents, but had them confused and thereby reduced the chance of having the meeting completely wrecked.

It was an incident in the autumn of that year that led me to make up my mind to leave Chesterton's Empire Loyalists.

In a BBC TV programme Malcolm Muggeridge was less than complimentary towards the Queen. What it was that incurred the wrath of Chesterton and the more dedicated monarchists escapes my memory. The League's view was that "a people who refuse to protect their Sovereign Liege, or to defend the Crown, which is the symbol of their own distinctive history, tradition and continuity, have ceased to be a nation and become a rabble."

I had no quarrel with this, nor do I today.

It was planned that Phil Burbidge and I should go to Muggeridge's home in Robertsbridge, Sussex, and when he answered the door we were to throw a bag of soot at him "We besmirch you for besmirching the name of Her Majesty the Queen" was the line we were supposed to take.

I had asked my new young apprentice, John Tyndall, to accompany me on this expedition, but he refused to go.

Fortunately, as far as I was concerned, when Phil and I finally located Malcolm Muggeridge's home the place was deserted.

Subsequently I made it clear that I would not go on a return visit. A.K. accepted my point that we should respect the privacy of a person's home, even if we disagreed politically with that person - "An Englishman's home is his castle," etc. However, he glowered and pursed his lip when I said the people would think it was just an over-reaction and would dismiss us as cranks. I added: "I would rather be called a Fascist bastard than a crank."

Reluctant to give up the substance of the League for the shadow of any new embryo nationalist movement, I spent the rest of the year contemplating my political objectives. Two days after Christmas I wrote to A.K. explaining why I had been non-active for two months and why I thought the League had a limited future.

"When I first approached the League, I thought: here is a fine patriotic movement that is attempting the impossible. Its whole tone was directed towards the 'thinkers' and intellectuals, quasi and otherwise, that one finds in the upper middle class ranks of Conservative voters. Yet these people would not do anything actively to 'Stop the Rot' (a League slogan) because they had too much to lose by associating themselves with something that was rather 'non-U'.

"... However, it was putting up a fight against the power of international finance capitalism, one world, one racism, and denigration of this country. If I joined, I thought, then I would do my best to see that more of our propaganda was directed towards those who stood to lose most: the working people."

I then acknowledged that Chesterton had given me a fair amount of freedom with street meetings, tours of market towns and production of *The Loyalist* to try and popularise the cause. I also emphasised another difference of opinion I had with the League, which was our attitude to Europe:

"Our Nationalism must transcend the narrow and outdated nineteenth century Nationalism that says 'Wogs begin at Calais' ... But our Nationalism must halt at Mosley's utopian European Nationalism of 'Europe a Nation' ... By political, economic and military pacts and treaties between sovereign states, Western Europe must present a unified front to our common enemies: Asiatic Communism and American finance capitalism ...

"... I am exploring the ground for the formation of a Nationalist Movement with the intention of contesting for power under its own name. I fully appreciate (*that was very presumptuous!*) the magnitude of this task."

I concluded by saying that I wished to remain a member of the LEL and assured Chesterton that I would continue to repay his loan. I also returned a cheque for £10 that he had sent to my wife and me as a Christmas present.

Surprisingly, in his reply Chesterton agreed with many of my criticisms.

"... It so happens that except for my distrust and detestation of the bureaucracy, I stand quite as far left as you do and have nothing in common with the 'true blues', who in fact are so untrue."

Chesterton knew how to play on my ego and kept me within his orbit for another three months.

The break finally came in April 1958 when I left in company with John Tyndall and several South and East London LEL members to form the National Labour Party. The choice of title was mine and was designed to appeal to patriotic minded people, and particularly those concerned over the effects of immigration, who had traditionally voted Labour. Tyndall was not happy with the title, but gave it his support. Surprisingly, Andrew Fountaine, with whom I had stayed in touch, was quite enthusiastic. As he had now sorted out his divorce he said he would consider accepting the figurehead role of President of the NLP, even though we had still not met. Chesterton made one final effort to woo me back into the fold. In a letter to me he said:

"I do not feel any deep conviction that the League, unless it has a big break, will get very far, but I do think that you are in danger of abandoning the substance for the shadow. The result could well be years of effort without making the slightest impact on the public mind. The loss of you would be grievous to us, and fragmentation of effort might be annoying, but quite honestly I think that you are going out into the wilderness and that nothing more will be heard of you in any serious political connotation.

"... Of course I would not wish to hide from you my recognition of your penchant for associating with people of markedly eccentric views whose membership of any movement would infallibly damn it."

In the event this turned out to be a portentous observation. Nevertheless, Chesterton ignored the fact that I had met most of the eccentrics on League activities where he too had tried to use them.

Although in my reply I acknowledged A.K.'s role as a prophet and soothsayer and expressed the wish that as the League was non-party we could co-operate on specific issues, I was surprised at the venom in his *Candour* articles condemning my action.

One complete distortion of the truth, which has now become established as fact by being quoted by most authors who have since written about the history of the extreme right, is that I stole, or attempted to steal, a list of LEL members from Chesterton's office. LEL members' names and addresses that came into my possession were primarily those who subscribed to my duplicated sheet, *The Loyalist*. There were others who had written to me personally over the previous two years and some, including R.K. Jeffery (the League's main benefactor) whose addresses I had written or seen printed on envelopes so many times on official League business that I had memorised them.

These were the people to whom we sent our National Labour Party literature. It would have been a waste of a stamp to send it to the retired Brigadiers, Colonial administrators and various members of the lower orders of the nobility that made up the rest of the League's membership.

Martyrs of Notting Hill was the front page headline of the first issue of *Combat*, published in the autumn of 1958 as the 'Official Organ of The National Labour Party'.

The line I had taken, as editor, was that the mainstream politicians and media had looked for scapegoats to blame for the seven September nights of violence. They first tried the Ku Klux Klan. But few could take such a bizarre movement seriously. They tried Mosley's Union Movement and then the National Labour Party, although neither movement had held meetings in the area prior to the riots. The answer they eventually found was to blame the 'Teds', and nine of their number, all aged around seventeen, were sent to prison for four years.

"We are the first to agree that the action of the young West Londoners - ever impetuous-youth was wrong ... Furthermore, the tragedy of those September nights was that many of the Negros attacked were harmless, law abiding people - nonetheless, still not welcomed as residents in this white country. As a landlord of a Notting Hill pub told one of our reporters, the coloured brothel keepers and drug pedlars disappeared from the district for a week.

We also made the point that:

"... the first reports that appeared of the rioting, particularly in the *Daily Telegraph*, gave something like a true account of what was happening. The razor slashing and hatchet wielding of Negros did at least receive nearly as much publicity as the bottle throwing of white hooligans. Then the story changed. God! The people were seeing through the lies of a decade. It must be stopped! Had the vast propaganda machines turned in vain?"

The NLP organised a petition, which received the signatures of quite a few West Indians amongst several thousand whites, calling for a reduction in the prison sentences. Two or three street corner meetings were also held in the area, at one of which Andrew Fountaine spoke wearing a bowler hat.

Audiences were nothing spectacular and I cannot recall us gaining more than two new members. Union Movement held one or two meetings with similar results.

The NLP had been formed in May, and a month later I was at last able to meet Andrew Fountaine, whom I hoped to persuade to become its President. I took the train one Saturday morning to King's Lynn, where Fountaine was waiting to pick me up in his Mercedes sports car. He was taller than I expected at six foot one and with his dark hair, brown eyes and straight nose he fitted my vision of a Norman knight. His ancestors had arrived with the Norman conquest and had lived in the Swaffam/King's Lynn area ever since. His forehead was rather narrow. Tyndall thought that this explained why Fountaine was usually slow to react mentally to changed circumstances, in spite of his in-depth historical education and general intelligence. Tyndall may have been right.

Andrew greeted me with his typical schoolboyish smile that instantly put you at ease. This, plus his inbred good manners, immediately made you feel welcome. Over lunch at Red Lodge we were joined by his then current lady friend, he having been divorced some twelve months previously. In the two hours or so political discussion that followed, his eccentricity on some issues and his tendency to concentrate on the five per cent where he disagreed with some person or action, rather than the 95 per cent area of agreement, soon became apparent. It was easy to see why he and Chesterton could not get on (and surprising, therefore, that later they were to tolerate each other for nearly two years in the National Front).

He agreed with our approach to "the decent working people" of the towns and cities, particularly using the immigration issue, as the bulk of his class were "bloody useless and would vote for a baboon as long as it was Tory blue." However, he was going to stand as a National Independent in a forthcoming Parliamentary by-election in Norfolk South West and would make his decision on joining us or not after the result.

His mother was an arch-Conservative and was highly displeased at Andrew having left the fold. His father, Admiral

122

Sir Charles Fountaine, had died in 1948 and his mother now lived alone, apart from a handful of servants, in Narford Hall. When the election came the mother had half-a-dozen Conservative posters facing across the road where the face of her son appeared gazing at the Hall from half-a-dozen National Independent posters.

I was shown the Hall after our early afternoon discussion and given a quick tour of the estate. Andrew had great pride in his tree conservation work and his perpetually gnarled hands bore witness to the many he had personally planted. By the time of his death this was around three million.

Over dinner, and two bottles of Chateau Lafite claret, I tried to get him to talk about his war experience, but he would say little other than that he was wounded as a result of a Japanese Kamikaze attack off Japan in 1945 on the aircraft carrier *Indefatigable*, where he was the gunnery officer. He was invalided out of the Navy as a result of his wounds but was denied a pension because it was then discovered he had joined the service by subterfuge. In the thirties he had been unable to follow the family tradition of passing through Dartmouth Naval College because they found he suffered from glandular fever. On the outbreak of the Second World War he managed to get into the Navy by persuading a friend who resembled him to take the medical on his behalf. He rose by his own efforts from Ordinary Seaman to Lieutenant Commander. He saw the flash of the atomic bomb which was dropped - unnecessarily as he thought - on Nagasaki.

Perhaps a good example of his unpredictability in political action lies in the fact that at seventeen he drove an ambulance for the Abyssinians, who were under attack by Mussolini in his attempt in 1936 to expand his African empire. Eighteen months later he was fighting for General Franco's forces in the Spanish Civil War.

Another good example came in 1968, when Fountaine was then vice-Chairman of the National Front. He felt great sympathy for the way the boxer Muhammad Ali was being abused in the United States for opposing the Vietnam war and also racial intermarriage. As this opposition also put pressure on Ali's training facilities, Fountaine wrote to him and said that he could bring his complete training staff to Narford and set up facilities on the estate. The offer was politely declined.

I left my weekend meeting with Andrew Fountaine with a cheque for £25. Contrary to a widely held view, this was one of the few occasions that he was able to donate funds to a political movement. Although the 6,000 acre estate meant he was rich on paper it was all tied up in the family trust. I doubt if his total donations to the NLP, the BNP and the National Front came to much more than £1,000.

I made one trip to help Fountaine in his 1959 election campaign, which was followed by a visit from John Tyndall. Tyndall's bull headedness and well known inability to compromise meant that the two did not take to each other. However, as Tyndall said then and on several occasions since: "John, you just can't dislike the man."

Andrew Fountaine received 780 votes as a National candidate in the SW. Norfolk by-election. True to his word, he then took up the offer to be President of the NLP.

Throughout my forty years of on and off relationship with John Tyndall his honesty and complete lack of deviousness compensates for his stubbornness and outspokenness. It was, therefore, not surprising to learn that one of his ancestors was burnt at the stake as a heretic against the prevailing orthodoxy of his day. This was William Tyndale (1490-1536), the religious reformer and first publisher of the English Bible, who spent much of his life embroiled in the flames of controversy and met his fiery end in the Netherlands at Vilvorde. In the seventeenth century, a branch of the family settled in Ireland. From this branch came Professor John Tyndall (1820-93), physicist, natural philosopher and spare time mountaineer. The present John Tyndall's paternal grandfather was a District Inspector in the Royal Irish Constabulary. Although the family home was then in Co.Waterford, they were strong Unionists, and the grandfather spent much of his life fighting 'the rebels' in both the North and the South.

John Tyndall's parents, like the son, were both born in England. My wife and our young family and I were taken to meet them on several occasions for Sunday tea during 1958-59. It was not long after this that his mother, a particularly charming lady, was widowed.

Our political relationship in the NLP was never plain sailing. My flippant sense of humour and often lack of gravitas with the members would sometimes annoy him. I think he thought there were occasions when they should stand to attention in my presence. My quick temper, which would sometimes lead me into verbally abusing him, did not help either.

At one Sunday lunchtime street corner meeting in St. Matthew's Row, Bethnal Green, I was being heckled non-stop by two Sikhs. The members present just found it amusing, where as I was hoping they would tell the Sikhs to go away. Seeing that the meeting was degenerating into a shambles, my patience lapsed and I leapt off the platform. I ran at the Sikhs and placing a hand on each chest propelled them round the corner with the admonition to *Malem Jow* (Go away). Probably surprised to hear my attempt at Hindi, they did so. John Tyndall laughed. "John," he said, "I admire your courage but that was a bit undignified." He was probably right. But I felt that somebody had to act.

Some of the members and supporters were the epitome of "the salt of the earth." Others you would certainly not take home to meet mother; whilst yet others were on the criminal fringes.

One of the latter, with Rasputin eyes and a hair line that started half an inch above his eyebrows, said that as we grew we would need to call on some hard men to defend us from the reds and the Jews. He knew such men and offered to take me and a few others to meet them in a Dalston pub after one of our meetings.

The 'hard men' turned out to be a minor East End gang, a forerunner of the Krays, led by a Sid Bullen. He and his gang were apparently auxiliaries to 'Italian' Albert Dimes, who fought West End territorial wars in the late forties and early fifties with Jack Como, alias Jack Spot, who was Jewish.

After a few drinks and what passed for pleasantries, Bullen explained what the deal was. In exchange for their help in "sorting anybody out" when we needed it, we would provide some of our more pugilistic supporters when they needed them. I made a few non-committal remarks and said I would have to talk the matter over with some of our other senior members and we would be in touch again through "Rasputin eyes." I felt that an outright "no" might mean we would have some difficulty leaving the pub in one piece. Needless to say, the outcome was a definite "no."

No doubt Chesterton would have said this was another example of my "penchant for mixing with lunatics and criminals".

* * * * *

Colin Jordan had departed from the Empire Loyalists almost a year before I left to found the NLP. He had been the instigator in the formation of a nebulous neo-Nazi minded organisation called The Ring, of which the infamous "Mr G." was a member. Its sole (even soul) activity seemed to be the painting of bridges and viaducts calling for the release of Rudolph Hess. This was not to be confused with the overt Northern Ring which was mainly concerned with the promotion of the culture and history of the North European people, and was non-political. Jordan was to become a member of this body later.

Although both Peter Ling and Dick Tynan gave early support to the NLP, Jordan opposed its formation.

In a letter to me giving his reasons for doing so he said:

"What do you think you are likely to achieve? You can go and stand at street corners and indulge in your speaking and hand out the products of your writing, and you can do it night after night, week after week and month after month, and for all the immense amount of time and trouble that this will cost you ... you will never reach many people anyway. Secondly, of those who do listen to what you have to say and read what you write only a few odd ones will show any response and fewer still will be of the slightest calibre.

126

"Your trouble, John, seems to be that you are still far too much given to democratic ways of thinking, and that you have not yet managed to get the democratic obsession for head counting out of your system."

Nevertheless, it was not many months after writing this that Jordan was resuming his activity in, and then leadership of, the White Defence League, formerly the White Defence Force. Initally, this began to grow in membership, particularly in Birmingham and Coventry, and probably peaked at about 200 members.

Meanwhile NLP membership was slowly growing in London as well as acquiring a scattering of members and supporters in Nottingham, Sheffield and Liverpool. In May 1959 we contested our first council elections in London. Rupert Simpson gained some six per cent of the poll in Tufnell Ward, Islington, and John Walker four per cent in Mile End Ward, Stepney. Elated by these minor successes we applied for permission to hold a public meeting in Trafalgar Square, which was granted. Conscious of our small numbers to support our meeting, I contacted Colin Jordan and invited him to be a speaker and bring as many WDL supporters along as possible.

Surprising though it may seem in the politically correct climate of the end of the twentieth century, the theme of the meeting, proclaimed on a twenty-five-foot long banner, was "Keep Britain White."

Half an hour before the meeting was due to take place more than a thousand people were already waiting. The two hundred or so National Labour supporters and WDL members present asked themselves: "Are the gathering crowds friend or foe? Would the meeting be a fiasco, as the less confident had prophesied?"

The answer came when the "Keep Britain White" banner was hoisted on the plinth of Nelson's column to commence the meeting. From a knot of some two hundred assorted Communists and Left-Wingers (virtually all white) came a howl of rage followed by chants of "No colour bar in Britain."

They were drowned by a louder chant of "Keep Britain White."

I opened the meeting, followed by Colin Jordan and then Andrew Fountaine. Reading through a synopsis of my speech thirty-nine years later (as given in the Autumn 1959 issue of *Combat*) I was pleased to note that the manner in which I stated my opposition to coloured immigration was virtually the same as in my interview for the BBC2 *Windrush* series on the history of immigration shown in May-June 1998.

"We are not race haters. We love race! The National Labour Party is the only party that champions the values of race: African, Asian, as well as European... The true race haters were those who were bent on mongrelising the British people. They, and the old parties who have allowed this situation to arise, are the people we hate, not the coloured people."

The report said that great play was then made of the fact that in four national press polls seventy-five per cent on average had said stop coloured immigration. The chant of "seventy-five per cent" was taken up by large sections of the crowd. The meeting ended peacefully with no arrests being made. The police estimated the crowd at 3,000; we reported it as 5,000.

A second Trafalgar Square meeting was held on 6th September that year. Apart from heckling, it again passed peacefully, as did a Mosley meeting around the same period. Our speakers were Andrew Fountaine, John Tyndall - who by now had become quite a forceful, though rather strident speaker - and myself. I did not ask Colin Jordan again as there seemed little point in providing him with a platform to bolster his own competitive movement, which I knew was now losing Midland members to the new NLP Midlands branch. This was verified in a placatory letter to me from John Tyndall of 20th August following one of our arguments.

"... The most significant things I have to say to you ... concerning the state of affairs in the WDL ... the whole Jordan edifice is collapsing ... Do not be in the least bit surprised if C.J. comes to you shortly with an offer of reconciliation on the terms put forward by us earlier on this year. If you wish to know what the trend of opinion is in WDL circles, I will tell you. It is far more pro-Bean than pro-Jordan. Believe me, your stock has climbed considerably of late. They are beginning to see your point."

I bided my time, knowing that the only asset Jordan could offer was the building in Princedale Road, West London, which was about to be given to him by the widow of Arnold Leese, a virulent pre-war anti-semite. Overtures to her had been made on behalf of the NLP by a third party, but Mrs Leese considered that I "was not Jew wise."

Early in 1959 we were given the facility to hold indoor monthly meetings, including our first AGM, at the Black Horse public house in Kentish Town. The landlord was William, 'Bill', Webster, who was well known in North London for speaking out against immigration. He and his brother Charlie Webster, who also ran a North London pub, were former professional boxers.

Having obtained six per cent of the poll as an independent in a local ward by-election, Bill Webster was keen to stand for the St. Pancras North Parliamentary seat in the forthcoming October General Election. He agreed to stand as an NLP candidate, putting up his own deposit and with the Party funding his election literature. A shop was hired as election committee rooms, with Bill offering to pay the rent, which in the event he failed to do.

He was a passable street corner orator with a rough and ready wit. To those who asked the question: "If a person of immigrant stock is born in this country, surely that makes him British?" Webster would reply: "If a cat has kittens in a kipper box that don't make 'em kippers." At one meeting an African was getting rather irate at Webster's delivery and started jumping up and down. Looking round at the rest of the audience he said: "I feel sorry for you lot if there's ever a food shortage round here. He'll 'ave you in the pot!" He knew it was good for a laugh.

Some authors of articles and books on the extreme right of that period had said that the NLP had given support to Mosley's simultaneous election campaign in Notting Hill. This was not so. We felt that Mosley was attempting to cash in on the anti-immigration campaign that the NLP had started, having previously hinted that it was a side issue. There were some NLP supporters who had a foot in both camps and decided to support the bigger name - Mosley.

We needed all the help we could get in St. Pancras North, with its reputation as a Red stronghold. Hundreds of Bill Webster posters swamped those of the other candidates on the hoardings. Women supporters and elderly males addressed all the election addresses. Thousands of extra leaflets were delivered. For every outdoor meeting of the other parties we held ten. Against the wishes of some of the 'action men' I organised a canvassing team of those supporters who could string more than three sentences together. A mile long cavalcade of marching men and women with flags and banners, seven lorries, a loudspeaker van, and some thirty cars all decked out with "Vote Webster NLP" posters, toured the area on the Saturday before polling day.

As I said to Andrew Fountaine and John Tyndall, the NLP had come a long way in eighteen months from six founder members and £3 4s 6d in the kitty. I was deluding myself. Outside of the area probably not more than two per cent of the British population had heard of us.

Webster polled 1,670 votes, around five per cent of the poll, with the Communist candidate some five hundred votes behind. But the national press publicity went to Mosley with his 2,821 votes, eight per cent, in North Kensington, although he, too, lost his deposit.

The highlight of Bill Webster's election campaign as far as my political life was concerned was the battle of St. Pancras Town Hall. Ten days before the polls the Movement for Colonial Freedom had booked the hall for a meeting to be addressed by Mrs Lena Jeger, the Left-Wing Labour MP for St. Pancras South and Kenneth Robinson, Bill Webster's Labour opponent in St. Pancras North. It was decided we would visit the meeting in force on a heckling foray. At heart I knew it would probably end in violence, but it should make the national press. My supposition was right.

The NLP members arrived in small groups hoping to be admitted. But the stewards had got wind of what was planned and barred admittance. Then Bill Webster with some fifty of his personal followers arrived on the back of two lorries. He had armed some with bags of soot. "That's for the white renegades," he said. And some with bags of flour. "That's for the blacks."

A charge was made at the scores of stewards now guarding the one open door, which I must confess to leading. By weight of numbers and some well aimed fists entry was soon gained to the hall vestibule. Here, fierce fighting with fists and boots ensued as the stewards barred our way into the main hall. One steward had armed himself with a heavy metal ashtray stand and had felled two or three intruders - one minus two teeth - before he was overpowered and hit with the ashtray. In a corner was a young Indian (for some reason I believe he was in fact a Sri Lankan) being punched by a Webster man. He was bleeding profusely from the nose and mouth and looked as if he was about to pass out.

"Leave him alone. He's had enough," I told the Webster man. He did, and changed his attention to another steward.

As I turned away from the young Asian, I was wrestled to the ground by a steward, who then sat on top of me whilst two others started to kick me. Two or three NLP members came diving in to the 'rescue', but ended up in a writhing mass with the stewards, all on top of me. I lay there, covered in soot and flour, gasping for breath and unable to move.

Fortunately for me the Police arrived at this vital moment, like the US Cavalry. Seeing my predicament, they were initially very concerned for my well being. "Are you alright sir? Would you like a check up at the hospital?" After talking to some of the stewards their attitude changed and I was one of the ten NLP members and Webster supporters arrested, including Bill Webster and half his close family.

The objective of making national press publicity was achieved, with three national dailies putting the story on the front page.

131

"Riot at St. Pancras Town Hall. Candidate arrested with Candidate's brother, son and election agent (that was me)" was the headline in the *Daily Express*. On appearance at Clerkenwell Magistrates' Court the following morning, all ten were charged with disturbing the peace. NLP member Gordon Callow and I were remanded on bail for a further hearing: the other eight members and supporters being fined there and then sums of between five and ten pounds.

On the second appearance in court I found that charges of insulting behaviour, threatening behaviour and assault were now being levelled. No doubt this was because eight of the stewards needed hospital treatment. In reply to my questioning, the police doctor stated that the more serious wounds had been caused by fists, and not by boots or the ashtray stand, which the stewards had accused me of using as a weapon.

When it came to his turn to give evidence, the young Asian I had rescued volunteered the statement that I had told the others to leave him alone and, for which I was particularly grateful, that he had not seen me hit anybody. As a result I was found guilty of threatening behaviour but acquitted of the other two charges. Although it was a first offence I was sentenced to one month in prison.

* * * * *

Although I had sat in police station cells for a few hours on several occasions as a result of various political activities, arriving at Brixton Prison was an entirely different experience. I wouldn't be going home in the morning, and in fact not for thirty mornings and nights. What is more I would not be home for our tenth wedding anniversary. As for the children, they were in bed usually by the time I arrived home, so they would probably not even miss me: a supposition that turned out to be correct. And would there still be a job to go to after I got out?

I filed through the showers with the rest of the new arrivals and presented myself to the prison doctor, who proceeded to look down, and up, all our orifices. "Any medical problems?," he asked. "Not that I know of, sir."

Gordon Callow, who had been found guilty of assaulting a steward, hoped he might be able to share a cell with me. As he had previously suffered from tuberculosis the doctor decided that he would have to have a cell to himself. I think Gordon found that, not being a hermit by nature, the disadvantages outweighed the advantages.

As orders were shouted for us to fall in line, still naked, to collect our prison clothing, I could see that this was giving some of the new intake problems. I decided to deal with it by imagining that I was back in the Navy and that all the prison officers were like the navigating officer on the *Bulawayo*; a bit of a zealot.

Brixton Prison was, and still is, for men remanded in custody and awaiting trial, and first offenders over twenty-one who have received a sentence of six months or less. As I sat at a table in F Wing eating a basic, but edible, meal for supper, I looked round at my fellow 'cons' and asked myself: "What am I doing here? I am not a thief, a bank robber, a rapist, nor did I attack old ladies to steal their pensions."

But I knew that this line of self-pity would not get me anywhere. I had played a leading role in a political riot and the law of the land had given me a month inside in consequence. And if it had not been for the evidence of the young Asian I would probably be facing three months. It was not nine months in Landsberg, and I was not Adolf Hitler, so it was not really the opportunity to write my particular *Mein Kampf*. I would relax when I could, crack a few jokes, and hopefully come out refreshed after "doing my porridge."

Following the supper, the new boys were taken off to their cells. Although most cells housed three prisoners, but built in the nineteenth century to house only two, there was only one other occupant in mine. He was a West African. This was to be part of my corrective punishment, I thought. He did not talk much, but when he did it was difficult to follow his form of English. I gathered that he was doing time for stealing car radios.

133

I found it very difficult to sleep. It was not helped by the fact that my companion talked to himself. Whether it was in his sleep or not I do not know. Eventually I dozed off but was awakened by loud breaking of wind as he sat on his chamber pot. Although he put a lid on it, the stench was pretty potent until I eventually drifted off again - probably semi-asphyxiated.

The relief to hear sudden voices, many footsteps and then the jangling of keys as our door was opened around 6.30 am. was indescribable. This was slop-out time, when each man carried out his pot to the lavatories. As on most other nights I had only peed in mine. I soon learnt that a good way of retarding the smell if you had to use it in the night was to light a piece of paper and drop that in your pot before putting the lid on.

Following breakfast - yes, porridge with an almost meat-free sausage and a chunk of bread, my name was called out by a prison officer. This was Mr Knight, our landing officer in F Wing. With Gordon Callow and three other new boys and myself lined up in front of him, he told us: "If you don't give me any trouble I won't give you any." We found he was a man of his word.

"Right, Bean, follow me. I am going to take you to your new little home." This was a great improvement. It was two cells knocked into one and accommodated four prisoners, and was my "little home" for the remaining 29 nights.

My fellow guests were a Wandsworth Borough Council dustman and a Brighton barrow boy, who were both doing three months for not paying maintenance to ex-wives, and a Greek Cypriot (Peter the Greek) who was doing six months for a bout of what we now call 'road rage' when he hit another driver with a starting handle. His story was that he was attacked first and was only defending himself. Living with him for a month gave a good insight into his character, and I was inclined to believe him. He was also more intelligent than the other two and, despite his accent, more literate in English language than they were.

I was given two regular jobs. The first was to be responsible for handing out razor blades to remand prisoners in the ablutions block in the morning and, most important, collecting them afterwards. This did have its problems with some of those on remand who were naturally violent. More than once my polite request: "Can I have the blade back, please?" would be met with the reply: "How d'yer want it? In yer right f.....g cheek, or yer left?" I would try to laugh casually, as if it was just a joke, and say: "Well, I have to do this bloody job, mate." It always worked.

Another remand, whom everybody referred to as Raffles, was a Mayfair cat burglar. A good looking man, he was even equipped with a David Niven moustache, which he would trim neatly every morning with my razor blade. Very well read, he liked to quote from Edgar Alan Poe's *The Raven* and, probably to impress me, pose as something of a philosopher with a few quotes from Descartes and Nietzsche. Winking at me and looking at his fellow remands, he would say: "As old Neetsh put it, they're all flies in the market place, and they all have a vote the same as you my old sport. So you are wasting your time."

My other job was to help collect the food from the kitchen and then dish it out to my fellow cons. This had potential problems with those prisoners who would glare at you and, in a whisper, so that the nearby prison officer could not hear, ask for a larger portion. I just looked at their plate and pretended I did not hear.

One lunchtime, as two men in the queue got nearer I could hear that they were talking about Mosley, and it sounded as if they were supportive. "Are you Mosley supporters?" I asked.

"What if we are?" said the nearest, challengingly.

"Good for you," I replied. "I am National Labour Party. I got nicked at the St. Pancras Town Hall do. Here you are, have some more duff."

I gave them both an extra helping of spotted dick. Thus largesse with Her Majesty's suet pudding helped to cement a radical right friendship, albeit a temporary one.

On the half hour's exercise every day, which entailed walking round the prison yard in a circle, I would be joined by Gordon

Callow. Then the keener of the Mosley supporters would join us, and after a while a Folk Deutsch, whose parents had been born in Poland but had to leave in a hurry in 1945. Most cons' conversations would be centred on sex, food and the various jobs they had pulled off. For us it was about sex, food and politics.

One day, to liven up our circular walking, we decided to march. And to march we needed a song. So, to the tune of *Die Farne Hoch* (the Nazi anthem), we sang the old Mosley Blackshirt song: "Comrades the voices of the dead battalions, of those who fell to make Great Britain Great ..." The Folk Deutsch chap sang in the original German.

Liberal readers may think that this confirms their worst suspicions, but we did it partly as a joke, partly as our protest that we considered ourselves political prisoners and not criminals, and partly to relieve our boredom. After a few days of this, word must have come down from above. The Senior Prison Officer in charge of the exercise yard, whom we called Tojo because of his physical similarity to the late Japanese war leader, called us four over and said: "Alright you Nazi nutters, we don't want any more of the funny songs and your marching. You walk like everybody else."

Two inmates on our landing who did not walk like everybody else were two homosexuals (the word 'gay' then still meant 'full of mirth'). One was white and the other a light brown West Indian with a great sense of humour and who out-camped the white. At slop-out time he would mince along the landing above us, wearing his towel like a sarong, waving at all the cons below and blowing kisses to the screws. To roars from the cons of "give us a wiggle chocolate bum," he would gyrate his hips and blow more kisses.

Thus this cameo floor show would play its part in helping to pass the day. At 6.30 pm after supper we would be 'banged up' in our cells for the next twelve hours. Peter the Greek and I were lucky. Around 8.30 pm we would be let out by a prison officer to go on the cocoa round. He was on one round, I was on another. This brought regular bonuses when we called on the remands. The prison officer would open the cell door and I would ladle out a mugful of cocoa for those who wanted it. As the remands could have food, sweets and cigarettes sent in from outside, the more friendly types, particularly 'Raffles', would drop a cigarette, or a sweet, or an orange surreptitiously in your hand. The prison officer knew what was going on but turned a blind eye to our perks.

Being in a cell to himself, Gordon Callow was always eager to see me on the cocoa round. On one evening call he was holding himself up by gripping the bars of the cell window so he could see out. Assuring Mr Knight that he was not trying to do a runner he told us he was looking for the phantom female flasher. This was alleged to be either a prison officer's wife or daughter, who would stand in the nude at the window of their nearby quarters facing Callow's side of F Wing. He said he never did see her and reckoned it was a wind-up by some of the cons.

Returning to our cells Peter the Greek and I would pass some of our perks over to the other two, but kept any cigarettes for ourselves. To light them, as matches were in short supply, we had mastered the art of splitting one match into four with a razor blade. It meant that you had to keep your thumb behind the head as you struck it and remove it quickly at the point of ignition. I had a dead area on my thumb for weeks afterwards.

Any serious reading with books from the prison library during the long evenings in the cell was almost impossible, due to the constant babble from my three colleagues. Prior to the cocoa round Peter and I would do some exercises, usually press-ups followed by pull ups by our finger tips on the I-beam that had been put in the ceiling when the two cells were knocked into one.

The other two found this amusing but did not participate. We usually managed to obtain a couple of newspapers from the remands, a day or two old. Mostly it would be the *Daily Mirror* or the *Sketch*, but occasionally I would go up market with a *Telegraph* from 'Raffles'.

It was into my second week in the cell when the Brighton barrow boy came up for release. He was replaced by one of the world's unfortunates, a quiet simple soul of around fifty who had left his native Norfolk to work as a barman in a London Club. He said that he had been in the habit of borrowing £10 from the till on a Tuesday and paying it back when he got paid on a Friday. A spot check on a Wednesday had revealed that the till was £10 light, and the result was that he got two months inside. To complete his tale of woe he said that his mother had been drowned in the great floods of 1953 that inundated the Norfolk coast. He would usually cheer up when I regaled him with the tale of the four and twenty virgins who came down from Inverness, followed by a few filthy limericks. Unfortunately, he would then repeat four or five times, every night, in his Norfolk accent:

"There was a young boy of North Walsham
Who took out his bollocks to wash 'em.
His mother said 'Jack, if you don't put 'em back
I shall tread on the buggers and squash 'em'."

* * * * *

It was drizzling with rain that Wednesday November morning as I stepped through the prison gate into Jebb Avenue, Brixton. In my pocket was the bus fare to Thornton Heath that I had been given, plus two shillings for a breakfast. The air was sweet after the noisome smell of a prison cell for four. And no more slopping out. That, for me, was the hardest part of prison.

It had not shaken my resolve to continue radical right political action: on the contrary. As eager as I was to get home and see my wife and children, my mind was going over the decision I had reached in prison. For any further progress to be made, we must have a proper HQ, even if it meant combining forces with Colin Jordan, who now had the building at 74 Princedale Road. With Andrew Fountaine's backing and our greater membership we should be able to control his more extreme utterances.

CHAPTER 7
'HOLD ON TO YOUR COBBLERS'

Whilst I had been inside, NLP members Carl Harley and Terry Savage had been successful in finding us an 'office' to rent. It was a basement below a shoe mender's shop in City Road, North London. Led by my wife, members had cleaned out the twenty years of dirt and made it quite presentable. We were there two months before Left wing pressure on the landlords forced us to quit.

Another problem was that Bill Webster, disappointed with his vote at the General Election, decided to withdraw his support from the NLP and join Mosley. He also refused to pay a number of election bills which he had promised to cover. All bills were eventually paid from the NLP's dwindling funds but it meant that, as his election agent, I was late in making a return of election expenses and incurred a £50 fine and was debarred from being an election agent for several years.

With no premises and debts exceeding our assets, in January 1960 I had a private meeting with Colin Jordan at 74 Princedale Road to explore "future co-operation."

It soon became clear that his White Defence League was of secondary interest to his connections with the Northern League and his desire to take that body over so that it would become a "pan-Nordic" organisation actively campaigning throughout North West Europe, the United States and the old British Dominions to "preserve the race and culture of the Nordic peoples." I had no great problem with this but thought then, and even more so now, that we could not afford to be selective and should concentrate on trying to preserve all European cultures. As Jordan was so keen on his "pan-Nordic" organisation, I thought this could be used to my advantage. I suggested that in any new joint movement we should have an external department which he should head. I would be the National Organiser of the UK party and he the Deputy National Organiser. Jordan politely pointed out that with Andrew Fountaine as the President backing me up and I retaining the editorship of *Combat*. I would have all the power, which was not a fair exchange for his 'dowry' of the building. I said I would go away and talk to Andrew Fountaine about the alternative of him being the National Organiser and I being the Deputy.

Whilst these negotiations were going on I received a letter from John Tyndall resigning from the NLP. Essentially it was down to his intolerance of all aspects of democracy at that period in his youth, coupled with the firm belief that only he knew the full answer to the problems facing our race and nation. This is borne out by the following extracts from his letter.

"... Some months ago I began to sense that your latent Liberal tendencies were finding a sympathetic ear among some members of the movement. These people were giving you just the kind of moral support you needed to justify them.

"The present position has utterly vindicated my belief. I feel that it would be carrying modesty to the extreme to admit that I had anything to learn, politically speaking, from these Liberal agitators, and I quite frankly admit to times when I have felt better judgement than yourself on certain issues.

"This, in brief, is my accusation against you, John: I indict you for your failure to maintain firm leadership and discipline in the ranks of the movement you have created, and for succumbing to the temptation always hovering before the politician to compromise yourself for the purpose of securing the agreement of the mob. I do not interpret this as cowardice in the strict sense of the word, because I have had ample enough proof that that is the last accusation one could make towards you. Rather, I think that you have made a psychological blunder of the first magnitude by believing that the kind of people with whom you are dealing have any real regard for the spirit of conciliation. They have not.

"But of course in face of all this criticism you will claim, "but we have to attract members!" Yes, John, but let's face it, have we attracted them? Can we honestly claim that the present two hundred or so after nearly two years existence is anything to shout about? I personally do not think so. Even if that two hundred or so was a tight, disciplined body-all hundred percenters it would not be much. But when they exist as they do, as a happy-go-lucky club such as I am forced to say the NLP is, then I seriously doubt that they present any real threat to the old order."

In retrospect Tyndall was able to put his finger on my principal weakness in my politically active days: lapses at critical moments in giving firm leadership. But it would appear that it has taken him his forty years of political struggle since then to appreciate that, if you are trying to seek political influence through the ballot box, then you must have a democratic movement that tolerates and utilises all types of people. It would appear to me that his present British National Party is not that dissimilar in its approach to the National Labour Party of 1960.

In balance I was sorry to see him go. Apart from Andrew Fountaine and myself, he was the only other public speaker in the movement, even if his delivery was rather dour. He also had more intellect than Andrew, although he lacked Andrew's extensive historical knowledge at that time. The down-side was his extremism, including sometimes openly expressed support for aspects of Nazi Germany. This had already led to several arguments when I deleted such references in his articles for *Combat*.

An advantage of Tyndall's departure was that, if I merged forces with Jordan, he would no longer have a fellow extremist as an ally. I was sufficiently confident (perhaps conceited would be a better word) to think that I would be able to control Jordan, particularly as I knew I could count on Andrew Fountaine to back me.

This was without doubt the biggest political mistake I made. Within three months of the merger John Tyndall was back in the movement supporting Colin Jordan, as was Peter Ling. It is surprising that it lasted as long as two years before I led the successful campaign for their expulsion.

The National Labour Party and the White Defence League amalgamated on February 24th 1960 to form the British National Party. Jordan fancied called the movement The Racial Nationalist Party, but gave in to the title favoured by all NLP National

Council members. He was the National Organiser and I his deputy, retaining the editorship of *Combat*, which was to be the BNP's official organ. Andrew Fountaine was the President, with Mrs Leese, the owner of the building in Princedale Road, appointed as Vice President.

For the first few months there was a good spirit of solidarity within the BNP, with membership doubling that of the former NLP. Branches were formed in East, North, West and South East London, Birmingham, Nottingham, Liverpool, Blackburn, Sheffield and Leeds, even if some of these branches only had half a dozen active members.

It was also the time of Sharpeville – termed a 'massacre' by the liberal-left and a 'riot' by the radical-right. This led to left wing movements in Britain organising a boycott of South African goods, which turned out to be a fiasco, and numerous meetings, including Trafalgar Square, which were better supported by liberal-left activists.

The biggest meeting was in Trafalgar Square on Sunday February 28th, with the BNP not yet a week old. BNP members turned up with posters and leaflets proclaiming "Stand by White South Africa," whilst a BNP loudspeaker van toured round the Square with a similar message. Also in attendance were many Mosley supporters and Sir Oswald in person, with Bill Webster from St.Pancras North standing by his side (see front cover photograph). BNP and Mosley's Union Movement members were soon forced to become allies for the day, as fierce fighting took place after members of the anti-fascist Jewish 43 Group pointed out known right-wingers to the meeting stewards. Skirmishing continued all the way down Whitehall and then Victoria Street as Mosley led his men back to their HQ at Vauxhall Bridge Road.

Mosley dominated the press and TV coverage of the event, but the BNP was also mentioned. We felt quite satisfied at the publicity gained within our first week. However, it led to a bitter attack upon the BNP, and me personally, by Jeffrey Hamm, Mosley's loyal lieutenant, in their paper *Union*. The message was clear: there was to be no co-operation among the radical right as far as they were concerned.

At a heckling foray at a Boycott meeting at Hampstead Town Hall, Colin Jordan was again to show that, whatever his faults, it did not include a lack of physical courage. He was hit on the head with a starting handle by the car driver of one of the speakers (the South African Solly Sachs) and knocked unconscious. Jordan was detained in hospital with a wound requiring six stitches. No charge was ever made against the perpetrator of the assault.

In the following months Jordan would usually be present at any heckling offensives against left wing and mainstream politicians (designed to get publicity) but would not be present at our own street meetings or placard demonstrations. Much of his time was spent on the 'External Department' where he was busy building up contacts with European, American and Australian groups that ranged from the purely cultural, to radical right and to others that were neo-Nazi. This preoccupation with 'white world solidarity' was a dominant theme at the BNP's first Trafalgar Square meeting held on May 29th. His secondary theme was an attack on 'Jewish finance', which led to the only strong heckling of the meeting. I ignored it in my speech and so did Andrew Fountaine.

In hindsight this was the time when Fountaine and I should have acted, particularly as we would have had the support of a majority of senior members. We did not, saying it was just one of Jordan's things which we will eventually talk him out of. What is worse I now see that I began to go along with some aspects of what Jordan was saying and started writing in *Combat* articles about 'Jewish dominated International Finance', reports with headings such as 'Jewish violence' in Leeds, North London or elsewhere. This even got as far as an article, under my name, condemning Israel for its capture of Eichmann in Argentina in that it violated Argentina's sovereignty. At least it had the saving grace of ending with: "Neither *Combat* nor the British National Party wishes to condone any atrocities that may have been perpetrated against the Jews."

143

I can remember Jordan saying with a smile: "What did you have to put that bit in for?"

One of our venues at that time for Saturday afternoon street meetings was near to Shepherd's Bush tube station. It was here that I felt another side of my emotive behaviour: fear.

I was on our portable platform speaking to a crowd of twenty or thirty, and with five other members present selling *Combat*. There was some occasional heckling, which we always welcomed as it helped to draw a crowd. The crowd was then joined by four Irish working men who had obviously been spending their lunchtime downing a few pints of the black stuff. They soon made it clear that they objected to my call for the need to stop immigration, and were deaf to my argument that it did not include fellow North Europeans whose Celtic, Viking and Norman blood also ran in the veins of those of us born in England.

With cries of "Remember Cromwell and the Black and Tans, you f......g bastards," they rushed the platform. A large fist hit me full on the side of the face, and I felt a tooth loosen. I fell to the ground with the collapsed platform on top of me. As an Irish Navvy's boot went into my ribs I lost all desire to discuss the kindred racial antecedents of Irish and English. I wanted to get away.

I ran round the corner. But I had not made more than thirty yards when I realised that the last thing I saw was our five members standing there trying to fight off the Irishmen. I ran back again nearly as fast as I went. Two policemen had arrived and had brought an end to Anglo-Irish hostilities. I reassembled the platform and continued the meeting, speaking with a lisp from my swelling mouth. Fortunately, after another ten minutes, during which our members managed to sell a dozen or so papers to the expanded crowd, the police stopped the meeting.

I never knew whether the members noticed the quick departure of their deputy leader, for nobody ever mentioned it. Perhaps they allowed for the fact that at least I came back.

Regular meetings were still held in St.Matthew's Row, Bethnal Green, and were an outlet for paper sales. Deptford in

South London was also becoming a good meeting area, with BNP candidates picking up ten per cent of the poll in local elections. The Nags Head in North London's Holloway Road was always a lively pitch on a Saturday afternoon, as the BNP had commandeered it from the local Communists. As well as being a regular speaker at all these London sites, I also addressed public meetings in Birmingham, Southampton and Liverpool. I cannot recall Jordan speaking at any London street meeting, although he did like to go to Leeds, where the strong local Jewish population was showing particular hostility.

The liveliest meeting place of all was at Earls Court on a Wednesday night. By mid-summer of 1961 it was attracting crowds of up to four hundred strong, with fighting frequently breaking out as Communists and Liberal-Left students tried to break up the meetings. I recall that John Tyndall particularly liked the headline of the *West London Observer*: "A Melee of Boots and Flying Fists at British National Party Meeting."

A regular heckler was a local journalist called Christopher Farman. Writing in the *Guardian* in the mid-eighties he reminisced about the various political meetings held at Earls Court in the sixties, with Communists one night, Mosley's Union Movement another night. "But Wednesday nights," he wrote, "that was when you had to hold on to your balls! That was BNP night." Neither then, nor on reflection, could I dislike him. Surrounded by his own coterie of supporters he would reserve his main heckling for me. As I mounted the platform after the opening speaker, a typical comment from him would be:

"Ah, here comes Siegfried, the Superman, who will try and kid us he has a brain."

"Well, it's better than having half a brain, Brunhilde," would be my reply, or something looking equally inane in cold print, but fitting to street corner rhetoric.

On another occasion he made a telling point when, pointing to one of our members of rather unprepossessing appearance, he yelled out: "How can you talk about Keep Britain White when one of your supporters here, this untermenschen, hasn't seen soap or water for a year!"

This brought a howl of laughter from much of the audience, not least a West Indian bus conductor standing on the corner and enjoying himself. A few minutes later there was a rush to the platform by some of the more militant opponents, who were then fought off by the BNP members. In this skirmish, Farman received a kicking from our diminutive and unwashed member.

"That's for calling me an 'unmention'," he said.

In May 1961 Jordan's work in the BNP External Department and his Northern European Ring bore fruit. A 'Northern European' camp was held on part of Andrew Fountaine's estate near Swaffam in Norfolk. Delegates arrived from the American National States Rights Party, and from Sweden, Germany, Austria, France and Italy. According to the national press at that time, some twenty others were either stopped at the English ports or prevented from leaving their own countries.

It was hyped up in the media as some sinister rally of neo-Nazis, but in reality it was just a five day holiday break for most of us, some fifty in all, with Jordan and a few of the overseas people taking themselves very seriously.

The official opening ceremony was the lighting of a wooden sunwheel, an ancient North European emblem and also the badge of Jordan's BNP. A photo dutifully appeared in *Combat*. But no report of Andrew Fountaine's short speech of welcome was given. In essence, this was that he hoped we would all enjoy our brief return to our roots and to get away from the influence of the Welfare State "that governs our lives from the cradle to the grave; from the erection to the resurrection." This was classic Fountainism and was greeted with mirth by most of the UK members present, although not Mr Jordan.

There was a torchlight procession, led by Jordan's newly formed Spearhead, whose original function was to steward meetings and lead marches. They, with some of the overseas people, were keen participants in the programme of lectures on the policy and history of the various radical right groups. Others, who tended to gravitate around me, were keener (as was Tyndall) on the physical exercise of hiking, swimming, boxing and football. We were also the keenest to get down to the local pub. Rupert Simpson, BNP North London organiser, called our group "The Beerhead," as distinct from Jordan and Tyndall's Spearhead.

On our return from one pub visit, full of alcoholic enthusiasm, we devised a new game of "storming the red platform." This was picked up by some journalists and writers of various books on the origins of the National Front as an indication of our intent to form a revolutionary fighting force. It was nothing of the sort. It was really the Beerhead showing the Spearhead that they could be just as effective in defending a platform without dressing up in quasi uniforms.

During that summer the Spearhead, all dressed in white shirts and dark ties, and including four or five drummers, led five marches in London and one in Birmingham. Jordan and Tyndall made sure that the ties did not match so that the Spearhead members did not infringe the Public Order Act in regard to wearing political uniforms. One of the most effective marches was a torchlight march to New Cross, then in the former London Borough of Deptford, from Peckham. Up to fifty members of the public joined in en route (see front cover photograph).

At this period concern started to be expressed to me by several senior members over new trends in the Spearhead. They were turning up for 'ideological training' meetings at Princedale Road dressed in grey shirts, Sam Brown belts and jackboots. The next step involved visits to a virtually deserted area near Wrotham in Kent that had been a small wartime military camp. Here, Spearhead members in full regalia would practice marching and unarmed combat and receive further ideological training, which bore more resemblance to the views of the Third Reich than the original BNP.

Initially I had tried to ignore the Spearhead, perhaps hoping that it would fold up. Then Jordan said that even if my other duties meant that I had no time to participate in the Spearhead, I should at least give it some acknowledgement. He made his case in a typically lengthy letter in the manner of the headmaster

147

going out of his way to explain a point to a favoured pupil whom he felt was letting him down.

At the same time Senior members such as Carl Harley and Terry Savage of the HQ Propaganda Production Unit, Rupert Simpson, North London Organiser, and Ken Merritt, Deptford Branch Organiser, were urging me to take action on the danger presented by the Spearhead of not only infringing the Public Order Act on uniforms but giving the public the impression that we were aping Mosley's pre-war Blackshirts. This was why the Public Order Act was on the statute books!

I decided that the first thing I must do was to attend the next Spearhead visit to Wrotham. This would be July 1961.

Making sure I was dressed in casual clothes I rendezvoued with Ken Merritt at New Cross Gate station, where we were to be picked up by Tyndall, Jordan and others in the party's Landrover. Ken, who was also my unofficial minder, was wearing a sombrero and open-toe sandals. Tyndall and Jordan were not amused. Arriving at Wrotham, we indulged in some basic keep fit exercises and a glorified game of tag, in which the object was to try and catch Peter Ling, a powerful runner. Nobody did, although I got near enough for a few seconds to breathe down his neck before he pulled away.

I believe that it was immediately after this effort, when I was sitting down regaining my breath, that I spotted two men observing us from one of the derelict wartime huts. One of them had a camera. The other I recognised as a Special Branch officer whom I had seen on a few occasions observing our Bethnal Green street meetings. I waved to them and shouted "Good afternoon." They did not return my greeting but moved away quickly.

Jordan, and to a lesser extent Tyndall, thought that I was imagining things. After searching the now deserted huts they decided to continue with the afternoon's programme. I said I would observe, but not participate. Ken Merritt participated and excelled in the unarmed combat, but contrived to be always out of step in the marching.

Shortly after this, Colin Jordan wrote in a *Spearhead* circular:

"Most, if not all *Spearhead* members, will be aware that there does exist within the ranks of Racial Nationalism (as he would have preferred to call the BNP) an element which has from the outset been hostile towards our formation and all for which it stands. As long as this hostility took the form of unfriendly detachment it caused no concern to us ... Of late, however, it has become increasingly clear that this hostility has manifested itself in the form of a calculated attempt to attack and undermine the morale of several Spearhead members ... It is a make-up which hates the spirit of military chivalry, which is an essential characteristic of Nordic man, and seeks to insert in its place an ideology which grafts the hammer and sickle onto the image of our Aryan Sunwheel."

In reality, the basis of this hostility was centred on the fact that many of us were critical of certain Spearhead members, whose activity for the BNP was solely confined to dressing up, listening to arcane lectures on our 'Aryan roots', and occasionally supporting a march to a street meeting. Our comment that this did damn all to convert the ordinary people to joining our ranks led to us being dismissed as Bolsheviks. Our criticisms were not personally addressed at Jordan or Tyndall, who until then were very active in the overt activities of the BNP. However, it was realised that without Jordan and Tyndall's drive and leadership abilities there would be no Spearhead.

The Spearhead issue was the final straw that led to the 1962 split in the BNP.

The origins of that split really go back to two earlier Jordan-inspired campaigns that led to some members questioning whether the BNP was becoming neo-Nazi. Several, including some good activists, voted with their feet on the matter. The first campaign was to 'Release Hess'. This entailed BNP UK activists putting up stickers and painting walls calling for the release of Rudolph Hess, with Jordan co-ordinating a similar campaign with various overseas Right Wing groups through his Northern European Ring.

Hess, who was Hitler's Deputy, flew to Britain in May 1941 on his abortive peace mission. He spent nearly fifty years of the rest of his life in prison until his mysterious death in Spandau Jail, allegedly by hanging himself. He had no part in any crime committed by the Nazis against Jew or Gentile. Yet he was sentenced to life imprisonment because of his senior position. For this reason I certainly believe that by 1961 Hess should have been released.

This was the feeling of nearly all Senior Members, but most held the view that, even if we had a million members protesting, Hess would still not be released. And as we only had a few hundred, better to concentrate on the issues that were gaining us members and not those that would lose members.

Then came the capture of Eichmann and his subsequent trial in Israel. I had lengthy discussions with Jordan, and sometimes Tyndall, trying to persuade them not to take it up as a propaganda issue, otherwise the media would present us as supporting the gassing of Jews. Although only present at one meeting, Andrew Fountaine supported my view.

A compromise was reached. If Eichmann was brought to trial then so should Menachim Begin, leader of the Irgun Zvai Leumi, for the murder of British police, soldiers and civilians in then Palestine, and the massacre of Arab civilians at Deir Yassin. The British soldiers killed included the hanging of Sergeants Paice and Martin. BNP leaflets, stickers and posters were produced with this theme.

The compromise was also extended to *Combat*. As its founder and editor, I objected to Jordan turning the whole issue over to Eichmann and Begin. Instead it was mainly confined to the middle page spread as a "*Combat Supplement*." As the particular issue only had eight pages in total, this fooled nobody.

Against my better judgement, in April 1961 I agreed to drive the Land Rover round Central London carrying posters proclaiming that Menachim Begin was wanted for murder. Other posters said that as Eichmann was to be brought to trial then so should Begin.

Passing the Princes Theatre, where unbeknown to me a Jewish meeting to commemorate the Warsaw uprising was being held, the Land Rover was hailed by a Police Constable sent forth by a group of senior Police Officers standing by the Theatre. When warned not to come back I asked how long the ban applied. Thereupon all the occupants of the Land Rover, including Jordan and seven members sitting at the back were arrested. I found out later that Jordan knew beforehand that the Jewish meeting was taking place.

In court, the police maintained that they did not instruct me to stop but I had stopped outside the Theatre of my own volition, adding for good measure that all the occupants of the vehicle were waving their fists and shouting abuse. I can honestly say that from inside the cab I did not hear anybody shouting. We were fined a total of nearly two hundred pounds more like two thousand today.

The incident was widely reported by the media, but as I feared, little mention was made of the majority anti-Begin posters. In the main we were presented as friends of Adolf Eichmann, trying to insult Jews gathered to mark the courage of the Jewish fighters in the Warsaw uprising.

For several years after this event I had a recurring dream, more of a nightmare, where I was driving an open lorry through the streets of an unrecognisable city. People walking by would stare at me then turn their backs. I turned my head to see what was on the back of the lorry. I saw that it was full of emaciated corpses dressed in concentration camp clothes. That was the dream, but in the world of reality I was sacked from my job as a result of the publicity.

During my sojourn in Brixton my employers at the technical journal publishing house had given me a month's leave of unpaid absence. Perhaps partly in the hope that in future I would keep a low political profile, within six months I was promoted from deputy editor of one journal to the editorship of *Petroleum*. My secretary was a very competent Jewish young lady, with a good sense of humour. Her uncle was a Labour MP. She was literally in tears after reading the press reports of my latest arrest and explained to our directors that she had previously thought I was a nice person to work for but could not possibly do so now as I appeared to be so anti-Semitic. I tried to assure her otherwise, but to no avail. The directors suggested that the best way out was for me to 'resign' and they would give me a good reference. I accepted this as probably the best for all concerned.

Thus the various seeds of discord in the BNP had been sown.

At the Party's Annual Conference in London on January 27th 1962 Andrew Fountaine and myself made it clear in our speeches that we were not happy with the drift to neo-Nazism under Jordan's leadership and hoped he would reverse this trend. In a tortuous speech it eventually became clear that he had no intention of doing so, other than to rein in the Spearhead so as not to contravene the Public Order Act. Eleven of the sixty two delegates present walked out uttering words to the effect of not wishing to be associated with the Nazis who had taken over the BNP. Andrew Fountaine and other senior members looked at me in expectancy, hoping that I would go into the attack on Jordan and his supporters there and then. I decided that this was not the right moment to do it, with representatives of provincial branches present, as it could wreck the BNP completely. Instead, I asked for a meeting of the National Council to be held within a fortnight to discuss Jordan's proposals.

My supporters had now grown and included Jack Lelieve, the Deputy London Organiser, who had previously been a Jordan supporter. Lelieve was a New Zealander who had been a lieutenant in the Australian Army fighting the Japanese in the Pacific. He was with the Australian-American ground force that inflicted the first defeat upon Japanese troops, in Papua New Guinea at the end of 1942. He joined the NLP as a result of our first Trafalgar Square meeting and, as a single man, dedicated himself completely to the radical right cause up to the formation of the National Front.

The National Council met on February 10th. At the outset Andrew Fountaine assumed the Chair, overruling Jordan who claimed the Chair as his right as National Organiser. Fountaine's first demand was that the Spearhead be disbanded as it had become divisive for the Party as well as infringing parts of the Public Order Act. Jordan refused to do this and we knew then that the parting of the ways was inevitable.

A vote was called for to expel Jordan, Tyndall and the Spearhead officers and to appoint me as the new National Organiser. It was carried by two votes.

The rest is history. The BNP tried to democratise itself to the public, with some success, and to the media, with very little success. Jordan, with a diminishing band of UK supporters, was able to become 'The Leader' of a National Socialist Movement.

The author (left) with Andrew Fountaine at BNP social camp at
Narford, 1962, with Celtic cross party flag
(Photo courtesy of *Telegraph Group*)
154

Having aligned himself with Jordan (which he was later to regret), it was John Tyndall who was keener than Jordan in trying to retain the British National Party title for their faction. Following a few weeks argument, Jordan agreed that we could keep the BNP title, if he could have the Landrover. Apart from being a reflection on his sense of priorities, it also meant that he was acquiring a mechanical wreck. Andrew Fountaine immediately loaned us another Landrover which had been employed on his estate.

On April 20th - Hitler's birthday - the National Socialist Movement was launched.

It was announced to Jordan's fellow Neo-Nazis around the world in the *Northern European*:

"Recently, the democratic nationalist faction, having secured the leadership of John Bean (editor of the party organ *Combat*) and Andrew Fountaine (nominal president) staged a crisis, demanding that National Socialism be treated as something which had failed and finished, and that a more insular policy be adopted, or they would split the party. Faced with a choice between loyalty to National Socialism and our comrades in struggle throughout the world, or the mere maintenance of party unity, the National Socialists of the BNP, led by Colin Jordan, immediately rejected the demands of the Bean-Fountaine faction which thereupon departed from the organisation."

Once the break was made, the only other members of the BNP National Council to support Jordan and Tyndall were Denis Pirie, Peter Ling and Roland Kerr-Ritchie. The latter was a standing joke amongst the 'democratic' faction. He had more than a passing similarity to a goose-stepping version of Kenneth Williams, although not quite so camp. His main contribution to 'the cause' seems to have been the production of a 300 page duplicated 'book' entitled "*Facts the Jews Fear.*" It had no chapters, less than twenty paragraphs, and the average length of a sentence was 500 words. I don't think the Jewish Board of Deputies lost much sleep worrying over its impact. I never met anybody who had progressed beyond page 3: it was unreadable.

All branches, with the exception of Birmingham, had stayed with the BNP, together with such National Council members as Carl Harley, Terry Savage, John Corney, Jack Lelieve and Rupert Simpson. Jack Lelieve had been resident warden of the old HQ at Princedale Road, as well as office manager, and Rupert Simpson also slept there as an additional guard. Both had to find new abodes, which temporarily meant staying with me, much to the disgust of my nine-year-old son, who had to give up his bedroom to them.

It was back to square one as far as a Party HQ was concerned. A forwarding address was obtained in the West End for nearly a year until left wing opponents threatened to burn the place down. A small lock up building in Stoke Newington was then rented for Jack Lelieve, Ken Foster and three or four other trusted members to work in on the Party's administration. Its address was never publicised. My home address and phone number were on all BNP literature, with my wife being subjected to more than her share of abusive phone calls. As in the provincial branches, active members met in private rooms above pubs to plan *Combat* sales drives, leaflet campaigns and local election campaigns.

In April 1962 the BNP fought two wards in Deptford's Borough Council Elections, with Deptford Branch Organiser Ken Merritt obtaining ten per cent of the poll and another member obtaining eight per cent, with both beating the Conservative candidates. In Tufnell Ward, Islington, three BNP candidates, Terry Savage, Rupert Simpson and Ken Davis averaged seven per cent.

Street meetings were continued on the regular pitches, with Earls Court again being particularly lively.

The climax of the spring campaign was a Trafalgar Square meeting on April 29th at which Andrew Fountaine and I were the only speakers. The audience was well up to the average of previous meetings, and with none of the extreme utterances from Jordan and Tyndall, they were more attentive and stayed longer. There was no violence or even organised heckling.

Special Branch officers were always present at large meetings, and most of the ordinary street corner meetings. As we tended to gravitate to the pub afterwards, mainly through lack of an HQ, some of them would also come in. They were usually playing the role of being friendly, particularly after the departure of Jordan, but we knew that this was in the hope of acquiring more information on our planned activities. Even though they assured us how they much preferred our company to the Left (mainly because the Left did not go into pubs after meetings), we knew that in the main they would do us no favours; although there was the occasional exception.

Looking through an old 1962 diary of mine I saw that in the April pages I had written in "Sergeant Pinkney, Scotland Yard, Ext 1108." Having spoken to me a couple of times after meetings going back to NLP days, after the April Trafalgar Square meeting he came up and said he would like a word on the quiet with me. He told me, in his slight Welsh accent, that we had split with Jordan just in time. "You were right not to have anything to do with the Spearhead. They will be facing real trouble soon."

On July 1st Jordan and his NSM ensured that no Right Wing movement would ever again be allowed to exercise freedom of speech in Trafalgar Square. (I tried to exercise this freedom three years later with an impromptu meeting, without police permission, the day Ian Smith declared UDI in Rhodesia. In twenty minutes I was arrested.)

A large crowd of Jewish Communists and other left-wing groups were waiting before the meeting started. Jordan soon had them hurling missiles when he said: "More and more people every day are opening their eyes and coming to see that Hitler was right. They are coming to see that our real enemies, the people we should have fought, were not Hitler and National Socialists of Germany but world Jewry and its associates in this country." Tyndall referred to Jewry as "like a poisonous maggot feeding off a body in an advanced state of decay."

The militant left wing Jews (later to call themselves the 62 Group) and their allies stormed the platform and the meeting

157

ended in a riot, with the NSM members lucky to escape with their lives.

Jordan was sentenced to two months in prison (later reduced to one month) and Tyndall for six weeks for 'insulting words likely to cause a breach of the peace', later reduced on appeal to a fine.

On July 22nd Mosley was due to hold his ninth meeting in Trafalgar Square since 1959 and no doubt hoped that it would be as peaceful as the rest. Seven thousand assorted 62 Group supporters, Communists and other opponents were waiting before the meeting commenced. Fierce fighting broke out as the Union Movement members defended Mosley and the meeting was stopped after fifteen minutes. There were fifty-six arrests.

At our regular street meeting sites, such as Bethnal Green and Earls Court, the 62 Group turned up in some force. I made sure that our speakers made no references to 'Jewish Finance' and were careful not to make disparaging remarks about Afro-Asian peoples whilst still calling for a halt to immigration. The result was that with one exception the police ensured that our meetings were allowed to continue. The plus side was that the noise attracted a bigger audience, with larger collections and more paper sales.

The exception was an Earls Court meeting where, as opposed to witty interjections from opponents such as Christopher Farman, the 62 Group, kept at bay by the police, were trying to halt the meeting with non-stop chants of "Smash Fascism!" On several occasions they tried to break through the police cordon. Getting rather impatient, with my words being drowned even though I had a portable loud hailer. I referred to the 62 Group as a "rat pack." The police officer in charge thereupon told me he was stopping the meeting and arresting me for using insulting words that might lead to a breach of the peace. In court I was fined fifteen pounds.

The thirty or so BNP members present left the meeting in a body, which had become a necessity. Owing to the intervention of traffic, Jack Lelieve, Bert Mitchell and two other members got cut off from the main body. About fifty of the opposition then attacked them, using boots and knuckle-dusters. Fortunately, they were rescued by the return of most of the BNP members and a passing police van.

Around this period individual BNP and Mosleyite activists were being beaten up by 'persons unknown' lying in wait for them, usually on their way home. There were even cases where intruders broke into their homes and beat them with iron bars and other weapons.

On Tuesday nights it was my normal practice to meet up with London activists in a private room above a pub in the Holloway Road. Apart from drinking beer, one of the main purposes of the meetings was to plan our public meetings so that we no longer appeared at the main sites on a regular, predictable basis, thus confusing the enemy. Code words were adopted which told members, when they rang me, where the meeting site would be and when.

One Tuesday in November 1962 I had been on a factory visit in Leicester for my trade journal and, to the amazement of my wife and children, went straight home on my return to London. The children vaguely recognised me. It was around midnight when I was awakened by voices immediately below my bedroom window. "We're friends of John Bean's. He asked us to call round any time."

I recognised one voice as a 62 Group member who was prominent at demonstrations against our meetings. I crept along the hall to the telephone, but instead of using my cigarette lighter to see 999 on the dial I foolishly turned the light on. I heard footsteps running away.

Apparently they had had a tip off that I always came home late on a Tuesday and were laying in wait for me. My Special Branch contact had told me that we had a "spy" in the movement and he was almost certainly the informant on my movements. A neighbour coming home late had seen the group in my garden fiddling with the ground floor windows. When the police arrived they confirmed that an attempt had been made to force the windows.

No arrests were made.

At one of our Bethnal Green meetings I had the opportunity to actually get into conversation with a 62 Group supporter. I pointed out that we had expelled Jordan and his supporters because we were opposed to his Nazi sympathies. Futhermore, there was now nothing in BNP policy which was anti-Jewish. Why then were his people attacking us? His reply was that never again would they allow Jews to be pushed into the gas chambers. And they aimed to smash not only open Nazi movements but any nationalist movement that might harbour anti-semites. I could understand the logic of his argument and with the passage of time I can see that it was part of the penalty of having been associated with Jordan.

Over the August Bank Holiday the BNP held its second camp on Andrew Fountaine's land at Narford. Unlike the first camp, it was for relaxation and an opportunity for London activists to get together with those from the Midlands and the North. In addition, wives, girlfriends and children were welcomed. The only overseas guest was an Italian, who is still a personal friend.

Over the same weekend Jordan had organised a camp in the Cotswolds to which several overseas neo-Nazis had been invited. The most notorious was Lincoln Rockwell (later to be assassinated), Leader of the American Nazi Party. He had arrived in Southern Ireland and was smuggled over the border by Jordan and then into England before the camp began. The purpose of the camp was to announce the formation of the World Union of National Socialists, with Jordan as world Führer and Rockwell the Deputy. Unfortunately the Deputy World Führer could not stand the pace and, after hiding in Jordan's Coventry home, gave himself up to the police. He was then deported. Few other overseas delegates managed to get into the country.

The bizarre proceedings surrounding the activities of the world Führers gave them considerable media coverage. Some of this rubbed off onto our own camp, with the *Daily Mail* again being in the forefront for inventiveness. The lanes between Swaffam and Narborough were congested with journalists' cars as they peered behind bushes and through trees looking for Americans in white sheets burning fiery crosses, Italians in black shirts, and goose-stepping Germans. Feeling sorry for their lack of success, Andrew and I invited them to come into the camp ground. Some still thought that the family holiday atmosphere was a cover to hide more sinister goings on. This was reflected in their articles about plans being hatched to organise race hate campaigns in the Midlands and the North. At least, in the main, they distinguished us from the Neo-Nazis. This was particularly so in the *Guardian* (then the *Manchester Guardian*), who though being profoundly out of sympathy with our views, have always been very factual in their reports on any Right Wing activity I have been involved with.

It was only a few days after the August Bank Holiday camp that I made another naive mistake. This was to talk to *Daily Mail* reporter Eric Sewell in a pub after one of our Earls Court meetings. The outcome was a lengthy report in their issue of 10th August 1962 with a heading of "I am the Goebbels of Britain's Nazis" appearing under a scowling photograph of me. Although three days later the *Daily Mail* published a short extract of a letter I had written denying that I had made this claim, it was reported by several authors, such as Paul Foot, in their 'exposés" of the radical right. Apart from £500 donations from other sources, it also personally cost me another £500 in barristers' fees in seeking advice on whether to sue for defamation or not. The view was that, because I had been associated with Jordan, a jury would be prejudiced against me and we would be unlikely to succeed at that time.

Eric Sewell's *Daily Mail* investigation Report began with some nonsense describing me as a mystery man, little known outside the 'Fascist fringe', who "for ten years has been a ringleader, policy maker and behind the scenes puppeteer of all the anti-coloured revolutionary parties that have sprung up in Britain under the banner of racialism.

"Mr Bean, an Aryan blond (*it must have been the August sun - author*), told me 'If you want to equate this thing with Nazism, I am Goebbels!' "

161

Needless to say I was shocked, and still am after a lifetime of experience with reporters, that anyone could so distort one's comments. When Sewell, or Sewer as I used to refer to him, said to me: "If Jordan is now the world Führer, who do you now see yourself as?," I told him that as we had rejected Jordan and his Nazi viewpoint it was just not relevant for me, or any other senior BNP member, to try and compare ourselves with the Nazi leaders. I can remember saying, which was confirmed by Jack Lelieve: "I reject all the past Nazi leaders. Half were psychopaths and the other half were evil."

"I can see that, John," said Sewell, "but off the record, if you were forced to choose to become one of the Nazi leaders, which one would it be?"

I fell straight into the trap. "Well, off the record, not to be quoted, but in your example, as I never fancied myself as a Führer, but rather the drummer boy trying to wake people up to what is going on, I suppose I would say Goebbels."

Not having £20,000 to spare to seek justice in the Courts, that is how, and without a club foot, I became known as the 'Goebbels of Britain'.

Having opened the Pandora's box, Jordan and Tyndall were sitting in their cells whilst Mosley and the BNP were being subjected to the violence orchestrated by the militant Left and the 62 Group. One outcome of this was that there was a limited amount of interchange between BNP and Mosley supporters attending each others' meetings, much to the dislike of Jeffrey Hamm of Union Movement. For example, three Mosley supporters had attended the BNP August camp.

The violence at Mosley meetings and the personal attacks on Mosley himself at Ridley Road, Dalston, and Belle Vue, Manchester are well documented, including in Mosley's autobiography *My Life* and Martin Walker's *The National Front*. On page 44 of his book Martin Walker states:

"John Bean was also talking of the prospect of a 'National Front' of like minded bodies, with the numbers to protect themselves, and a political organisation which meant that the rallies and public demonstrations would be just one tactic of a strategy, which included standing in carefully chosen by-elections, and building up a local group in each place."

Walker's observation was basically correct, and whilst we still had to hold some rallies and public demonstrations in order to gain publicity and let people know we were still in existence, it was at that time that the BNP began to build up its local groups in Deptford and, particularly, Southall.

On the same page Walker also states that earlier in the year, i.e. immediately after the split between Jordan and myself but before Jordan 'outed' himself as a full blown Nazi, Sir Oswald Mosley had approached us through an intermediary (a Miss Mary Taviner) and offered to make us national organisers on a par with Jeffrey Hamm. Walker states: "Bean and Jordan were too close to their own leadership struggle in the BNP, and too mistrustful of Mosley's policies, for the negotiations to advance to the stage of a meeting with Mosley."

This, no doubt, was true of Jordan. But what Martin Walker did not know, or anybody else other than Lelieve, Harley and Savage, is that I did have a private meeting with Mosley.

The meeting with Sir Oswald was over tea at the Eccleston Hotel near Victoria. I had briefly shaken hands with him after hearing him speak at Kensington Town Hall twelve years before. This time I was given the full Mosley hypnosis treatment, with the opening and lowering of the eyelids which made his pupils appear to dilate. He proffered his hand. As far as I can recall he said: "How nice to meet you, Bean. I was amazed to find that you were once in our movement, yet your talent was not recognised and they let you go. We must make amends and see that your organising and speaking abilities are fully utilised as a senior officer within my movement."

Incongruous as it may seem, I was then asked to help myself to a cucumber sandwich. That I remember well.

I felt flattered at his offer (other than the cucumber sandwich) and could feel the effects of his charisma. I hastened to point out that unlike the Empire Loyalists, Jordan and Tyndall, I could go a considerable way with his views on Europe but felt it premature to call for 'Europe a Nation' whilst international

163

finance capitalism still controlled the economies of Europe. I suggested to him that de Gaulle's 'Europe of Nations' or even a Confederation of Nation States would not only be more practical but would also attract some of the former British nationalists who supported him in the pre-war BUF days.

I cannot recall his precise answer to this but it was non-committal and on the lines that, as I was half-way there, there would be no problem on that score on my joining his movement, or rather re-joining.

I told him that there was another, more important, factor which had led me to leave his Union Movement in 1953 and prevented me from accepting his offer. This was that his past actions had labelled him as an anti-Semite, even if he was not today. Because of this he would never be able to obtain power through the ballot box.

At this his expression changed and I noted some anger in his voice. He thought this was a little odd, given that I had been associated with anti-Semites for the previous few years and that the label would also stick to me. Unfortunately I was to find that Mosley was right in this context.

I made some attempt at explaining my idea for co-operation in public rallies and elections - my concept then of a 'National Front' - but it was plain that he was not interested.

The meeting ended and I knew that I had been in the presence of a greater intellect than I was to find anywhere in my political odyssey. I was never to meet Oswald Mosley again.

Owing to the violence that Jordan had initiated with his April Trafalgar Square meeting, the BNP meeting in the Square booked for September 2nd was cancelled by the authorities. Instead of adopting a low profile until the storm passed over and concentrating on leaflet campaigning and spot street meetings in the two main branch areas of Southall and Deptford, I decided to call a substitute meeting for September 2nd in the heart of enemy territory: Ridley Road, Dalston. If it came off, we would gain considerable publicity. If it did not, there would still be some publicity.

Peaceful Mosley meeting in Trafalgar Square, 1959,
addressed by Raven Thomson

Peaceful BNP meeting in Trafalgar Square, 1961, addressed by
John Bean

I had hoped that we would be able to muster up to 150 supporters for the meeting. The writing was already on the wall when the night before a briefing meeting for the plan of action was held in a private room above a pub near Highbury Corner. Less than forty people turned up, and one of them I was certain was a 62 Group spy. I should have cancelled the Ridley Road meeting there and then. It was obvious that we were on a good hiding to nothing. But a mixture of vanity and stubbornness decided me to go ahead. If we did not the Right Wing in general would think we had 'lost our bottle'.

Our rendezvous the following day was in a small square off Balls Pond Road, Stoke Newington. Around fifty members and supporters had gathered there. There was no sign of any opposition in the immediate vicinity, although we had reports that several thousand Communists, Yellow Star and 62 Group members had occupied the pitch in Ridley Road, some ten minutes walk away. By arrangement, Andrew Fountaine and I set off to walk to the nearby Police Station to be instructed where we were to hold the meeting. We had Ken Merritt from Deptford, and Derek Ainsworth, a six foot six ex-policeman from Leeds, as bodyguards. Nevertheless, as we walked towards the junction with Kingsland Road my steps were leaden and I felt sick. I thought: "What the hell are we doing here? I should have called it off."

We made the Police Station without being spotted. The Superintendent in charge of the event informed us that it would be impossible to go ahead with the meeting in Ridley Road as it was 'occupied'. He offered us an alternative street site a mile away from Ridley Road and warned us that if there was any immoderate language he would arrest the speaker and close the meeting. I told him I had no problems with that.

As we left the Station and retraced our steps to the Kingsland Road junction we saw several BNP supporters running towards us, most of them bleeding from the head and face. Five minutes after we had departed two or three hundred 62 Group supporters had made a pincer attack upon our people from the side streets. Outnumbered five or six to one, and with some of the opponents wielding sticks and iron bars, our people did not stand much chance. Several were taken to hospital to have head wounds stitched, including Jack Lelieve, John Frankland, and a sixty-year old pre-war nationalist, Bill Barnes. His son, Paul, who had just joined the BNP with his friend Bill Baillie, had managed to stand over his fallen father and with the hard core of our more street wise supporters hold off the attackers until the Police arrived.

It was nearly two hours before we could get our meeting under way. Understandably, our supporters were now reduced to not more than twenty. This rose by two when Jack Lelieve and John Frankland reappeared with their heads swathed in bandages.

The Landrover had been immobilised and the loudspeaker equipment wrecked during the attack in Balls Pond Road. I proceeded with the meeting using lung power and an orange box as a platform. With something like a thousand opponents yelling abuse, it was pointless. We managed to make a tactical withdrawal whilst the police were still present.

We received our publicity, both on TV and in the national press. But we were presented as the instigators of the violence, and in consequence we lost as many members as we gained. I had made a major mistake, but at least learnt by it. From then on I opposed all 'coat trailing' meetings and marches in areas offering little support. The time and energy was better spent in building up branches where we had support, such as in Southall and Deptford. The failure to learn this message of 1962 was my reason for finally leaving the National Front in 1978.

The end of the turbulent year saw the Spearhead Trial at the Old Bailey. Jordan, Tyndall, Dennis Pirie and Kerr-Ritchie were found guilty of 'organising, training and equipping Spearhead in such a manner as to arouse reasonable apprehension that they were organised and trained to be employed for the use or display of force in promoting political objectives, contrary to the Public Order Act, 1936.'

Jordan was sentenced to nine months, Tyndall six months, and Pirie and Kerr-Ritchie received three months apiece.

* * * * *

1962 had seen the Cuban missile crisis, which in reality was created by President Kennedy's naivety in world politics by siting nuclear missiles in Turkey, which resulted in Khrushchev reciprocating with missiles in Cuba. The BNP's reasoned anti-Communist stand gained a few more supporters; similarly with our concept of "workers' partnership in industry." This fully supported industrial capitalism, whilst restricting finance capitalism, and called for participation of workers' elected representatives with the management and the shareholders in the running of a company and ensuring, and sharing in its profitability. Whilst supporting the Trade Unions, it was felt that this would also keep them out of Communist control. This viewpoint was one of the factors why some Empire Loyalists and people such as Martin Webster, later to become dominant in the National Front, decided that we were Left Wing.

The six years of Harold Macmillan's Government and his "winds of change" had seen the final abandonment of Empire. The BNP also held the view that with each surrender of a little more independence from the United States, all reputedly in the defence against Communism, we had slowly become a US satellite. Our answer of a third force of Britain and the old Dominions working through pacts and alliances with Western Europe and keeping the balance between Communist Russia and the unbridled capitalism of America, met little opposition except from those who saw reds under all beds and those who thought 'wogs began at Calais'.

In 1963 greater emphasis was being placed on private meetings of supporters and invited guests. Amongst these would be a number of middle-aged to elderly people, predominantly women, who invariably found our Third Force concept unpalatable. For some reason, they also had odd views on many subjects in which they claimed that 'the Jews' were brainwashing us all by putting fluoride in our toothpaste. Beer was also being tampered with and was to be avoided at all costs. In fact virtually everything was being tampered with, usually by 'the Jews'. To

168

think now that one had to make time to talk to them as a source of paper sales and small financial donations is embarrassing, and even distasteful. Many years later I heard Denis Norden use an expression that was very applicable to these people. To understand them you needed a degree in psychoceramics - the study of crackpots.

In regard to paper sales, in addition to bulk sales to the branches *Combat* now had several hundred subscribers including a hundred or more overseas, mainly the USA. Around this time we received a subscription from a young Frenchman who had just left the French Parachute Corps. His name was Jean Marie Le Pen.

A significant development on the international scene was the rise of the Black Muslim movement in the USA, which in a year or so was also to gain the support of Cassius Clay (Muhammad Ali). My view then, which I have no desire to alter today, was expressed in an article in *Combat*:

"This movement has been attacked by the Kennedy regime and the press in both the USA and this country for its racial views. But does it not perhaps contain the basis of the way out of the growing racial problem in America?

"The Black Muslims have a sincere belief in the destiny of the American Negro as a racial unit. They are thus firmly opposed to intermarriage with whites and attack in forceful language those whites as well as blacks who are working for multiracialism. They lay down a very strict code of moral behaviour for their members to follow and say that they want to see the Negro develop his own way of life and not just imitate the white man's. Most important of all, they advocate that the black American be given two or three States of his own in the USA to develop as his own area. This is, of course, apartheid. In consequence we now witness a new phenomenon in post war politics: a group of coloured people actually being attacked and abused by the liberal multi-racialists! We say good luck to the Black Muslims!"

Back in Britain, in 1962 the Macmillan Conservative Government had made some response to the rising rate of immigration by passing the first Commonwealth Immigration Act, which was opposed by the Labour and Liberal Parties. On the doorstep in such areas as Southall and Deptford our members found that the "restrictions" promised had nibbled away at our support. When the 1962 immigration figures were released in February 1963 it showed that 181,000 citizens from the Coloured Commonwealth had arrived in Britain in the last six months after the passing of the Act, compared with just over 100,000 in the whole of 1961. Furthermore, to hide the true state of the problem, the official figures only mentioned the nett gain of immigration over emigration. The emigration number also included those native Britons who were emigrating to Canada and Australia.

Backed up with a special leaflet, the BNP was able to explain the Tories' trickery with the immigration figures on the doorsteps in Southall. The result was immediate and spectacular. In the April Council elections the BNP fought two wards for the first time. In Hambrough Ward BNP candidate Jack McConville received 27.5 per cent of the poll, pushing the Conservative into third place. In Glebe Ward, Southall Branch Organiser Ron Cuddon gained 13.5 per cent.

The progress being made in Southall was primarily due to Ron Cuddon's approach. He was one of the first to see the futility of the 'coat trailing' meetings which ended in violence. Instead, he built up a local team of ordinary men and women, none of whom had been connected with 'extreme' politics, who worked methodically talking to people on their doorsteps who shared the same disquiet at what was going on, and the same feeling of being let down by the orthodox parties. There was also considerable, but not unanimous, support from the Southall Residents' Association, who tried to act as a non-political pressure group, looking after white residents' demands on restricting the number of Asian immigrants.

I accepted the BNP's Southall Branch invitation for me to become its prospective parliamentary candidate. I had originally been picked to fight Deptford, but the cause here was not helped when one of the Deptford Branch activists received prominent local press publicity on a charge of planning a bank robbery. At his trial at the Old Bailey, the Judge decided that it was really a 'prank that went wrong' and he received a suspended six month sentence. Nevertheless, the harm was done to the BNP's prospects in Deptford.

By January 1964 the success of our Southall campaign led the sitting Labour MP George Pargiter to call for "a complete ban on immigration to Southall," much to the consternation of his party nationally. Later, the Tory group on the local council was calling for a fifteen year qualification period before immigrant families could go on to the council's housing list. Ron Cuddon, the BNP's most able branch organiser, was able to exploit this situation to our advantage. He even persuaded Arthur Cooney, Southall Residents' Association Chairman, and Doris Hart, treasurer, to nominate the BNP candidates for the council elections.

Nationally, the BNP had lost the support of some young male activists whose main attraction was the excitement of confronting "the enemy" on demonstrations and meetings in opposition territory. We also lost most of our national media publicity as a result of withdrawing from confrontational politics, although occasional references were made to our Southall and Deptford campaigns. If we had had the funds and the same quality of branch organisations that existed in Southall, the BNP could have become a mass movement.

When the General Election was held in October 1964 I received 3,410 votes, 9.2 per cent of the poll, which was the highest vote recorded by any minority candidate since the Thirties. We had hoped for 5,000 votes but with the national swing to the Conservatives in immigration areas and the Southall candidate coming out strongly for further restrictions on immigration, it was a more than satisfactory achievement.

Primarily because of the "bank robbery" smear, the BNP did not contest the Deptford seat. Instead, it gave its support to an independent standing mainly on a "stop immigration" platform. He received 2,386 - 8.5 per cent.

Some concern was expressed in the House of Commons that "an openly racialist candidate" in Southall should have received almost as many votes as the Liberal's national average. But their main "shock and horror" was reserved for Peter Griffiths, the unknown Tory who won Smethwick against the national swing to Labour from Patrick Gordon Walker, Labour's Foreign Secretary designate. In opposition, Gordon had led the attack on the Tories' 1962 Commonwealth Immigration Act.

Harold Wilson, who had become Prime Minister, made the mistake of prophesying that Griffiths would be treated like a leper in the House of Commons. His main justification for this was the suggestion that Griffiths had adopted the electioneering slogan: "If you want a nigger neighbour, vote Labour." This slogan was in fact invented by Mosley's Union Movement Birmingham Branch Organiser at that time. We heard that BNP members were also using the slogan and although I did not approve of it, I must confess to turning a blind eye to its use.

Not having a candidate in Smethwick in 1964, a number of Birmingham area BNP members did help Griffiths in his campaign. We had begun to appreciate the usefulness of tactical voting. In some respects Griffiths' victory was a victory for us.

* * * * *

A few months later, in January 1965, Gordon Walker thought he saw his chance to return to the House of Commons. There was a by-election in Leyton, East London, which Labour held with an 8,000 majority in the previous October. The BNP's East London members had an efficient and highly active Area Organiser, Ron Tear. He asked me to stand as the BNP candidate, which was announced in both local and national press. Ten days later it was announced that I was withdrawing as a candidate. The reason given was that a canvass had shown that whilst immigration had become a strong issue with the electorate, it was very unlikely that if I had stood I would have obtained the nine per cent of the poll achieved in Southall, and as the BNP's chief representative I would appear as an unsuccessful carpetbagger. However, there was another reason, which was touched on in the local press but, surprisingly, never taken up by the national media, or by any of the subsequent authors of books on the history of the radical right.

The Conservative candidate was Ronald Buxton, who in the event won the seat by the narrow margin of 205 votes. Prior to my withdrawal as a candidate he telephoned Andrew Fountaine (BNP President) twice asking him to persuade me not to stand as it would "split the vote." Buxton then sent Fountaine a confidential report on Buxton's attitude to immigration. Fountaine did not show this report to the local press, nor to me, as it had been given to him in confidence. But he told me over the phone that Buxton said that if elected he would call for a moratorium on further immigration for two years whilst an extensive study was carried out on its immediate and long term effects.

This was good enough for us. Andrew Fountaine telephoned Mr Buxton and told him that the BNP was withdrawing. He expressed his thanks at this and asked whether the BNP would continue to campaign in the by-election. When told we would, he replied with words to the effect that this would be a great help.

As a result 8,000 BNP "Stop Immigration" leaflets, plus numerous stickers, were distributed in Leyton, and our members led the heckling of Patrick Gordon Walker's meetings. The Labour Party had called upon the 62 Group to supply auxiliary stewards at these meetings, which led to all hecklers, including those who were not BNP, Mosleyites or Jordan supporters, being set upon with fists, boots and chairs. The resultant violence was widely reported by the national media and the actions of the stewards generally condemned. Colin Jordan, again showing his physical courage, was viciously attacked. The *Daily Express* described this as "Nazi methods against the Nazi leader." This was Gordon Walker's last meeting. When it started, the majority of the audience were cheering the Labour speakers. When it ended, many had walked out in disgust and those who remained were silent.

We did not expect public acclaim from Ronald Buxton for securing his return as MP for Leyton, but we did not expect to be abused by him in the local press *after the event.*

In view of the vote we showed we could attract at Southall, even the most cynical viewer of our chances must admit that had we stood we would have been likely to have gained more than 205 votes (Buxton's majority) from Tory voters. Hence our claim at the time: *"We won at Leyton!"*

Stewards and assorted radical right hecklers come to blows at Leyton by-election January 1965

The author and Peter McMenemie at a Hitchin meeting, 1965

A poster parade in Deptford with John Tyndall, front left

CHAPTER 9
BIRTH OF THE NATIONAL FRONT

We greeted the news that the new Labour Government was going to bring in a Racial Discrimination Bill with mixed feelings. It proposed a fine of up to £1,000 and two years imprisonment for "threatening or insulting speeches and pamphlets intended to stir up racial hatred."

On the credit side it would curtail those morons whose opposition to immigration was based on verbal abuse and physical attacks upon non-whites. Our political opponents had had some success in equating such people with those, such as the BNP, who opposed the *policy* of allowing non-European immigration to continue. To this end we had used the slogan "Keep Britain White" as an expression of a socio-political opinion and not as an insult. Now it was to become illegal.

The Bill, as with all the additional clauses that have been added over the past thirty years was, and is, undemocratic. It undermined Britons' rights of free speech and freedom to associate with whom we choose. There were already laws in existence that curtailed public speakers, and publishers of leaflets, from using threatening or insulting language. In effect the Bill was to alter our legal system whereby a public speaker could be imprisoned because he said something contrary to Government thinking on immigration, even if no disturbance whatsoever occurred at the meeting at which the 'offence' was committed.

It was our opinion that the main purpose of the Race Bill was to suppress discussion of immigration. The passage of time has not altered that opinion. It certainly had no effect on the gradual growth of BNP membership, except that the hooligan element which we had been plagued with in the past began to drift away as we dispensed with provocative marches and concentrated on peaceful pickets - such as in support of Rhodesia - and doorstep politics. This was substantiated in an article by Colin Cross, then an accepted authority on Right Wing politics, in the June 3rd 1965 issue of *New Society*.

After dealing with the hopes and failures of Sir Oswald Mosley's Union Movement and Colin Jordan's National Socialist Movement, Colin Cross stated:

"It is possible, however, that the true future of British racialist politics lies with the British National Party, which is the only organisation formally to have broken away from the Fascist traditions of the 1930s ... In the past three or four years it has advanced at a quicker rate than any other racialist organisation. It is smaller than the Mosley movement ... but it is so closely tailored to current racial tension that it possesses a definite potential.

"The break with pre-war Fascism is almost complete. The BNP has no 'Leader' whom it puts forward as a potential dictator and it avowedly works within the Parliamentary framework, declaring that it seeks power in just the same way as the orthodox political parties seek power. Bean, the leading personality, says he regards himself as 'the drummer boy' awakening public opinion rather than as 'the new Charlemagne'. That this line of policy has won success is clear from the results."

Throughout the summer and early autumn of 1965 the BNP became increasingly involved in pickets, poster parades and street meetings in support of Ian Smith's attempts to retain European civilisation in Rhodesia.

On October 11th, immediately following Rhodesia's declaration of independence (UDI), I was at our regular Sunday meeting pitch in Cheshire Street, Bethnal Green. Following the meeting I put it to the members present that, after a snack of a cheese or ham roll and a pint in our customary watering hole, we should depart to Trafalgar Square and hold an impromptu meeting in support of Ian Smith.

Equipped with a battery operated loud hailer, I scrambled on to the plinth in the Square, knowing that as official permission for Trafalgar Square meetings was denied to the BNP (but not to Africans opposing Ian Smith) it would not be long before I was arrested. Accompanying me were Bert Mitchell, holding the Union Jack, and Mike Briggs (a recruit from the Mosleyites)

178

with a banner previously used outside Rhodesia House declaring: "Stand by Ian Smith."

A large crowd quickly gathered and within minutes cheers and applause were coming from sections of the audience. A constable came up and our members told him that he could not have been informed that permission had been granted for our meeting. Obviously, he did not believe them. Within a quarter of an hour two police vans arrived and the three of us were arrested, but not before the crowd had grown to around a thousand.

Initially, Bert Mitchell and I were locked in the close confines of the small police box in Trafalgar Square. We could hear the chanting outside from BNP members, other right wingers, and several Rhodesians and South Africans: "Free Speech for Britons." "Stand by Smith, the Man with Guts." "Ian Smith for Westminster, Wilson to the Tower!"

At Bow Street Magistrates Court the following morning I was fined ten pounds for the crime of speaking without a permit. Mitchell was fined two pounds. The fines were easily covered by donations received from the crowd in the Square, to say nothing of the *Combat* sales.

This marked the beginning of a twelve month period when *support* for the BNP rose considerably, although actual membership increased only slightly. But that new membership included some good calibre people. One in particular, who had joined in the early days but resigned over Jordan's extremism and then rejoined, was Philip 'Maxwell'. He was a thirty-year-old middle management executive working for a multinational company. Because of his job he used the pseudonym of 'Maxwell'. Only Andrew Fountaine and I knew his true name. He had a keen analytical mind and soon became a member of the BNP's National Council. Another new member was Major General Richard Hilton, who had been running the Patriotic Party. He became the BNP's Vice-President. Bernard Simmons, a former judge in the Colonial Service, also joined us as an active member.

A lot of the general support (as opposed to membership) at this period came from young Rhodesians, South Africans, Australians and New Zealanders - women as well as men - who swelled the crowds at meetings, with marches from Earls Court to the West End becoming five or six hundred strong.

It was also of significance that these pro-Rhodesia activities were attracting the individual support of some Mosleyites, Empire Loyalists and supporters of John Tyndall's Greater Britain Movement: Tyndall having parted company with Jordan and, more importantly, his Nazi beliefs. It was here that the seeds of a national front were planted.

In October 1965 I received letter from John Tyndall, which had also been sent to Sir Oswald Mosley and A.K.Chesterton of the Empire Loyalists. In essence it recognised the differences in principle and policy of the three organisations and accepted that they would remain. Nevertheless, he said, a joint enterprise could be organised to stage a large public meeting confined to the issue of supporting "our kinsmen in Rhodesia." Mosley did not reply to Tyndall's letter. Chesterton did, but declined the offer of co-operation at that time. After a week's consideration I wrote to Tyndall making these points:

"If you or I were to make application for an assembly hall I am certain it would be refused. However, if you get one of your members to make an application on behalf of some non-existent body, e.g. "Support for Rhodesia Committee," perhaps we may be lucky. If this came off I would then be prepared to speak as an individual, together with any other person with the exception of Colin Jordan. This I must stress would be solely on the grounds that it was a meeting organised by a body with no official connection with the Greater Britain Movement, or the BNP, and I would state at the commencement of my speech that my appearance on the platform did not necessarily signify approval or disapproval of any other political views held by the other speakers. Naturally we would publicise the meeting to our members and supporters."

Without the numerical support of the other two movements, nothing further came of Tyndall's plan, although some of his members continued to support our meetings.

* * * * *

The February 1966 General Election saw the BNP fighting three seats: Southall, Deptford and Smethwick. My vote in Southall fell to 7.4 per cent with 2,768 votes, against 3,410 in 1964. Gerald Rowe in Deptford gained 1,906 votes, 7.0 per cent. In Smethwick, Roy Stanley, a twenty-three-year-old, received 508 votes, just 1.5 per cent. Andrew Fountaine wrote a strong letter castigating me on my decision to allow Stanley to stand, particularly as the campaign was ill-prepared.

On reflection he was probably right in his objections. However, my decision was based on the need to show provincial members that the BNP was not just a London and Home Counties movement, plus the fact that it gave the Birmingham Branch electioneering experience.

Importantly, as the Tory MP, Peter Griffiths, had said little in the House of Commons on immigration after using that issue to capture the Smethwick seat from Labour in October 1964, I felt it essential to show the electorate that it was the BNP that stood firm in calling for a halt to immigration, as opposed to the wavering opposition offered by some Tory MPs. Griffiths lost the seat to Labour by more than 5,000 votes.

The decline in the BNP's 1966 vote was partly due to the 2.8 per cent national average swing to Labour. Perhaps more important was that 1964 was a vintage year for protest votes on immigration, with independents and minuscule parties all over the country picking up 500 to 1,500 votes merely if they let it be known to their local newspapers that they opposed immigration.

The public in 1966 were still just as concerned with immigration but they found from their 1964 experience that their protest vote had been of little use in bringing it to a halt. The public may act like sheep but they are not fools. They knew that such a measure could only come about from a party with some Parliamentary representation. With only three candidates in the field, the BNP was unable to present that image.

Mosley's Union Movement fielded four candidates in the 1966 election. In Ardwick, Manchester, their candidate received 796 votes; in Handsworth, Birmingham, 1,337; and in Islington South West, 816. In Shoreditch Sir Oswald Mosley made his last appearance as a Parliamentary candidate and obtained 1,126 votes. The Union Movement average was only 3.78 per cent.

Two months later in local elections six BNP candidates in Sheffield, Leeds and Canterbury averaged 7.4 per cent of the poll: remarkably consistent with the General Election results of 7.4 per cent in Southall and 7.0 in Deptford.

That summer demonstrations and marches, particularly in London's West End, in support of Ian Smith's Rhodesia, continued to attract several hundred supporters. Although invariably followed by TV cameras and reporters, the media was silent. Those marches attracted a fair number of attractive young Rhodesian and South African girls and women, who in turn attracted more young Brits than before. An outcome was the formation of the BNP's National Youth Movement, headed by Charles Kiely of Birmingham. But that was the solitary swallow to make the BNP's summer. Most of us in the hard core of activists felt we were running as hard as ever merely to stand still. After seventeen years of non-stop political activity and simultaneously trying to earn a living to sustain my family I felt mentally exhausted. Being laid low with hepatitis B for two months did nothing to help.

Some long standing members drifted away. Arguments between National Council members became more frequent. Those between Andrew Fountaine and myself were kept private and I found that his unpredictability, plus my volatility, made them more frequent. The common front we enacted in public was based on our personal friendship that had evolved over the years. My wife and I were the only witnesses at his second marriage in 1962, which the four of us them celebrated in excellent style at the St.Ermines Hotel, near Caxton Hall. Our visits to Narford Hall in Norfolk became less frequent by 1966.

The message was clear. The BNP could stand still and wither on the vine or expand by combining with other right wing groups preferably radical right. The pro-White Rhodesia campaign had shown that this was possible, but to achieve it would probably require my handing over the role of National Organiser to somebody else.

* * * * *

By this time my relationship with A.K.Chesterton had greatly improved as we began to exchange letters, although many of his old guard Empire Loyalists were still distrustful of the "young whipper-snapper" who had gone off to form the NLP. Chesterton knew that his younger people, now almost his only activists, were supporting BNP demonstrations. My Deputy National Organiser was now Philip 'Maxwell', who began regular contact with both Chesterton and his 'aide de camp' Austen Brooks.

Meanwhile John Tyndall continued to distance himself from his Nazi juvenile past and seemed to have regretted his connections with Jordan as much as I had. In his publication *Spearhead* he wrote an article headed "Where is the Right?" In it he condemned "the little men who talk about uniting Britain, the white race, Europe or whatever you prefer, cannot even unite themselves."

I telephoned him and we had a private meeting. At our meeting I was somewhat surprised to learn that he had already had a meeting with Chesterton in his Croydon flat. It appeared that Chesterton realised that his Empire Loyalists were slipping away to join the Monday Club and/or the Anglo-Rhodesian Society (for whom the BNP had provided stewards), with younger members joining the BNP or even Tyndall's Greater Britain Movement, and he was ready to merge the LEL into a new non-Fascist movement of the Right. It was agreed by Chesterton and then myself that Tyndall's presence at the

183

formation stages would be more of a hindrance than a help because of his past utterances and his jail sentences. However, he would encourage GBM members to join as individuals, offer support for any new movement in *Spearhead*, and sit on the sidelines until he could join.

Tyndall's work in bringing about the founding of the National Front was significant. Understandably, he was annoyed that this was not acknowledged at the time, because of his past.

I reported to BNP National Council members details of my non-committal meeting with Tyndall as Philip Maxwell did with his meeting with Chesterton and Austen Brookes. Most were enthusiastic, except Ron Cuddon. He became very agitated and said that "a neo-Nazi plot was afoot" and that he would not have any part in discussions with Tyndall or Chesterton. Maxwell, Bernard Simmons (the former High Court Judge) and I tried to assure him that this was not so, but he resigned and switched his allegiance to the Racial Preservation Society (RPS).

Starting in 1965, the various non-party immigration control organisations in the Midlands and the South were loosely linked in the RPS. The driving forces were Robin Beauclair, its Chairman, and Alan Hancock and his son in Brighton. It was supported by such movements as the Southall Residents Association (who had given me some help during my two election campaigns) and Tom Finney's English Rights Association in Birmingham. Most important, the RPS had attracted a number of financial backers and was able to bring out various broadsheets such as *RPS News*, *Midland News*, and *Sussex News*, most of which were given away free. The level of much of their propaganda content made *Combat* look like a haven of intellectual thought. And what was most galling was that one of the main financial backers, Raymond Bamford, had previously been helping me to meet the printers' bills for producing *Combat*. We even published Bamford's series of articles on "The Discovery of the Race Soul," which brought forth the comment from some less discerning readers of "up your hole with the race soul."

A.K.Chesterton, in a letter to me, was more analytical: "I read his article with fascination and wonder, pondering over each lovely sentence to savour to the full its gorgeous pseudo-intellectual meaninglessness."

One of the BNP's senior members was Ted Budden of Brighton, who was also closely connected with the Hancocks and the RPS. Ted Budden arranged a meeting in Brighton between Philip Maxwell and myself, Robin Beauclair, Alan Hancock and a James (Jimmy) Doyle, an Arthur Daleyish antiques dealer who had begun the Southern Group of the RPS. I recall feeling euphoric the night before this meeting. It seemed very likely that Chesterton would bring his forces and, more importantly, his financial backers into the new movement, which meant that we would have a central London office and at least one full time paid administrator. Now there was a good chance of bringing in a fair number of the RPS people. My moving down the line from principal official would give me more time with my family, as I had promised my wife, and allow me to concentrate on *Combat*, which had not been published for three months because of outstanding printers' bills.

The Brighton meeting went well with all favouring an amalgamation of forces. It soon became apparent that Doyle and Beauclair visualised that they would be running the show, particularly as I made it clear that I did not want to be a principal official. Philip Maxwell played his hand skilfully, telling them that the time to talk about whose role was which was after the members of each body had agreed to merge and, most important, whether or not Chesterton's LEL was to come in with us. Titles suggested were the British National Democratic Party and the National Democratic Party. I favoured the National Front. It was agreed that the next step was for a joint meeting of the RPS officials with the full BNP National Council to be held in London on August 6th. Maxwell would draw up a working programme for the amalgamation of the BNP and the RPS to present to the meeting.

I felt quite at ease at the thought of working with Alan Hancock and even the impetuous and politically naive Robin Beauclair, and I already knew Ted Budden's reliability. James Doyle was another matter. My instincts told me he was not to be trusted. He talked glibly of the money he could raise, without ever showing evidence of how he was going to do it. He had no track record of political action and no political standpoint that one could tell. All he had was an apparent hatred of blacks. Important to me was that when he spoke to you he dd not look at you but through you. I was not surprised to read two years later that he served a three-year prison sentence for receiving stolen goods.

Perhaps my years of experience in dealing with the different personalities of the radical right, which had more than its fair share of odd-balls, had given me an insight to character that Maxwell did not then possess. For in a letter to Doyle immediately after the meeting he wrote: "We will propose that I be appointed Executive Director and possibly retain, for the time being, the responsibilities for Information and that you be appointed Finance Director (I hope you'll agree to this - I think your talents in this direction are exceptional)."

Philip Maxwell's true abilities were apparent in the working programme he devised for the joint meeting in London, and which I approved with hardly an amendment. I suggested that he took the chair at the meeting and knew that the time was imminent for me to stand down and recommend to the National Council that he should become the National Organiser. My stepping down would probably remove the last barrier for Chesterton to be able to swing his Empire Loyalists into the new movement.

In my speech to the joint delegates I emphasised that "there must be a spirit of compromise on all our parts. However, without wishing to introduce a sour note, there can be no compromise as far as we of the BNP are concerned on policy, particularly its racial content. We are prepared to cross T's and dot I's differently, or even rephrase various points of the policy we have previously pursued, but we have spent six years evolving this policy and evidence shows that it is what is needed for a Nationalist movement.

"As the first gesture of compromise, I wish to make it clear that I am fully prepared to stand down in any new movement from my present position as the principal officer of the BNP. It will have great advantages for a new Radical Right movement to have as its leader a man who did not once 'ride with Colin Jordan'. However, I think that my active experience, unbroken since 1949, has taught me a lot and I want to see that experience and knowledge put into practice. In consequence, I hope you will not be pushing me too far down the line initially. This is also important so that we get the overwhelming majority of the BNP members to follow me into the new movement. Naturally, what happens later when other people show their ability is a different matter.

"On the question of the title for the proposed new movement, British National Democratic Party had been suggested among others. I now favour National Front. Particularly as this would suggest a true union of nationalist movements. And when we have seen if we can effect unity of the BNP and RPS I know that proposals will be made this afternoon in regard to another movement."

All BNP National Council members were in favour of going ahead with the merger if approved by a majority vote of Senior Members. Having originally favoured the 'Democratic' title, Andrew Fountaine eventually supported the proposed title of National Front, particularly as he had founded his National Front Movement in 1950 when he was expelled from the Conservative Party. In the latter years of his life he was to delude himself into proclaiming that the National Front of 1966 onwards was a continuation of the movement he founded.

The next step was for me to resign as BNP National Organiser and nominate Philip Maxwell as my successor. He was unanimously elected by the BNP National Council.

It did not take Maxwell long to discover the measure of James Doyle. In an October BNP members bulletin informing them of the progress made in seeking the fusion of the BNP, LEL and RPS he wrote.

"... at our Council meeting on Saturday 15th October your National Council, including our former National Organiser, Mr John Bean, decided unanimously to recommend in the strongest

187

possible terms to the Senior Members that the BNP be merged with the League of Empire Loyalists and with certain Branches of the Radical Preservation Society (excluding Mr Doyle, the Chairman of the RPS, with whom we have found it impossible to work)..."

In the same month a further step towards the founding of the National Front was taken when Philip Maxwell in his new role as BNP National Organiser was invited to address the LEL at its Annual General Meeting. His speech on the urgent need for Right Wing unity was extremely well received by the delegates. The immediate outcome was the setting up of a joint working committee to merge the BNP and the LEL to form the National Front. By this time Chesterton also had come to support us on the title. I understood later that Tyndall had indicated to Chesterton that he too favoured this title. Tyndall had made it clear to me in a letter of 18 April 1966 that this was his choice of title.

The actions of two new BNP members, each for different reasons, came near to wrecking the attempt for Right Wing unity.

As a former High Court Judge, Bernard Simmons was readily accepted by us all, with respect for his intelligence and sincerity. He soon began to publish his own duplicated bulletin, *Truth*, generally in support of the BNP but with views that were very much his own. Philip Maxwell, Ken Foster (the National Secretary) and two or three others were keen to co-opt him onto the National Council. My view, partly supported by Andrew Fountaine, was that no matter how excellent he may have been as a colonial judge, he should first serve an apprenticeship in practical politics before we gave him office. As my plans for giving up the driving seat were now under way I withdrew my opposition and he was co-opted.

One of Bernard Simmons' first actions on joining the National Council was to propose the training of defence squads to keep order at indoor meetings. Later, when the negotiations with the LEL were at an advanced stage, he suggested that it should be called National Action and members would wear political insignia. When Chesterton heard of this, with all its connotations of the 'Spearhead trial', he understandably hit the roof. At one of our regular lunchtime meetings in Fleet Street Philip Maxwell suggested that as the BNP's regular meeting stewards under Ken Merritt and Ron Tear were very much 'John Bean men', as the new National Organiser, he would propose that I should head the National Action group and thereby prevent it going into a paramilitary direction. I agreed to this, which did not endear me to Mr Simmons but certainly placated Chesterton.

I then made sure that the idea was gently dropped.

Even more potentially damaging to the merger negotiations were Simmons' meeting with John Tyndall and writing an article for his journal *Spearhead*. Having coaxed back Ron Cuddon to support the merger, he again resigned in consequence and was followed by half the Southall Branch, plus Charles Kieley, National Youth Organiser, and others. In his letter of resignation to Philip Maxwell of 12 December 1966 Simmons wrote that his letters and article for *Spearhead* were motivated by "a desire to improve the journal *Spearhead*, by criticising anti-semitism and other attitudes with which I profoundly disagree, and by disseminating more useful matter among a new readership for me."

There were some who thought that Simmons was a plant by the opposition to prevent the merger taking place. I disagree. He was a sincere patriot but a political tyro.

I did not have this opinion of the BNP's other new broom, Gerald Kemp. Some, in hindsight, suggested that he might have worked for M15, or some other Government agency, and his role was to cause dissension in the fledgling National Front before it got off the ground. It may have looked that way, but I doubt it. More likely, he was one of those political dilettantes who were later to play a major role in the downfall of the National Front. He lived in West Drayton and joined the BNP in the summer of 1966 following his retirement from the Army as a Warrant Officer. His nearest active branch was Southall and he immediately began to criticise the running of the branch and its organiser Ron Cuddon, who had organised such a skilful campaign over three years. Following my stepping down as

National Organiser he was co-opted onto the National Council before October was out. This brought him closer to Fountaine, whom he courted assiduously. Andrew being Andrew, incapable of deviousness, told me that I must have upset Kemp because he insisted that I was holding the movement back, was an obstacle to any merger with the LEL, and had outlived my usefulness. He emphasised my weakness in regard to any in-depth organisational planning - which was true - and my preference for impetuous action, which Andrew had himself criticised me for many times in the past. Being bogged down in organisation detail in the past would have meant little action to hold young members' interests and the inability for fast reaction to political events that gained the BNP its much needed publicity. Nevertheless, Kemp had more than a germ of truth in his objections to me, and the other motivators in the Party, and skilfully played on Andrew Fountaine's doubts.

Kemp originally sided with those who suggested, like myself, that after Tyndall had served a long sabbatical and had showed that he rejected his Jordan era Nazi beliefs, he should be allowed into the new movement. However, finding that Fountaine would not tolerate Tyndall, he quickly changed sides. Kemp's next move was to get close to Chesterton. He was soon taking tea with A.K. at his South Croydon flat.

In late October I had advised BNP National Council colleagues that as much as we wanted unity we must not allow the LEL to dictate terms. They were out of touch with the public and the BNP had shown that it had more appeal to the electorate. Therefore we must stand firm on key policy issues such as employees and employers partnership in industry. The LEL's key asset was money, a London office, and A.K. Chesterton's brain. All this was conveyed to Chesterton, who wrote me a long letter from South Africa on 1st November asking whether we should call off the whole idea of a merger. The only person who could have passed my comments on to Chesterton was Kemp.

I stood by my comments to Chesterton, being as tactful as I could. Because of our past association and respect for each other any animosity was overcome. The merger was back on course.

On December 15th 1966 the British National Party organised a private meeting at the Caxton Hall, Westminster: private, because public meetings were denied to us throughout London. As well as BNP members, Empire Loyalists and RPS members had been invited. When we arrived a howling mob of Communists, Maoists, 62 Group supporters and Young Liberals were there to greet us. Some less dedicated supporters of the meeting were frightened off by their presence, but close on three hundred still got into the hall.

The purpose of the meeting was to announce to BNP members the formation of the National Front. Speakers were Andrew Fountaine, followed by myself, then Philip Maxwell, and Austen Brooks for the Empire Loyalists. A united platform hid from the audience the tension and friction the speakers had been subjected to over the previous months. Their enthusiasm for the National Front was soon reciprocated by the audience, with only one voice of dissent to my recollection.

At the close of the meeting there were nearly a thousand opponents outside. The police advised us to usher the audience out of a side door. Three BNP members, two of them middle aged, were attacked, one receiving a fractured jaw, at the nearby underground station. Although the police detained one assailant no charge was made.

The speakers at the meeting, escorted by a hard core of younger and fitter BNP members under the charge of Ken Merritt and Ron Tear, marched away through the back streets to Victoria Station, followed initially by a handful of opponents. When they had received sufficient reinforcements to outnumber us by three to one, they attacked, some throwing bottles. As we ran past a dustbin, I suggested to Merritt that we ought to empty it, to make sure it did not contain any more ammunition for our pursuers. It produced four or five empty bottles which were hurled at the enemy. Thus, taking advantage of many dustbins en-route, we arrived unscathed in Victoria Street to be met by several van loads of police. Merritt complained to the police that we had been attacked with bottles - "No officer, I didn't throw any back" - and ten of our opponents were arrested. The only one to be charged was a Tony Bloom, a Young Communist, who was later shot in a pub argument (non-political) in St. Pancras.

* * * * *

In the next issue of *Combat* I pledged my support for the National Front, although I held no executive position at that time. I pointed out that: "With the possible exception of the point on the Commonwealth and, in my view, the unfortunate dropping of the BNP proposal of a European Confederation of nation states, NF policy is basically the same as that of the BNP."

I was particularly pleased that A.K.Chesterton had persuaded the LEL people to accept Point 9 of the NF's objectives:

"To ensure that just profits, salaries and wages, founded on a fair partnership between employers and employees, are guaranteed by maintaining the principle of private enterprise within a framework of national guidance, wherein employees would be genuinely represented in all matters pertaining to hours, wages, production and working conditions. Consumer interests would also be represented to ensure protection from monopolistic and other malpractices."

Point 8 dealt with immigration:

"To preserve our British native stock in the United Kingdom, to prevent inter-racial strife such as is seen in the USA, and to eradicate race hatred, by terminating non-white immigration, with humane and orderly repatriation of the non-white immigrants (and their dependants) who have entered since the passing of the British Nationality Act, 1948."

This was feasible in 1967 and also legal to say so. Under the welter of race relations legislation that has been introduced since then, it is no longer legal to say this, such has been the erosion of freedom of speech.

I concluded my article with this advice to the National Front: "Experiences over the past twelve months have fully justified the caution I have always taken in regard to 'miracle men'. They come forward from out of the blue and immediately see where we have gone wrong, usually with the statement of the obvious, and to the accompaniment of half a hundredweight of draft programmes, new constitutions and numerous memos instructing us on the right path forward. Of course, such men are invariably sincere, intelligent and dedicated - at least for a while. However, because they have distinguished themselves in their profession, some people imagine that this means those abilities are automatically transferred to the very different field of *practical applied politics*.

"I trust that the National Front will ensure that all prospective 'miracle workers' must first present their credentials of having served a political apprenticeship before being given too high a position of office."

This advice was soon forgotten and within a decade the National Front paid the price.

One of the many pro-Ian Smith demonstrations organised by the BNP, 1966

Another of the pro-Ian Smith demonstrations, 1966

John Bean, addresssing the inaugural meeting of the National Front in 1967

A K Chesterton addressing the inaugural meeting, 1967

CHAPTER 10
KICKING THEIR WAY INTO THE HEADLINES

In January 1967 National Front Members Bulletin No. 1 was issued. Its opening paragraph read:

"The National Front, which consists essentially of a union of the former British National Party, the League of Empire Loyalists and elements of the Racial Preservation Society, is now in being."

It announced that headqurters had been established at 11 Palace Chambers, Bridge Street, opposite the Houses of Parliament, with a full time staff. The old BNP headquarters at 1 Windmill Row, Kennington, which operated behind the title of Kinsman Books, would continue as a subsidiary headquarters for evening callers.

Members were informed that the NF would be run by a Policy Directorate which would lay down official policy and hold the power to expel members. I was concerned that this did not include a true BNP member. The Chairman was A.K.Chesterton with Aidan Mackey (ex-LEL) and Gerald Kemp as Vice-Chairmen. The Executive Directorate would be responsible for administering the day to day work of the movement. The Chairman was Andrew Fountaine, with Philip Maxwell and Austen Brooks as Vice-Chairmen.

To Maxwell and I the choice of Fountaine as Chairman of the Executive Directorate was acceptable in principle but in reality his commitments to running his estate in Norfolk meant that he was not able to "administer the day to day work of the movement."

Ex-BNP members, who still constituted four out of five of the new NF's active members, were expressing strong opposition to Kemp being the only so-called "ex- BNP" officer of the Policy Directorate: a view also held by the ex-GBM members now joining the NF. They felt that I should have a more senior role. I gave my opinions to Maxwell, who in late February wrote to Chesterton still in South Africa during our winter months to alleviate his emphysema. He made several points in favour of my becoming a member of the Executive Directorate, including these:

"I know that at your AGM you stated that the LEL would be joining the BNP minus John Bean, though in a context which personally I certainly took to mean the BNP without John Bean as its leader. Subsequently you agreed that in time John should assume a position in the National Front suited to his abilities, if he wished.

"None of us is perfect ... But surely it is the man as a whole that we must judge and above all what he can contribute to the Nationalist cause. I have yet to meet someone of John's generation who can match him as far as political ability, knowledge, dedication to the Nationalist cause and fundamental honesty of purpose are concerned. John gave up the leadership of the BNP quite voluntarily because of the severe strain imposed by personal problems and additional work at the BNP office. He is now prepared to serve as a member of the Executive Directorate. In my opinion it would be utterly absurd for us not to accept his services.

"There may still be one or two people in the LEL who still dislike or mistrust him for something he did eight years ago but three quarters of the membership of the NF at least consider him to be a first class fellow."

At the next meeting of the Executive Directorate I was co-opted as a member. With the increasing pressure of his own family ties and from his employment, plus his disillusionment at the continual behind the scenes arguing and knife sharpening, Philip Maxwell became less and less involved. I realised that my own plan to be less active would have to go on hold in order to keep the support of our BNP activists. Having got on well with all the ex-LEL members on the two Directorates, and finding them sincere and open in their genuine support for the NF, I accepted Chesterton's offer to take over Philip Maxwell's post as Deputy Chairman of the Executive Directorate when he tendered his resignation that May; which, no doubt, was in his mind when he wrote to Chesterton in February.

An intensive NF leaflet campaign was started that Spring, including one opposing Britain's entry into the Common Market. Municipal elections were fought in several areas, with lukewarm support from Chesterton. However, he was cheered up when seven NF candidates in Sheffield obtained an average of nine per cent. Elsewhere, in Islington, Ealing, Leeds, Canterbury and Dover the vote was between four and seven per cent.

New members were beginning to join. This support was not just confined to those who opposed immigration. It was coming from those who were concerned at our decline on the world stage which had reduced us to a satellite of the United States, with the offer of becoming part of a Federal Europe as the only apparent alternative.

As the swinging Sixties progressed, there were others who were attracted by the NF's opposition to the undermining of the nation's moral standards. Home Secretary Roy Jenkins, ever more liberal and the archetypal champagne socialist, was in the vanguard of those who claimed to be 'advancing our civilisation' by hastening our moral decline. For some this was epitomised by the passing of the 'Queer's Charter', which legalised homosexual acts in private for those over twenty-one.

However, there were others on the Radical Right who were in full support of the legalisation of homosexual acts. This included a Mosley supporter who organised a delegation, including two or three NF followers, which supported a mass rally in South London in support of the new Bill. The rally organisers were somewhat perplexed when the group unfurled a banner proclaiming *Fairies for Fascism*!

Another prominent Radical Right homosexual was Peter Ferguson, a former naval officer and long term Mosley supporter with a great 'campish' sense of humour. The likeable Ferguson's sexual proclivities were apparently shared by 'Harry' Bidney, the founder of the anti-fascist Jewish 43 Group and later the 62 Group. It is said that when they met either in conflict at a Mosley meeting or pursuing their social life at West End clubs catering for their shared tastes (including Bidney's Golden Whip Club), it would be in an atmosphere of armed neutrality, with a smiling Ferguson enquiring: "How's your love life, Herschel (Bidney's real forename)?"

* * * * *

In May, Austen Brooks, Chesterton's loyal lieutenant, suffered a severe nervous breakdown and was sent on a long holiday by the ever generous Chesterton. A wartime junior naval officer (he was at the D-Day landings), he was courteous to friend and foe alike, wrote with clarity in his articles for *Candour*, and was the first to welcome me back into an executive position in the NF. Twelve years of leading the Empire Loyalists unique brand of demonstrations, which were never violent, had taken its toll. The in-fighting that went on in the first few months of the NF's foundation, and which was to become endemic for the next twenty years, finally broke him. He never came back to active politics.

I suggested to Chesterton that Ken Foster, who had been the BNP's only part time employee as National Secretary, could take over part of Austen's work at the HQ in Bridge Street, certainly for manning the office and dealing with enquiries. In the long run this did not turn out to be successful as Foster, dedicated and loyal as he was, in no way measured up to Austen's intellect and found the job beyond him. Foster was a very private man and I suspect very lonely. Everywhere he went he carried a large holdall: in the NF office, at meetings, and in the pub. One evening in St. Stephen's Tavern near the office, he left the zip of his holdall half open. From the gap appeared a guinea pig. Away from the political circle it was probably his only companion. We saw less and less of poor Ken Foster after that, although Chesterton would recount the guinea pig incident with much humour at soirées I attended at his flat. "John has this penchant for mixing with strange company."

A visitor to the Bridge Street HQ at this time was Martin Webster, although he was not made welcome by the ex-LEL members, who referred to him as 'Tubbs' due to his bulk. As a late teenager he had joined the LEL just after Tyndall and I had left to form the NLP. Together with two ex-grammar school contemporaries, Paul Barnes and Bill Baillie, he was highly active with the League until disillusionment with its policies set in. He next surfaced in Jordan's National Socialist Movement and then as a leading member of Tyndall's Greater Britain Movement (GBM), whilst Barnes and Baillie joined the BNP and soon gravitated towards its 'work hard, drink hard' sector. Because of his verbal abuse of the Empire Loyalists following his departure, he seemed to be more disliked and distrusted by the rank and file, but less so by Chesterton, than I had been. For me, he had a saving grace of a great sense of humour. Although joining in the laughter at his jokes and mimicry in the St.Stephen's Tavern, Barnes would warn me not to trust him, adding: "In any case he's as bent as a nine bob note."

In 1989 (twenty-two years later), when Andrew Fountaine and I were reminiscing over the fatal flaws in the foundation of the National Front, he showed me a copy of an astounding letter written by Chesterton to Gerald Kemp on 29th October 1967. In it Chesterton wrote:

"I now want to tell you something in the strictest confidence. In all matters affecting the internal security of the NF you are the absolute boss. However, in dealing with outside contacts and particularly other movements I have always operated an independent intelligence service, which has proved of great value. Its members do not normally belong to the Movement which makes use of their services. Unknown to anybody else, my chief intelligence officer now and for some time past is Martin Webster (A.K.C. Then gave his address). I am advising him to call upon you for any help he may need and you are also at liberty to call upon him. Martin has asked me to give him a letter of authorisation but, as so few people know the meaning of discretion, I am suggesting to him that he deal only through you, should the services of anybody else in the Movement be required in any given ploy. You could then cope with the situation without letting Martin's identity become known."

This explains why Chesterton's relations with Tyndall and his GBM went so much more smoothly than his relations with Fountaine, Maxwell and myself. It also emphasised Chesterton's gullibility in dealing with certain people.

Another ex-GBM member taking an active role in the NF was Denis Pirie, who had been sentenced to three months at the Spearhead trial. I attended several meetings at Pirie's flat, partly political, partly social, at which BNP and GBM activists got to know each other. Webster was usually there. I can only recall Tyndall being there once.

At one of these meetings a new emblem, or logo, for the NF was being discussed, as the BNP's Celtic cross, with its Northern European historical roots, was not acceptable to the new Executive Directorate. Independent of each other, Pirie and I came up with the compressed 'NF' logo, which has since been painted on innumerable walls.

Tyndall was still not even a member of the NF, although in *Spearhead* in September 1967 he announced that the GBM would be discontinued and that its members and supporters should give 'wholehearted support' to the NF. In October he attended the first Annual Conference of the National Front at the Caxton Hall, Westminster, but did not speak.

At the Conference A.K.Chesterton gave some prescient advice which, although warmly applauded by the audience at that time, became forgotten within two or three years:

"Let us face this. We have an attraction for certain kinds of louts who, unless kept in check, can and certainly will wreck any movement. The harm these irresponsibles can do us may be incalculable.

"We are fighting a clever and immensely powerful enemy, and while we cannot match his resources, we can and must try to match his brains. The man who thinks this is a war that can be won by mouthing slogans about 'dirty Jews and filthy niggers' is a maniac whose place should not be in the National Front but in a mental hospital... We simply cannot afford to have these maniacs active in our ranks. A nation once noble and great

202

cannot be rescued from the mire by jackasses who play straight into their enemy's hands by giving the public that image of us that the enemy most dearly wants to be given.

"If scapegoats have to be found, do not look for them among the Jews or coloured people. Look for them among the six hundred odd traitors or dripping wets in the House of Commons. Look for them among the champions of Sodom in the House of Lords and in Lambeth Palace."

In the next issue of *Combat* I published an article submitted by John Tyndall. Headed *'Worms at War with Men'*, it attacked the Government's sanctions policy against Rhodesia.

The outcome was some typically idiosyncratic behaviour by Andrew Fountaine, in his capacity as Chairman of the Executive Directorate. He sent a memo to all NF Branch Organisers that they must not sell that issue of *Combat* because it contained an article from a proscribed person: John Tyndall. I decided not to make an issue of it, accepted Andrew's £10 donation to *Combat*, and was told verbally by several Branch Organisers: "We saw no memo. Must have been lost in the post." Nevertheless it did nothing to uplift my waning enthusiasm for the cause and the next issue of *Combat* was the last to be published.

In that final issue I reported the result of the March 1968 by-election in Acton, West London. Andrew Fountaine stood as the National Front candidate, its first Parliamentary election campaign, and obtained 1,400 votes (5.6 per cent). Although I had drafted his election address and canvassed for him at weekends, which I knew from Southall experience was essential work, he complained afterwards that I had let him down by not speaking for him. I had to remind him that he chose Gerald Kemp to do this.

Seven days before the election I was astounded to see the number of 'Vote Fountaine' posters in windows in most areas of the constituency. This support was also reflected in the canvassing returns. Based on my Southall experience it seemed that he would be well ahead of the Liberals, whose candidate gained 2,868 votes, and he looked likely to top 5,000. He then became the victim of a 'fascist' smear campaign. First, from an illegal leaflet distributed throughout Acton by the 62 Group. Second, from Liberal and Labour canvassers and loudspeaker cars. Third, from a scurrilous leaflet issued by the Liberals on the eve of poll. The Fountaine posters were soon taken down.

A.K.Chesterton had come down on my side without prevarication in regard to the banning of *Combat* and he stated in a letter, "It was evident that neither Andrew nor Gerald K. relished my championship of you. Once again I ask you to use your great influence to prevent the movement splitting in two."

I did as Chesterton said, but with less and less enthusiasm. I could see that we founders of the National Front had made a great mistake in having two Chairmen: A.K. on the Policy Directorate and Andrew on the Executive Directorate. The position was aggravated by the one having to spend half the year in South Africa and the other having to be coaxed from his estate in Norfolk. Such was Andrew's behaviour, like a loose cannon on his beloved quarter deck, that I realised that I should have kept him in his figurehead role that he performed as President of theBritish National Party. The trouble was that he could be so likeable and he was my friend, right up to the end of his life.

The clash between the two bulls, one old but wise, the other younger and more headstrong, was inevitable.

The catalyst was the student riot in France in May 1968 that threatened to bring down the French Government. It also spread to Berlin and Warsaw. Thinking it was to happen here, Fountaine sent a circular to all NF Branch Organisers warning them that civil war was imminent and that they should report with all branch activists to the local police station to put themselves at the disposal of the forces of law and order.

To some of us it was laughable. "That's just Andrew with another bee in his bonnet. Ignore it!"

Chesterton was furious and considered Fountaine's directive 'absolutely ludicrous' and placed a ban on it being sent out. However, Fountaine had it duplicated and posted from Norfolk.

This action also convinced Chesterton of changing the Two-

Directorate system into a One-Directorate system to obviate anything of the kind happening in future, thus ensuring a single, unequivocal chain of command.

A joint meeting of the two Directorates was held, but Andrew Fountaine strongly opposed the motion, refused to serve on the drafting committee or to share the executive duties with others. A vote was held and the motion was carried with only one other member supporting Andrew's opposition to it. I voted, with a heavy heart, for the motion. Fountaine then spent thousands of pounds, with Quintin Hogg as his Q.C., in taking the issue to court. The court found that under the first NF Constitution, his expulsion as Chairman of the Executive Directorate was invalid.

Kemp had backed Fountaine to the hilt on his irrational actions, which were threatening to destroy the NF. Without any prompting on my part he was then expelled from the Movement by the new Leadership Executive. Significantly, Chesterton had this to say about him in a letter to me of 13th May 1968:

"I quote from a letter of his (Kemp) of January 6, which is only one of several of the same kind that I received. 'Disruption. Here I must be blunt. There is only one blatant disrupter in the NF and that is John Bean, the self-styled Goebbels of the radical right. As long as he stays there will be trouble. The rest can be handled, but it may be necessary to weed out a few more at a later date and perhaps dispense with Birkbeck Hill altogether.'"

No.10 Birkbeck Hill was the Nationalist Centre, a building owned by Gordon Brown (alias Marshall), then a close Tyndall supporter, and another so-called antiques dealer. It was now the publishing office of *Combat* as well as *Spearhead*.

I felt quite flattered when Philip Maxwell said that Kemp's 'mission' was to take me out of the NF equation. If it was, he need not have bothered. The Fountaine/Chesterton clash had left me deeply depressed and I tendered my resignation from all positions of office whilst retaining NF membership.

At the AGM in October, which I did not attend, a vote was taken on the Leadership of the new NF Directorate. A.K.Chesterton received 316 votes and Andrew Fountaine 20.

The newly elected 'Leader' of the Party then proposed his team, which was accepted, but not voted upon, by the assembly. They included Denis Pirie, Martin Webster and Gordon Brown (Marshall) from the old GBM but still no mention of John Tyndall.

* * * * *

Whilst this turmoil was going on within the fledgling National Front, in the real world there was an event which was to act as a catalyst for its rapid growth. Enoch Powell stood up to speak to Tory activists in Birmingham on April 20th, 1968.

Contrary to popular mythology, he did not predict that rivers would flow with blood if immigration was not stopped. This was the key part of his speech:

"Those whom the gods wish to destroy, they first make mad. We must be mad, literally mad, as a nation to be permitting the annual inflow of some 50,000 dependants, who are for the most part the material of the future growth of the immigrant descended population. It is like watching a nation busily engaged in heaping up its own funeral pyre. As I look ahead, I a filled with foreboding. Like the Roman, I seem to see the Tiber foaming with much blood."

Here was a leading, respectable, orthodox politician saying what we had said for more than a decade. The effect was electric. It dominated the media headlines. Dockers and meat porters in London marched in support. "We back Enoch," read their banners.

I immediately phoned Chesterton and asked whether the dormant Free Speech Defence Committee, of which he was Chairman and we had formed a year before, would apply for permission to use Trafalgar Square for a rally in support of Powell (the NF, like the BNP, was denied the right to hold Trafalgar Square meetings). He readily agreed, but when the matter was discussed at the next Directorate meeting (prior to the split) Fountaine spoke vigorously against the rally. "We shall be slaughtered," he said. I said that with our contacts, particularly with the Smithfield Meat Porters, there would be enough meat porter and docker muscle there to make sure we were not "slaughtered." Andrew swung a majority his way and the rally was off.

National Front leaflets supporting Powell were distributed in their thousands. A hundred or more members were joining every week. At the Nationalist Centre in Birkbeck Hill posters were produced to hand out to the meat porters and dockers, some with the NF logo. Initially, I did nothing. I was enjoying family time, but also felt deep disappointment at not being able to influence the new opportunities for growth.

Late July I was phoned by Martin Webster, who asked me if I would come along with NF members to support a Smithfield Meat Porters' pro-Enoch' rally. I agreed and offered to meet him with my car at the Nationalist Centre.

There were five of us in the Consul 375. There would have been six but Webster's bulk meant that even three in the back was a tight squeeze. The others were Ken Merritt, my faithful 'bodyguard', Tom Nobbs, Merritt's right hand man, and another member who I cannot recall. We were well received, as usual, in Smithfield and apart from giving out NF leaflets, cemented our relations with most of the meat porters. The exceptions were the close supporters of Dan Harmston of Mosley's Union Movement, who were also trying to cash in on the Powell furore.

In Trafalgar Square on that same Saturday afternoon a rally was held against Powell by Left Wing groups. Some of the more militant members of the Young Communist League and International Socialists had made their way down to Smithfield, but seeing the strength of the meat porters' meeting had departed after some heckling. As I drove towards Ludgate Circus we spotted seven or eight Young Communists standing outside The Punch waving a YCL flag.

"Stop up there, John," said Merritt, "and leave the engine running." I pulled up near The Bell in Fleet Street. Merritt, Webster and the other two got out and Merritt turned down my rear number plate (on the Consul 375 it was on a hinge which pulled down to give access to the petrol cap). They walked casually back to Ludgate Circus and pounced on the unsuspecting young reds with a flurry of blows. Merritt stuffed an NF leaflet in one young red's pocket and grabbed their flag with the other.

With much chortling in the car at the capture of the flag, I drove up Fleet Street and the Strand and stopped at Charing Cross Station where Tom Nobbs and the unknown NF member went off to catch a train home. Although the anti-Powell rally had ended, there were still large numbers of rally supporters moving away in groups. With Merritt sitting alongside and Webster reclining in the back seat surveying the motley crowd with a cynical gaze, the traffic brought me to a halt again halfway down Whitehall. Suddenly it was a case of the 'biter being bit'. Webster and/or I must have been recognised by our opponents. Five or six young men were kicking the car and trying to pull open the doors. I pushed open the driver's door as hard as I could hoping it would knock the nearest one off balance. This partly succeeded. Then I literally saw stars as, half way out of the car, I was hit on the mouth by a bottle. I tasted blood and could feel bits of teeth in my mouth, but it was not painful, just numb. Merritt shouted "Get back in, lock the door and keep the engine running." Swinging himself round a lamppost he got both feet straight into an assailant's head. Webster, some six stone heavier than Merritt's eleven, stood by the rear door with his arms going round like a windmill.(Some LEL members had accused Webster of physical cowardice: I never found this to be so.)

The traffic in front at last began to move. I leant on the horn and Merritt and Webster leapt back in.

Arriving at the Nationalist Centre in Tulse Hill a gleeful Webster presented the Young Communists' flag, with a beaming Tyndall looking on. I was playing to the gallery with my bloodied face and broken teeth when Merritt, with a touch of *lese-majesty*, said: "Stick to the organising and producing *Combat*. You're bloody useless as a street fighter." It was good advice.

My wife was even less impressed by the results of the

afternoon's activities, and which by the evening were giving some considerable pain. Three days later we were due to go on holiday and she thought I had reneged on my word of gradually withdrawing from my leading political role. The resulting tension ruined the holiday, in spite of my extended dental plate containing two more handsome false teeth.

For the next eighteen months I concentrated on my technical editing and then technical PR work and was virtually inactive in the National Front. I did write articles for John Tyndall's *Spearhead*, which remained independent but in support of the NF.

This enabled me to put forward some of the old BNP views which had now become rather controversial to the Chesterton and Tyndall dominated NF. Typical was my article: "Europe: Can We Afford To Ignore It?" I called for a more flexible view towards Europe, although opposing entry into the 'financiers' Common Market. We could still retain our Britishness and control of our own destiny whilst recognising our common accord with our fellow Europeans.

Another article, "NF Must Win Labour Voters," was initiated by the desire to offset the imbalance of ex-Tories within the NF membership, many of whom were coming in via the Tory Monday Club. I suggested that a minimum wage be established and that this should be pegged to the cost of living index. We should support fuller employee represenation in the running of industries. Finance must become the true hand-maiden of industry instead of its master.

* * * * *

The initial spurt in membership following the famous Powell speech faded after some twelve months and in the late spring of 1970 serious dissension had again broken out on the Directorate.

Although Chesterton had his doubts about the NF's ability to fight ten Parliamentary seats at the forthcoming June election, he gave the contest his approval, if only to keep the support of the pro-election activists. I sent him my suggestions for the election campaign and received the following reply of May 27, 1970:

"Many thanks for your election campaign notes. These are excellent and need neither amendment nor addition. I will ask HQ to ensure that several copies are sent to each agent.

"When are you coming back? We miss you like Hell. Maxwell is a decent enough chap but in my view practically useless. If you could return to the fray, it would make all the difference."

Chesterton always knew how to play on one's ego.

The election results were appalling. Where around ten per cent had been gained in the same areas in the earlier Municipal elections, it dropped to an average of only three per cent. Although run off, my election campaign notes had not been distributed (not that they would have made much difference), probably due to the general inefficiency that abounded at the Fleet Street HQ and was only slightly alleviated with the appointment of John O'Brien as office manager.

Key members were beginning to line up for the making of a split. A so-called Action Committee was set up primarily by Gordon Brown (née Marshall) with the objective of ousting Chesterton, who they said was too old and out of touch with the new young movement. This gained the support of several key activists, but few thinkers or potential leaders. They included former BNP activists such as Ron Tear and John Cook of East London and the gifted Peter McMenemie who designed much of the NF literature, including *Spearhead*, at that time.

The remaining Empire Loyalists supported Chesterton, as did John O'Brien. Crucially, Chesterton could also rely on the support of Tyndall and myself, although neither of us held any official office, as well as Martin Webster and Philip Maxwell. With the possible exception of Maxwell, we did so for two reasons. The first was our recognition of his intellect, his long term track record and his undisputed knowledge of the machinations of the international money power, whereas the 'Action Committee' seemed solely motivated by their opposition to coloured immigration.

Our second reason was the question of substantial financial support. Chesterton had several wealthy contacts which had enabled him to finance *Candour* and the League of Empire Loyalists. His main benefactor was R.K. Jeffery an ex-patriate millionaire from Chile, who was reputed to have given Chesterton £70,000 until his death in 1961. Jeffery's will was mysteriously altered immediately prior to his death, which deprived Chesterton of his estate, said to be worth over a million pounds. The will was still being contested in the courts in 1970.

With the plan to oust Chesterton well under way, I wrote to him pointing out that they had some substance in their claim of lack of leadership and to offset this the NF should be more 'Radical' Right and less 'Reactionary' Right. I assured him that whether he took this advice or not, I would still support him.

He replied on 23rd June, 1970:

"... I accept without question your assurance about your use of the word 'radical', and never for one moment did I think that you were making a bid for the Movement's leadership. You have not only given abundant proof of your personal loyalty, but you are politically much too wise to attempt to take over the National Front in any context other than a battle for the Chesterton succession. This may sound conceited, but I only intend it to be realistic. Confidentially, should I be alive when the battle opens, you will have my full support."

The battle opened sooner than Chesterton visualised, and as I did not throw my hat in the ring he eventually switched his support to John Tyndall.

Gordon Brown secretly approached Tyndall and asked him to take over the leadership from Chesterton. Being loyal to Chesterton, he refused to do so unless that was the wish of the members in an open vote. Although they still had no leader and were incapable of producing one from within their ranks, the Action Committee circularised all NF branches condemning Chesterton, particularly for his "dictatorial methods and pettiness in the leadership." As Chesterton had opposed Powell's economic views in *Candour*, his new opponents had a point which we told him when they said in regard to Powell that: "Rightly or wrongly he is respected by a huge majority of the

British people and to attack him incurs the hostility of that majority."

On receiving a copy of this circular Chesterton wrote to Cmdr G.K. Rylands, the Chairman of the NF National Council (a figurehead body that hardly met) resigning his position as National Director and his membership of the National Front. Apparently Chesterton thought that the support of those who opposed the Action Committee was only lukewarm and therefore he had no choice but to resign.

In a letter to him in South Africa of November 27, 1970 I made these points:

"I feel that because a number of us tried to 'pour oil over troubled waters' and admitted the justification of some of the complaints made, but not the manner in which they were proffered, you have somehow felt that this signified luke-warm loyalty on our part. This is not so: it merely signifies the different manner in which I and others tackle problems of this nature. Although John Tyndall would have taken a stronger line than I did, the above is his view also, as it is that of Martin Webster and John O'Brien. Similarly, the fact that on my own volition I called a private meeting of people who also happened to be members of the Directorate, and took the chair at the meeting, did not mean any disloyalty on my part. It was motivated by the fact that as I still have some influence amongst a number of the longer serving Directorate members I thought it necessary to act quickly and get the 'rebels' to withdraw their insulting remarks about you and your so called sycophants and thus clear the way for an official Directorate meeting. In the event I succeeded, but now it all seems rather pointless as you have since resigned."

Tyndall wrote to Chesterton in similar vein.

Having been co-opted back onto the Directorate, I called a special meeting at the Great Eastern Hotel, near Liverpool Street Station, on Sunday, November 29th. It was booked in the name of Clare Macdonald, a new Directorate member. I got the majority to agree with me that we should ask Chesterton to withdraw his resignation. I was strongly opposed by Brown and three of his supporters. Rosine de Bounevialle, a loyal

212

Chesterton supporter from the LEL days, roundly condemned them and retorted that A.K. would never return until the Action Committee was expelled.

Rosine knew Chesterton better than any of us. She was right. A.K. would not withdraw his resignation and gave his reason in the December issue of *Candour*:

"If the right leader comes along and if the twilight creatures are relegated to the sewers, the NF will have no stauncher friend than me."

With Tyndall still playing his waiting game, the office manager, John O'Brien, was elected Chairman of the Directorate: another man from nowhere, shaken out of his conventional support for Conservatism by the immigration problem, and going nowhere. At least he was likeable, personable and honest.

Chesterton's subtle comment on his appointment was: "John O'Brien is far and away the best man for the job in as far as he was the only one willing to accept it."

Meanwhile John Bean was again deeply depressed and returned to his new job, including its social life, with enthusiasm.

Another social occasion was to undertake the role of godfather at the christening of Ken Merritt's daughter. The vicar showed no reaction at the announcement of her second name, Boadicea. I was told he had previously officiated at the christening of Miss Merritt's brother Caractacus Merritt.

"Well, I weren't gonna call 'im Leroy, was I, John?"

* * * * *

By the summer of 1972 John O'Brien, the office manager new boy who became Chairman after Chesterton's resignation, thought he could democratise the National Front and expel the key extremists, Tyndall and Webster. He was no match for their experience of in-fighting and soon found himself out-manoeuvred and out of office.

Although I was kept informed of the changing patterns resulting from the various taps on the NF kaleidoscope over the next ten years, I was rarely directly involved from 1972 onwards. I used my diminishing influence to advise Tyndall, Fountaine and others at private meetings. I soon found it was a waste of breath to try and advise Martin Webster.

As an extremely active activities organiser Webster stands credited with playing the major part in putting the National Front on the map. To achieve this he is alleged to have told a press reporter (one Christopher Farman of BNP Earls Court days): "We had to kick our way into the headlines." Webster disputes this, and says he used the word "crashing" rather than "kick." Nevertheless, as far as the public were concerned, what they saw between 1973 and 1979 was the National Front kicking its way into numerous local and national headlines, with the action there for all to see in several TV news programmes.

Its origins began when the heckling, often witty, carried out at opponents meetings in the early NF days by former Empire Loyalists and some ex-BNP members, was replaced with chanting and cat-calling. This accelerated after Chesterton's retirement.

Week after week from 1969 through to late 1973 teams of NF activists, first twenty, then forty, then sixty and eventually hundreds strong, would infiltrate and rowdily lambast every Left Wing meeting in London. The Central Hall, Friends Meeting House, Conway Hall, Haringey Town Hall, Church House and the London School of Economics all echoed at one time or other to the chanting, shouting, cat calling, irresponsible and irrepressible noise of the NF mob. Writing in *Spearhead* in March 1977, Martin Webster wrote:

"All this resulted in oceans of publicity from the Establishment's cynical presses which can't resist riot, mayhem, outrage, flour spattered Cabinet Ministers bereft of their pomposity, and bags of 'action' photos! Soon the London Activists became a 'travelling circus', and Left Wing occasions as far afield as Cardiff, Leicester and Birmingham were 'hit', the resultant publicity winning recruits in those places who soon formed Branches.

"... Once we started being able to mobilise Activists by the hundred we moved to a new style of activity: **marches**."

Marches were held in most Midlands cities and large towns, in Blackburn, Bradford and Huddersfield in the North, Bristol and Cardiff in the West, and in many parts of London. Initially, I was in favour of this tactic (although I did not participate in any march), in that the spectacle of waving flags and marching bands was making its impression on the public, and particularly the youth. This was reflected in the increased votes the National Front was picking up from the October 1974 General Election through to 1977.

Equally I must confess that *at the time* emotive romanticism had me supporting the NF confrontation with the left in the 'Battle of Red Lion Square', June 15th, 1974. Fifteen hundred NF supporters had marched through London's West End to a meeting in Conway Hall, Red Lion Square. Opposing them were up to 5,000 Marxist Leninists, Trotskyists, orthodox Communists and other Left Wing militants. The 'battle' that took place was between them and the police while the NF marchers were still twenty minutes away.

However, I did raise objections to the fact that some marches through immigrant areas were being perceived by the public, following media prompting, as coat trailing exercises that were provoking violence. In a letter to Martin Webster of November 1st, 1974 I wrote:

"Please find enclosed my form signifying assent to being co-opted onto the Publicity Committee of the NF, if approved by a majority of the Directorate. In regard to your request for comment on past publicity work, I would refer you to my earlier comments on the advisability of 'coat trailing' marches through immigrant areas. Also, my proposals for a public relations campaign already submitted to the Directorate via John Tyndall. However, one point in this that I would emphasise is my belief that great emphasis should be placed on personal canvassing as a regular, sustained activity in all seats that the NF proposes to contest at the next election."

For some reason I was not co-opted onto the Publicity Committee.

The need for caution was being voiced by others of the radical right. Bill Barnes (father of Paul Barnes) and a pre-war member of one of the Fascist organisations, was writing under the name of Athelstan in a private circulation news letter called *Nation*.

In the July 1974 issue the following advice appeared: "Has the time come for the National Front to abandon the romantic ritual of marches and rallies? Not completely, perhaps, but the march/rally/demonstration is heady stuff, to be used sparingly. The romanticists among us are stirred by the sight of waving banners, the beat of the drums, the chanting voices and the comradeship. But if we are to get the mass support to which we have a claim we must avoid the appearance of over aggressiveness, of 'trailing our coat tails', in short of 'fascism', the bogey of British political folk lore. ...

"Now we are politically credible let us seek to advance by political means. The Conservative, Liberal and Labour parties seldom find it advantageous to hold marches, rallies or anything other than indoor meetings. Should we feature them so frequently we stand the risk of being considered *jejune* and provocative, a sort of militarised Boy Scout movement with sinister undertones.

"The man in the street has a fear of party dictatorship. Economic tyranny he is enduring; financial dictatorship he has long endured; but the thought of a Martin Mosley or Oswald Webster as Gauleiter of Greater London moves him to terrified reaction to the benefit of the liberal democrats."

At the end of 1974 the 'populist' elements within the National Front thought they had found a new democratic leader in, a former Conservative from Blackburn who had left the party over immigration. He had presented a good image in the NF's Party Political Broadcast it had obtained by putting up 90 candidates that October. Above all, he was not tainted with a 'Nazi' past. Andrew Fountaine had also rejoined, following the death of A.K. Chesterton, which strengthened the populist camp. At a vote of the NF Directorate a tie was reached with ten votes apiece for Kingsley Read and John Tyndall. Gordon 'Brown' (Marshall), landlord of the NF HQ at Pawsons Road, Croydon, gave his casting vote for Kingsley Read.

216

1975 saw little growth in the NF, whose energies were now once again taken up with in-fighting. It was not just a question of conflict between the 'populists', who had much to offer, and the hard-liners personified by Tyndall and Webster, for there was growing friction behind the scenes between these two.

Tyndall, Webster and their supporters were not going to give up control of the movement that easy. Fired by their fanaticism, and with the stomach for hard work, control was regained in 1976. Kingsley Read, Roy Painter and other ex-Conservative populist's departed to form a National Party, which staggered on for a year or two, including staggering out of the pub.

Andrew Fountaine in the meantime had found himself expelled by Kingsley Read and on the latter's departure rejoined with Tyndall for the third time.

Fountaine's rather biting comment on his expulsions was expressed in a letter to me many years later, in April 1989.

"I was expelled three times from the National Front:
Once by Chesterton,
Once by Kingsley Read,
Once by Tyndall,
The first thought he was the Doge of Venice. The second was a drunkard. The third was a play actor whose summit ambition at one time was to be mistaken for Adolf Hitler."

I told Andrew that I thought his last simile was rather unkind.

He just grinned in his naughty schoolboy way.

Following the death of Read in 1985 I was not unduly surprised to hear that the 'anti fascist' magazine *Searchlight* had published a report stating that he had for some years been one of its undercover agents.

By the end of 1976 it was claimed that more than 4,500 new members had joined in that year. In early 1977 I had every reason to believe that membership had reached 15,000, which was its peak. However, NF membership suffered from the bathtub syndrome, as did the Mosley movement and the BNP to a lesser extent. The bath was never full because as fast as new members came through the taps others were disappearing down the plughole, mostly through disillusionment.

217

1977 was also the highwater mark for National Front votes. Over 400 candidates stood in the May County Council and Greater London Council (GLC) elections and gained nearly a quarter of a million votes. In London 91 candidates collected 119,000 votes and beat the liberals in 33 of the seats. In Bethnal Green & Bow and Hackney South and Shoreditch the NF gained 19% of the poll; Stepney & Poplar, 16.4%, and Hackney Central and Newham South both more than 15%. The average London vote was 5.3%.

In Leicester the National Front beat the Liberals in all but one of the sixteen wards in the city. They gained a total of 22,526 votes (13.2%). The percentage of the votes was in double figures in many wards in Wolverhampton, Birmingham, Bradford, Manchester, Preston, Bolton, Accrington, Nottingham and Derby, with 7% and 8% being commonplace.

"Unnerving" was how Labour Agent Ron Hayward described the NF vote. "The National Front is becoming extremely worrying," said Mrs Thatcher.

The far-Left continued to organise counter demonstrations against NF marches, usually 1,500 to 2,000 strong by this time, with much blood being spilt. In Lewisham the left attacked both police and NF marchers with bottles and bricks, but the image perceived by the viewer at home in front of the TV was that the NF had marched through an immigrant area deliberately to stir up trouble. The NF could justify their action by saying that they had gone to Lewisham (which includes Deptford) at the request of their local members and local voters opposed to mass immigration.

But they could not justify their action on Saturday 2nd July 1977 when 200 members and followers went to Lewisham to counter-demonstrate against Socialist Workers Party members demonstrating in support of a recently arrested gang of local black muggers. In the resulting mayhem more than fifty NF members were arrested.

I did not renew my National Front membership when it expired at the end of 1977.

* * * * *

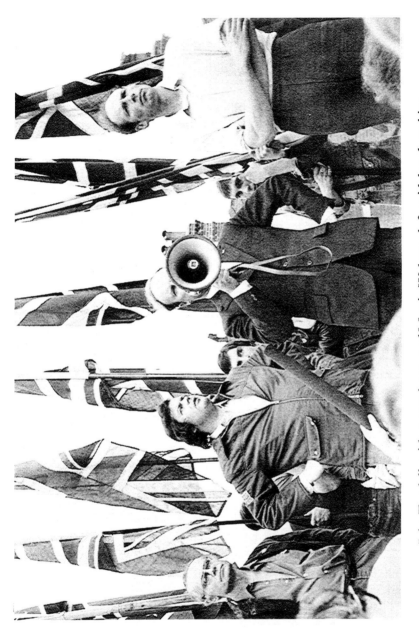

John Tyndall, with megaphone, and Martin Webster, left, with hands on hips, address a National Front rally, circa 1976

In 1978 the National Front at last acquired the lease of a substantial building for a national head office. This was, 73 Great Eastern Street, London EC2, which had over 20,000 square feet on four floors. A group of NF business men, led by Paul Kavanagh, formed National Front Properties Ltd, which acquired the building and then let it to the NF for a token rent.

Officials of the movement hoped that at long last there would be an end to the internal bickering and an improvement in organisation. An area which was suffering particularly was in the regular production of *National Front News*, a popular news-sheet that sold well to the general public. Martin Webster was still the editor and, befitting his character, the news-sheet would be produced when the muse took him.

He had also agreed to bring out a publication exposing the Communists and other extreme Left organisers behind the Anti-Nazi League, which had been formed in late 1977 to physically attack the National Front. When it eventually appeared, nearly twelve months late, it was quite effective in persuading some of the original sponsors of the Anti-Nazi League (ANAL) to disassociate themselves from this vicious, violent and subversive alliance of Marxist opportunists and agitators. Liberal MP Richard Wainwright withdrew all support *because of the lack of any democratically elected management controlling it.* Although a number of other original sponsors, such as Jonathan Dimbleby, appeared to distance themselves from ANAL after mid-1978, there were still enough gullible sports personalities, showbiz celebrities and academics around to give the impression that it was a respectable body devoted to maintaining freedom and democracy!

Incidentally, when Britain's No. 1 tennis player at that time, Buster Mottram, let it be known that he was a National Front supporter, obnoxious ANAL supporters, led by Peter Hain, demonstrated against him at Wimbledon, repeatedly interrupting his game.

By 1979 opposition to Tyndall, and Webster in particular, was again threatening to split the movement. Accusations were made of hysterical behaviour by Webster and his homosexual

220

cliques at Excalibur House. Others, including myself, although I was no longer a member, did not like the decline in Webster's *National Front News*, which seemed to concentrate on racialist abuse of coloured immigrants. The opposition centred around Andrew Fountaine. He announced that he would be standing for the Chairmanship of the NF at the forthcoming NF conference. In the meantime, as the movement's Regulating Officer, he suspended Martin Webster from office until the various complaints about his actions could be fully investigated. Seeing that Fountaine could possibly take his place as Chairman (in the event he did not obtain enough votes), Tyndall sided with Webster and Fountaine was expelled, yet again, with many key activists following him into the new National Front Constitutional Movement.

This further haemorrhage of the NF came on top of its disastrous 1979 general election results, where many erstwhile Front voters were wooed away by the siren voices of those of Maggie Thatcher's Conservatives who had promised to "tighten up on immigration control".

Some of the directors of NF Properties Ltd, the owners of Excalibur House, were still supporting Tyndall and Webster, with almost half supporting Fountaine's Constitutional Movement. The issue of who was to control the premises was soon resolved by a typical 'democratic' decision from the establishment when dealing with political tyros it does not like. The Secretary of State for the Environment issued an Order dated 10th April 1980 upholding the decision of the Inspector (under the Town and Country Planning Act) earlier that year forbidding the use of Excalibur House for any political purposes.

National Front Constitutional Movement (NFCM) members continued to use it for private meetings, but with a P.O. Box number for all literature. Later that year two Communists, brothers called Read who had joined the NF as moles, had tried to burn the place down but were caught redhanded by the police. One was given a suspended sentence, the other was discharged. In May 1981 while East London NFCM members were attending GLC election counts at Hackney and Tower

Hamlets, arsonists broke into Excalibur House and started a fire which gutted the top two floors causing £60,000 damage. No one was caught. The same night a young man, Anthony Donnelly, who had been actively helping local NFCM candidates, was murdered in Glyn Road, Hackney. He had been repeatedly stabbed. Three West Indians were charged with his murder.

Having given up my non-active membership of the National Front at the end of 1977, I reluctantly became a supporter (not a member) of the NFCM, under pressure from Andrew Fountaine and Terry Savage (whom I had known since National Labour Party days), who now edited its paper, *Frontline News*. I spoke at a meeting in a London hotel on 29th March, 1980 to launch *Frontline News*. The editor reported:

"Making an unfortunately rare but greatly appreciated appearance as a guest speaker, Mr John Bean, one of the founding members of the National Front, stressed the need for the National Front Constitutional Movement to recognise the fact that politics is the art of the possible."

He did not choose to inform his readers what specific part of politics I thought should be the art of the possible. Andrew Brons, by this time Chairman of the National Front, did when he wrote this in an NF publication, *New Nation*:

"I was brought into serious Nationalist politics after hearing John Bean, who was then (1965) National Organiser of the British National Party, address a meeting in Leeds and it was from that Party that I came into the NF at its formation in 1967. I had joined the BNP after becoming convinced that the man in charge of it was a hard-line British Nationalist who would not betray our principles under any circumstances. It was with horror and disbelief, therefore, that I heard recently that he had addressed a meeting of the 'Con Movement' Faction saying that the proposal for compulsory repatriation would have to be dropped because the British people would not stand for it."

I was sorry to upset Andrew Brons, as I liked him and thought he was one of the brighter people to join the movement. But I did say that in regard to repatriation, with the proviso that all illegal immigrants should be deported, and I stand by it today.

More important than what was happening on the fringes of the Constitutional Movement (which faded out after some three years), was the 1980 split between Webster and Tyndall. It was a parting of the ways waiting to happen and had been delayed solely because the other splits with the 'Populists' had kept driving Tyndall and Webster back together.

With the rump of the old National Front, Webster resumed the marches and made up for the loss of the comparatively more disciplined marchers with gangs of completely undisciplined skinheads and football hooligans, plus supporters of Colin Jordan's British Movement and its offshoot, Column 88 (Heil Hitler) and its psychopaths. Young bloods eventually ousted Webster, who went into political retirement.

In June 1980 John Tyndall formed the New National Front, which "aimed at quality first and quality second". Within two years the staying power of Tyndall had attracted around him the bulk of the residue of those British Nationalists who had survived the twelve years of the rise and fall of the National Front. Recognising that its fall was permanent and mainly due to the forces of self-destruction, he ditched the title and resurrected that of the British National Party. He even showed signs or moderation and was at last admitting the mistakes of his neo-Nazi youth. Whether this was but a tactical ploy or a genuine change of heart was not yet clear.

Ron Tear, left, with early NF poster parade outside
London's Rhodesia House

Fifty years on. The author at the derelict site of
Hayle Power Station in 1995

CHAPTER 11
REFLECTIONS

My political odyssey moved into calmer waters in the spring of 1973 when my wife and I moved to a four hundred year-old Suffolk cottage. We were in the vanguard of the phenomenon that became known as white flight. Although virtually non-active I was to remain a paid-up member of the National Front well until the end of 1977.

After twelve months I was prevailed upon to join the village Community Council. In later years I was then asked to stand for the Parish Council, but did not do so as the local press would undoubtedly find out my connections with the radical Right and start a witch hunt, which would be embarrassing to Wickhambrook's Parish Councillors. Nevertheless, whenever politics came up in the village I never hid my views, and most people knew where my allegiances lay.In April 1975 I became editor of the village magazine, *The Wickhambrook Scene* and held the post for eighteen years. I kept it non-party political, although one reader of Left Wing views told me during one of our many discussions in the local hostelry that it occasionally showed 'fascist undertones'. The furthest I ever went in expressing my views on the effects of immigration was in the November 1987 issue:

"Many of the newcomers to the village have come here to escape the pressures of modern city life and enjoy the community spirit that exists here. However, an unfortunate outcome of the mass move to East Anglia is that it has pushed up house prices so high that young local people just getting married find it extremely difficult, if not impossible, to even raise a deposit for their 'starter home'. Spare a thought for them. Have any of the politicians taken time off from telling us what they are going to do about the underprivileged in the inner cities to even consider the problems of our rural underprivileged, whose ancestors, going back to Saxon and even Celtic times, made this land?

"In no way can we blame the newcomers to our village, particularly as your Editor is one who sneaked in here fifteen years ago before the rush started. As I see it, many are driven out of the towns and cities because they have become unrecognisable from the immediate post-war years, when you could walk through some of the roughest parts of London or Birmingham without danger. The sixties and seventies policy of self-expression and rejection of old-fashioned discipline in the schools, and the home, has now produced its crop of self-centred hooligans, white as well as black. Coupled with this, the ever open door to immigration has meant that the cities are no longer composed of a homogenous people, of a common culture, but several conflicting cultures, with all the resultant problems of friction.

"Some may be shocked by my expression of the above view; now deemed to be most unfashionable by TV pundits and liberal politicians, if not even 'racist'. I make no apologies, and we should stop kidding ourselves that the situation in the cities is otherwise."

I did not receive any letters of complaint regarding this editorial but several verbal comments of approval.

One of the advantages of distancing myself from the political action in the eighties and nineties is that it enabled me to see more clearly the reasons for the decline and failure of the National Front. I believe there were six major reasons.

1. Following the 1977 high water mark vote gained by the National Front in County Council elections, Margaret Thatcher said: "The National Front is becoming extremely worrying". It soon became clear that what she proposed to do about it was to steal their clothing by subtle implication. People were beginning to say: "If we vote for Maggie at the next election she is going to tighten up on immigration". In fact, she never made a pledge to this effect but implied that something must be done to control numbers.

More importantly, former National Front voters began listening to the siren voices of those Conservative MPs who did speak out strongly in calling for tougher controls. Conservatives such as Tony Marlow, Ronald Bell, Harvey

Proctor, Nicholas Winterton and John Carlisle were particularly outspoken. Needless to say, only Nicholas Winterton holds a seat in the Conservative Party of William Hague.

This contrasted with the liberal immigration policies pursued by the Heath Government from 1970-74, whose admission of the Ugandan Asians in 1972 had been a great fillip to the Front's fortunes. In consequence the 1979 General Election saw former Front voters switching to Mrs Thatcher's victorious Tory Party in droves.

2. The almost continual internal warfare that beset the National Front from its foundation not only led to its haemorrhaging, as described in the previous Chapter, as various splinter groups were formed, but also sapped the energy of key personnel. The result was that very few other than Tyndall were able to survive the stress. Brilliant branch organisers such as Anthony Reed-Herbert in Leicester were worn down and finally gave up the struggle.

3. Marches and demonstrations have a part to play in politics when they are held for a specific reason and are disciplined.

Witness the huge 300,000 strong Countryside Alliance march in London on March 1st, 1998 - and which I was pleased to attend. Nevertheless, it is an easy transition from King Arthur's Camelot to a Nuremberg rally, as the Front was to find by the time of the Lewisham march in July 1977. They were perceived to be trailing their coat tails in immigrant areas, of being over-aggressive and provocative. The evidence was there to see on TV news programmes - admittedly selective evidence - that the marchers were behaving as their Left Wing opponents deemed them to be: as Fascists.

4. The smear leaflets put out by mainly Left Wing groups, but at Acton and other places by the so-called "Liberals", did have some effect in frightening off potential voters. I remember my indignation at seeing the first "National Front is a Nazi Front" leaflet with a photograph of myself standing alongside Colin Jordan at a BNP meeting in Trafalgar Square in 1961. It ignored the fact that I was instrumental in Jordan's expulsion because of his Nazi utterances. I too was a 'Nazi' by past association.

For many years similar smear leaflets would be handed out in thousands at election times showing John Tyndall dressed in his Spearhead uniform. No matter how often National Front candidates complained to the returning officer that virtually all these leaflets were illegal, and no matter how much Tyndall claimed that the uniform was a stupid act of youth, the smear campaign lost many potential votes.

Yet when Kingsley Read and the 'populist' element split away from Tyndall and Webster to fight elections as the National Party, they were surprised to find that, although they had never been associated with the old Jordan, Mosley or even Chesterton far-Right extremists, and thus considered themselves to be squeaky clean, they were still smeared and in most areas were well behind the NF vote. Similarly, in the 1998 Australian election, Pauline Hanson of the One Nation Party had no 'fascist' past yet she was soon dubbed a 'race hater' and 'Nazi' by Australia's own version of the Anti-Nazi League rentamob. And she still polled a million votes from those concerned with the rise of Asian immigration.

5. People interested in joining the NF did so primarily on the issue of immigration. When they wrote in for further details most found that they also had sympathy for some of the other NF views, such as opposition to Britain's membership of the Common Market; the return of capital punishment for child murderers and murderers of police officers; denouncing the international bankers who put profit before national interest and jobs. But when they looked through the pages of *National Front News* and *Spearhead* they would see other issues that did not appear in the general leaflets and the usually well-written election addresses. These would be articles on Jewish financial power, alleged Jewish control of the media and Zionist influences over British and American foreign policy. Particularly sickening to many people would be the articles nit-picking over the number of Jews who were done to death in Poland and Russia and in the Nazi concentration camps. There would also be numerous adverts for books and magazines from the so-called historical revisionists asking "Did Six Million Really Die?", and even

denying that the holocaust ever existed! It is small wonder that many would-be members decided that it was true after all. The National Front were anti-semitic, and they could see why they were being called Nazis.

Apart from this Jewish issue, by 1979 *National Front News*, under the editorship of Martin Webster, had moved away from condemning the *policy* of allowing immigration to continue, to open racial abuse on several occasions.

6. Finally, the National Front (like the British National Party who won the Millwall Council seat in 1993 but were subsequently unable to hold it) found that another reason for their declining votes from 1977 onwards was white flight. Many of the supporters who had given them 20 per cent votes in areas in East London, Southall, Leicester, parts of Birmingham, etc, had moved away to the suburbs, or down to the West Country or out into East Anglia.

In the above six major reasons for the decline of the Front I have not mentioned the physical attacks upon National Front supporters by first the 62 Group and then the Anti-Nazi League, because they had very little effect upon voting patterns.

ANAL (Anti-Nazi League) was formed at the end of 1977 with the specific purpose of organising and carrying out physical attacks upon NF supporters. This was made clear in the first press report on the formation of ANAL, which was by Chris Rowe in the *West London Gazette and Post* (8.12.77).

"A new left-wing movement in West London says it is prepared to use violence against the National Front. The Anti-Nazi League has been formed following the Front's emergence in Shepherds Bush. The campaign is being organised mainly by local leaders of the extreme left-wing Socialist Workers' Party. They are prepared to use violence to stop the NF."

Virtually all subsequent ANAL statements and literature echoed this commitment to violence. A classic example was a poster produced by ANAL in Bristol in June 1978. It was headed by a drawing of a brick smashing through the window of a National Front member's car while he was driving. Below the picture it stated:

"The following cars belong to members of the National Front. (Car numbers were then given.) If you see them cruising around here they're most likely looking for trouble. Do whatever you think is needed to show them they're not wanted - and ring 40898 to get more people to help you!"

Little or no comment was given by the media on this and many other examples of blatant incitement to violence - and no prosecutions were ever started, let alone carried out. Imagine the furore if the same posters were issued but the words "members of the National Front" were substituted by "supporters of immigration into Britain".

The call for violence was soon answered with attacks on NF meetings and marches all over Britain. NF women and pensioners were beaten up and hospitalised as well as the young men. At least some sections of the media started describing the vast collection of mallets, knives, clubs and staves that the police were taking off ANAL supporters. Following an NF rally at Bolton Town Hall in February 1978, the local evening paper showed a photograph of the weapons taken off their opponents.

There are also on record in numerous local press reports and complaints to the police (but seldom mentioned in the national press) accounts of organised attacks on individual NF, and later BNP, members. Again, just a few examples.

In 1978 the brother of Anthony Reed-Herbert, the NF Leicester Branch Organiser, narrowly escaped having his head blown off in a shot-gun attack. Anthony Reed-Herbert's wife received continual threats of violence against her baby daughter.

In March 1978, Mr. Philip Minor, the Chairman of the East Birmingham Branch of the NF, was forced to leave his Kitts Green council home after two fire-bomb attacks within a week.

In July of that year the home of the Organiser of the Walsall Branch of the NF, Charles Baugh, was subjected to an arson attack. In this fire, three people were trapped at the top of blazing stairs and only the fortuitous passing of a police panda car saved them from being burned alive.

This left-wing violence has still continued in the nineties. In 1995 the Press Officer of the British National Party, Michael Newland, was attacked in his North London home by four men posing as local council workers. He was beaten with an iron bar and received several broken bones and a fractured skull. No arrests were made. The BNP Chairman, John Tyndall, and his wife have been attacked on the streets by so-called Anti-Nazis.

The point we are making is that the left, and certainly Jewish groups who have a justifiable fear of the emergence of neo-Nazis, have the right to oppose and expose those they consider to be their opponents. But groups such as ANAL have indulged in Nazi terrorist tactics to do this, *with the tacit approval of the political establishment.*

* * * * *

Reflecting in Suffolk on the rise and fall of the National Front, I have often wondered whether I would have made any difference to its fortunes if I had remained in contention for executive office in 1970. If I had stayed, would the NF have given the militant opposition so many sticks to beat it with? Would there have been a score or more of NF councillors and perhaps even one or two MPs (as once looked likely) to give warning to the old parties that Britain wanted to remain British and not become a multiracial geographical area, a Mecca for those looking for a quick economic fix? Probably not; the liberal-left smear technique and the non-left media boycott would have still been in operation, even if slightly moderated.

Apparently the militant left think I might have had some influence on events. In April 1994, the 'anti-fascist' information magazine *Searchlight*, edited by Gerry Gable, former Communist Party candidate in Stamford Hill and an official sponsor of ANAL, commented on a letter I had published in the *Sunday Telegraph.*

"... Bean was the national organiser of the original BNP from 1960 until it became part of the newly formed National Front in January 1967. He also edited its paper *Combat*, one of the best publications ever turned out on the far right. Bean ...

231

wrote with both wit and hate. He was also one of the best street speakers the British far right had after Mosley."

In September 1997 I was approached by a researcher for Pepper Productions, who produced the three part *Windrush* series directed by David Upshall for BBC 2, to mark the fiftieth anniversary of the commencement of West Indian immigration. The lady researcher told me that she had spoken to "the *Searchlight* people" for my telephone number and they had told her: "Be careful in talking to John Bean. He is far too clever and will make racism sound reasonable."

Perhaps more important than this boost to my elderly ego is that it reflects on how it is now accepted as normal by the media to approach the crypto-communist, pro-Zionist, *Searchlight* organisation to supply the dirt on the nationalist right. Ben Lewis, the producer of the BBC 2 smear programme on the Nationalist Right, shown in early spring of 1999, told me that he went through the same *Searchlight* channel. Do they realise that they are mixing with persons who have broken into people's homes and offices to steal right wingers' documents? Gable himself has a conviction for trying to steal documents belonging to the historian David Irving while posing as a Gas Board official.

Incidentally, although David Upshall, a pleasant chap whose father came from Trinidad, spent one hour and forty minutes recording my views on early attitudes of the public to West ndian immigration, only two twenty second rather inane comments from me appeared in the *Windrush* programme. Perhaps what he was really looking for was some racial abuse from me - which he certainly did not get.

A similar situation occurred with the March 1999 programme The Lost Race, referred to above, which dealt with the decline of the National Front and the rise of the BNP. I was asked by Ben Lewis to give my views on the reasons for the NF's demise. During one and a half hours filming I dealt at length with the six points I have given earlier in this chapter, and emphasising that I was still an unrepentant opponent of the multiracial society. But it soon became clear by the questioning of the interviewer, Jolyon Jenkins (a sweet name for a 'sweet' person), that what he and Lewis were planning was a hatchet job on the BNP and on Tyndall in particular. Although at times I was critical of the BNP, I refused to provide the bullets that the BBC dirigist duo obviously wanted to fire. (The BNP, by some of their *past* actions, had made enough bullets of their own). Despite Lewis having parted with the £100 fee I had demanded, with or without the approval of his Executive Producer, Richard Klein, no part of the interview was shown in their resultant blatantly biased programme. Perhaps I should take it as a compliment that I was excluded.

I did not return the fee, but used it to help in the promotion of these memoirs.

As for the BNP, I assume they consoled themselves with the fact that everybody knows that most television documentaries are faked.

I was more pleased with my contribution to the BBC *Timewatch* programme on the history of immigration in Britain that was broadcast in April 1995. I realised afterwards that I had been able to reach more people, around two million, if only for ten minutes of the total programme, than I could in a full lifetime of street corner and hall meetings. Enoch Powell was, of course, the main, and only other, opponent of immigration on the programme, and was showing signs of the effects of Parkinson's disease that was to tragically end his life.

A quarter of an hour before the programme was recorded Enoch Powell arrived in the BBC hospitality suite where the participants in the programme, excluding the 'noble lords' (mainly old Labour hacks), were supping tea and nibbling sandwiches. They looked at Enoch in some awe. I walked over to him to introduce myself. He looked at me rather shyly when I said: "Well, whether you approve of it or not Mr Powell I am the only other person here who can be said to be on your side. I believe I have been invited because I gained some three and a half thousand votes in Southall in 1964 on a stop immigration ticket."

I was given an example of his legendary memory power when he replied in his crisp, West Midland tone: "Oh yes, I believe that was some nine per cent of the poll". He returned to sipping his tea. I moved away.

* * * * *

From 1980 onwards my friendship with Andrew Fountaine took precedence over our political - mainly tactical - differences. We were only forty minutes drive apart. At our meetings he would frequently raise the question of my retirement from the leadership cadre. His view was that it was a dereliction of duty. I should have sorted out my personal problems and come back to work initially with him and gradually he would have left more decisions to me as in our running of the old BNP.

As the eighties progressed he began to agree with me that the National Front, if not the West's radical right in general, was suffering Hitler's revenge. The bulk of the postwar population has been conditioned in the schools, colleges, universities and by the media and cinema to equate belief in racial cultural differences with National Socialism. Because Hitler based much of his creed on racial differences their logic says, therefore, that if you also believe that there are racial differences then you too must be a Nazi! It had as much relevance as saying that if you are a devout catholic then you support those who burned protestants at the stake - or vice versa.

The irony is that the greatest threat to European civilisation's existence in the 21st century stems from the birth in the 19th century of a man alleged to be its defender.

It was not only politics that Andrew and I discussed at our meetings, usually at Narford Hall, in the eighties and nineties. He had a keen interest in the use of hydrogen as an alternative power source and was convinced that its development was being held back by the vested interests of the oil companies. The interest went back to his days studying natural science at Cambridge University in the thirties. In 1990 he worked with Dr.Dennis Chaplin and Dr Alexandra Jenner of the University of East Anglia in the preparation of a syndicated article:

234

"Hydrogen to Cure Global Ills". It was referred to in publications world-wide, including some in-depth reports that I arranged in three UK trade journals.

This was not just a cranky interest of an English eccentric - which Andrew was. Readers can draw their own conclusions from these extracts:

"On the whole, the proportion of carbon dioxide in the atmosphere appears to be slowly increasing,' cautioned scientist J R Partington as long ago as 1937, the man Fountaine has regarded as an environmental prophet since his days at Cambridge. Despite many early warnings like Partington's, the environmental pollutants associated with fossil fuels have largely been ignored until of late.

"Until Fountaine's campaign to influence consciousness in the right direction this year, hydrogen has been sadly ignored as a safe and large scale energy provider. An ironic situation, says Fountaine, because it is readily available, non-pollutant and highly efficient.

"Fountaine's case rests upon the fact that once the initial cost of implementing the electrolysers (*electrolysis of sea water to give hydrogen and oxygen*) has been absorbed, hydrogen fuel will easily replace North Sea gas and help Britain to maintain her economic position in the EEC. In this perspective, he has been actively encouraged by Prince Philip, Duke of Edinburgh, with whom he has corresponded on the matter."

Also in the field of science he was an acknowledged authority on trees. Apart from having personally planted more than three million of them, he had his own arboretum at Narford, and had written many articles for the learned journals.

He had at one time shot game birds, but from the age of fifty he put his guns away. Although he had no need to wear spectacles, he said as he felt that he could no longer guarantee killing a bird outright with one shot, he would give up shooting. He also gave up fishing in his lake on the estate. I was also under the impression that he had not ridden with the hounds since he was a youth. He told me that "I have too much respect for the fox than to do that". However, he agreed with me that those who wished to hunt or shoot should have the right to do so. And in the case of hunting, if the fox had gone to earth, then that was the fox's right to survive that day. His last appearance on Anglian Television, three months before his death, was to speak in support of the right to shoot by those who wanted to and to condemn the government for its knee-jerk reactions in response to the Dunblane tragedy.

In the autumn of 1996, although suffering from the onset of lymph gland cancer, he drove me round the estate for the last time, in the same old battered Landrover that we had used in the 1964 and 1966 Southall election campaigns. As we left a young copse of Brazilian black walnut trees he had planted some five years earlier, he stopped by some caravans, a mixture of modern 'travellers' caravans and the old horse-drawn gypsy caravans. Men from the caravans strolled over to greet him smiling. "Hello Sir! How are you Mr Fountaine, Sir!"

"The buggers are stealing half the pheasants on the estate, but at least they will enjoy them. They have nowhere else to go so I let them stay here in the winter. They keep the place clean."

This was part of the enigma of Andrew Fountaine.

On the way back we drove deep into a wood, where he showed me a badger set. I was honoured by the fact that I was the only other person, apart from him and his wife, to know that the badgers were there.

The last time I saw Andrew Fountaine was in the Swaffam Cottage Hospital in August 1997. The ravages of his cancer had led to the amputation of his left leg. As I looked at his frail figure I wanted to cry. To hide this I said:

"Well, you have still got one leg you can get over, Andrew. And you never were a left-winger."

He gave a chuckle and his dark eyes lit up. "Yes, John. What do you think of that nurse over there? She has a lovely arse."

I noticed that although he was 78, and so ill, his hair was still dark, as were his eyebrows.

We talked for a while about politics and I told him that John Tyndall had said how sorry he was to hear of his illness - which was true. He grimaced at Tyndall's name, who was never his favourite person, and said: "He's to blame for it all going wrong with the National Front." I tried to reason with him gently that there were many outside forces that played their part in the downfall of the NF and that we should not put all the blame on Tyndall. After half an hour I could see that he was in considerable pain. He asked me if I would leave as he wanted to try and rest. We shook hands, and I knew it was for the last time.

A fortnight later my wife and I, together with Paul Barnes from the old BNP, attended his funeral at Narborough Church. Terry Savage, Carl Harley and our Italian friend sent a wreath, with their condolences. As far as I know, nobody else from political circles did so.

* * * * *

With the millennium upon us, I reflect upon the half century in which I have given support in one way or another to those defending the values of our race and nation. But who is left to champion the cause? Patriots with a conscience who have splintered from the old parties, such as those now supporting the UK Independence Party, busy themselves with opposition to a Federal Europe, but bow to political correctness by refusing to speak out against the open door policy on immigration. Some even attack those who do, hoping to curry favour by jumping on the "anti-racist" bandwagon. Such movements offer no salvation to our nation's problems and are doomed to failure.

The National Front exists (at least as I write) only in name and confuses the issue by putting up a few candidates at elections and splitting the nationalist vote.

Then there are the lunatics whose diminished mental capabilities mean that they can only express themselves through violence and a pathological hatred of Blacks, Asians and Jews. They are attracted to Combat 18 – the one and the eight being the letters of the alphabet, AH, Adolf Hitler. The liberal-left element that controls much of the media - and almost all of television - find such people extremely useful to smear the British National Party by subtle hints of association. Those of us who have grown long in the tooth in the field of radical right politics may be forgiven for wondering whether organisations such as Combat 18 are financed by the Anti-Nazi League or even Government intelligence: for Combat 18's actions serve only their interests.

Since writing this I have been told that The Observer has revealed that its leader had been working for Special Branch!

What of the British National Party itself? Up until the mid-nineties it stood little chance of a break-through, despite its transitory success in winning the Millwall ward by-election. The problem was that, until then, John Tyndall was both its greatest asset and its greatest drawback. His persistence, rock-like reliability and leadership had kept the movement going, but with almost imperceptible growth since its 1982 foundation. His past association with Jordan's National Socialism and the Spearhead uniform escapade still provided ammunition for the liberal-left to besmirch the BNP, although with the passage of time it became part of the law of diminishing returns. Nevertheless, his past, coupled with a rather dour demeanour, did cause many a potential supporter to think: "Yes, he could be a fascist".

Particularly since its 1997 election campaign, when it fought 55 seats, the BNP has shown that it is growing up; becoming more mature, with a subsequent increase in growth. Much of this has been due to the influence of a new generation of racial nationalists, as well as Tyndall learning from the past. This new generation has been quick to exploit the advantages offered by the electronic age, from fax machines, production of give away videos, to web sites on the internet, in order to break through the suppression of nationalist views by the establishment media. Digital TV gives the possibility of an even greater break-through in the new millennium.

John Tyndall rightfully points out that people should judge him on what he says and does now, or even over the past fifteen years, and not on what he said and did nearly forty years ago.

As I have pointed out in the early chapters, he was always a slow developer. The media forgives Jack Straw his extreme left wing associations of twenty years ago, as it did Denis Healey's former membership of the Communist Party when he took up office in Harold Wilson's Labour Cabinet. And it made little of the fact that Charlie Whelan, Gordon Brown's former press aide, was a card carrying member of the Communist Party until 1990, and that Peter Mandelson was a member of the Young Communist League.

I can understand criticisms of pro-Zionist policies, i.e. always putting the defence of Israeli actions before British interests in the Middle East, but I cannot understand, or support, sly digs at Jews that still appear, albeit with diminishing frequency, in some BNP publications. Because of this I am not a member of the BNP. Nevertheless, as there seems to be nothing else on the horizon, as long as the BNP continues its now more practical approach it has the potential of providing our salvation. Whether it realises this potential remains to be seen.

Whatever happens my support will only be given to those who appreciate that the continuance of our British culture, with its Irish, Scots, Welsh and English aspects, stems not from its geographical features but from its stock, its race, in the same way that the great civilisations of Japan, China, India, etc, stem from their stock and not their particular location on the globe.

Either through historical ignorance or as part of the liberal-left's socio-political agenda, teachers, TV and radio programme producers and newspaper columnists are telling our youth that prior to the great Afro-Asian invasion of the second half of the twentieth century, the people of the British Isles were already an admixture of many different races. Celts, most Roman legionnaires, Angles, Saxons, Jutes, Vikings, Normans, Huguenot refugees were all from varied tribes of the common North European race and all came from within a few hundred miles of each other. Their arrival on these shores bears no comparison with the post-1948 mass immigration phenomenon.

As the reader will probably have gathered by now, I am not making a case for a superiority of the European over the African or Asian. What is our yardstick? As can be seen by Asian children's performance in schools, in some aspects they are our mental superiors. It is not superiority, but a question of difference. Numerous psychologists, geneticists, anthropologists and other scientists have produced ample evidence to show that this is so, but until recently they have either been ignored or demonised as 'racists' and 'crypto-fascists'. To name but a few, I have in mind Professor Hans Eysenck (a refugee from Hitler's Germany), Dr William Shockley (the inventor of the microchip), Dr.Arthur Jensen, Professor Audrey Shuey, Professor C.D. Darlington, Dr Carlton S. Coon, Dr Henry E. Garret, Sir Cyril Burt, and more recently (1996) Herrnstein and Murray, who came under fierce attack by the American and UK liberal-left 'intelligentsia' after they published *The Bell Curve*. Their work, as others, suggested that in the common European gene pool there is a greater likelihood of producing people of superior intellect to blacks, and marginally ahead of most Asians. However, it should also be pointed out that this European gene pool can also produce some of the most intellectually *inferior* people. A classic example is Scotland. Out of its towns and cities come some of the lowest dregs of humanity. But the Scots have also produced, per head of population, the world's greatest number of scientists and engineers. It is their genes that we need for our continued existence.

I believe then that a good case has been made for showing that without exception a particular culture is always the product of the race. Nowhere in history has one culture truly intermingled with another to produce a new, separate higher culture. One either completely dominates the other or they mutually reject each other, with resultant spiritual and physical conflict. A key factor in the downfall of all great civilisations, whether it be the Indus Valley civilisation, Ancient Egypt, Greece, Rome, Aztec and Incas, is that this occurred when the founders of the particular civilisation passed from history through intermixture of subject-peoples and conquerors.

Here in Britain at the start of the third millennium there would be little threat to our culture, our way of life, if there were some

100,000 people of Afro-Asian stock scattered around the country. But what we have now is not so much a race problem as a numbers problem. The old party politicians and their media mouthpieces are still giving fictional figures of their being "only five or six per cent of the population who are immigrants," i.e. three to three and a half million. This figure is arrived at by totalling up all the known figures for legal immigration since 1950 and ignoring those born here of immigrant stock and also ignoring the number of illegal immigrants, because the exact figure is difficult to determine.

Illegal immigration, as distinct from so-called 'political refugees', is not just a problem of the present decade. As far back as 1960, according to a *Daily Telegraph* report, the Indian High Commission in London stated that there were 100,000 Indians living in Britain (*not* including Pakistanis or Bangladeshis) and 20,000 of them had come in on forged passports. This was when Asian immigration was still quite small compared to West Indian immigration. *And it has continued at an ever increasing rate for the past forty years!*

By 1996, according to a report by Ian Henry in the *Sunday Telegraph*, there were "an estimated three-quarters of a million illegals in London alone". The same report, July 28 issue, quoted a John Tincey, a spokesman for the Immigration Officers Union based at Stansted, as defining what has since become the new trend: "There has been a marked shift in emphasis from illegal immigrants to asylum claimants. All work is now concentrated on asylum claims."

By May 1998, Mike O'Brien, immigration minister at the Home Officer, stated that there were 51,000 asylum-seekers cases under consideration, 23,000 going through the cumbersome judicial appeals process, *plus* 40,000 who have been turned down "but have not yet left". Each case costs the Government (you, the tax payer) about £6,000.

From these and many other statistics in my possession it can be estimated that over the past half century we have accumulated some three million illegal immigrants and their descendants, and 'asylum seekers'. With probably at least seventy per cent of the adults seeking social security, housing benefit and health care (which their dependants also require), at a minimum total cost to the state of £6,000 per head per annum, this could be costing the country in excess of 15 billion pounds per annum - almost equal to the nation's defence budget! This does not take into account those among the three and a half million or more legal immigrants and their descendants who may not be in employment.

No wonder that the Government states that we need to build another five million new homes by 2016. This is equivalent to ten new cities in our shrinking countryside, each bigger than Sheffield. This is not necessarily to house asylum seekers or traditional immigrants, but to accommodate the increasing 'white flight' of the aboriginals of these islands as they get out of the cities and larger towns as fast as they can. The Government says that it will be necessary because our projected population in 2016 will be 61.6 million, compared to the present 60 million. In 1985 it was 56 million and in 1951 barely made 50 million.The average birthrate in Britain, having fallen below 2.1 per woman, the replacement value in 1976, is now only 1.74 children per woman. This figure includes the immigrant population, with Bangladeshi families having an average of eight children. It is safe, therefore, to assume that the birth-rate of the white population in Britain over the fifty years since immigration started averages at below 2.1 (replacement level). The ten million difference between 1951 and today can only be attributable to immigrants including up to a million whites, and their descendants. Futhermore, these figures do not include the loss of nearly one million Britons who emigrated to the old White Dominions, mainly in the fifties, sixties and early seventies.

In trying to ascertain the true number of people in Britain who are of Afro-Caribbean or Asian stock, a most significant news item appeared in the *Daily Star* of 20 April, 1993. It reported that an ethnic minority group was planning a telephone directory especially for their own people, to be called *Black Pages*, and that it would cater for a population of *seven million* (it was to include Asians as well as 'blacks'). Couple that statement with the figures I have given above and it would appear that 21st Century Britain has a non-European population of at least eight million: more than thirteen per cent of the population, as opposed to the much outdated figure of five to six per cent.

In arriving at this figure I have not only tried to take into the equation a more realistic estimate of the number of illegals over 50 years, *and* their descendants, but also a more realistic interpretation of the official government figures for legal immigration in the sixties and seventies. As Enoch Powell pointed out at the time, often these figures were heads of households only, and did not include all dependents. Again, with the passing of the 1962 Commonwealth Immigration Act, the Home Office resorted to the device of giving *nett* immigration gains from the Commonwealth as a whole. For example, in the first complete year after the passing of the Act, the nett intake was given as 34,523. However, the total number of immigrants was 333,243. Of those who returned home, over half were Australians, New Zealanders and Canadians completing an extended visit to the 'old country'!

Of the approximately eight million non-whites living in Britain today, the majority are under twenty. Among the white British population the majority are nearly sixty, a figure that is repeated throughout the rest of Europe. Furthermore, according to the 1995 Social Trends Survey produced by the Government's statistical service, the number of British women who are childless had almost doubled in the previous twenty years to 37 per cent. With the growth of feminism and 'girl power' since then, encouraging women to place careers before families, it is likely that a quarter of all British women born since 1965 will never produce babies. It is ironic that in the post-war age of affluence, public sanitation and improved medical care, the aboriginal British population is declining at its fastest rate since the Black Death.

It is the same story in the world at large. At the start of the 20th century, whites made up more than thirty per cent of the world's population. Today the white race only makes up eight per cent, while only two per cent are white females of child-bearing age or below. At the turn of the century, America's non-white population was about seven per cent; today it is around 37 per cent and climbing, thanks to a sharply declining white population and a huge rate of Third World immigration. The same will apply to Europe in another thirty years or so.

Ian Holmes, writing in *Spearhead*, September 1997, had this to add:

"... the white people who are having the most children are usually the most unfit, unproductive and unintelligent. Encouraged by the welfare state, people who have difficulty even looking after themselves are breeding, while the best elements of our people are abstaining from having children, encouraged by a system that teaches that it is better for intelligent women to pursue meaningless careers rather than raise the next generation of our people. Growing numbers of highly educated and intelligent young women are now choosing to be sterilised in their early twenties, in order to concentrate on their work."

Further statistics reflecting on immigration rates (illegal or otherwise) and birth-rates came with the Government's publication in September 1996 of an analysis of the 1991 Census. This stated that Britain's ethnic minority population "grew at a rate forty times faster than the white majority in the ten years to 1991". This mainly Asian population explosion cannot be explained by their higher birth-rate alone. In fact it would be biologically impossible. It must be that immigration, and almost certainly illegal immigration, was far higher than we were told - apart from the fact that not many illegal immigrants would have put their names down on the 1991 census returns!

The analysis also verified the point I have made about the shrinking white birth-rate when it revealed that over the decade, the population rose by 2.5 per cent. But two-thirds of this increase was due to minority ethnic groups, with the white population contributing only 452,000 - less than one per cent.

"While the white population remained almost static, ethnic groups saw rises of between 24 and 95 per cent. This was due to a 'high level of fertility' among most ethnic minority groups."

Statistics published by a London Research Centre associated

with London University Institute of Education just before Christmas 1997 revealed that white children had become a minority in inner London. In the twelve inner London boroughs white children made up 45 per cent of the roll in primary schools - 47 per cent overall. The report added: "The higher birth-rate in black and Asian communities suggests that the proportion of whites in inner London schools and parts of the Midlands will continue to decline."

In its issue of February 6th 1998, the *Daily Telegraph* reported that forty per cent of Birmingham school children were of immigrant origin.

For those readers who do not share my enthusiasm for preserving our British and European culture and are happy to accept a multi-cultural Britain and the likelihood of multi-racial grandchildren, then let them at least consider that apart from island city states such as Hong Kong and Singapore, England and Wales with a population density of over 800 to the square mile now equals Holland as the most densely populated area in the world. That alone, plus the cost to you as a tax payer, will surely persuade you that immigration must come to a halt. It must now be apparent to you that Jean Jacques Rousseau was right when he said: "A home for everyone is a home for no one".

If you share my view that it is the continuance of our people that is at stake, for we have nowhere else to go, then sweet words, designed not to give too much offence, of: "We must tighten up on immigration restrictions" are not enough. All further immigration of non-EC citizens, excluding any *genuine* asylum seekers, must be stopped. Immigration control staff must be augmented to track down the illegals who are here and return them to their country of origin.

And what of those people of West Indian, African and Asian descent who either came into this country legally or who were born here? A practical, and humane, answer was given by Mike Newland, a BNP spokesman, when interviewed on Radio 5 in October 1998.

First, he pointed out that, fundamentally "it's all a question of numbers". Therefore, said Mr Newland, once we've got rid of the illegals and the bogus asylum-seekers, then deals can be done with the huge numbers who would leave voluntarily in exchange for generous resettlement grants. "We would be prepared to make exceptions for law-abiding non-whites, allowing some to stay once the number was reduced to a level at which they did not threaten our identity."

In support of this we have Bernie Grant's findings of a couple of years back that at least forty per cent of Londoners of West Indian origin would go to the West Indies straight away in return for the air fare and a generous lump sum for each family.

The money for these "generous resettlement grants" would come from the savings that I have shown could be gained on the handouts currently being given to bogus asylum seekers (many of them white) and the claims by illegals.

It should not be overlooked that there are a growing number of young blacks in Britain, whether Rastafarian or supporters of the Nation of Islam, who fervently believe in racial separation and provide the backbone to the Back to Africa movement both here and in the USA. They should be supported. They are our friends.

With a return to pride in our own country and in our own history, many Moslems would prefer to return to traditional Moslem countries. The Trinidadian writer V.S. Naipaul (a non-Moslem) in his book *Beyond Belief* indicates that this would be a likely outcome when he writes:

"Islam seeks as an article of faith to erase the past; the believers in the end honour Arabia alone; they have nothing to return to." He adds that Islam requires the convert to accept that "his land is of no religious or historical importance; its relics were of no account; only the sands of Arabia are sacred."

Needless to say, those advocating the above course of action to try and save our nation as a historical entity can expect the full wrath of the politically correct and the race relations inquisition. 'Racist', they will cry. Racists we may be, but race haters we are not. We know that one of their first acts, circa 1970, was the subtle etymological shift of the noun 'racialist' (someone who believes that race largely determines a life pattern) to 'racist', presumably because it has a useful alliterative connotation with 'fascist'!

There is a possibility that some true 'race haters' of the new millennium (and not necessarily of the white variety) might employ race-specific weapons - genetically engineered to single out and decimate only the members of selected ethnic groups, or ensure that the child of a racially mixed marriage only inherits the genes of a chosen parent. This would be possible as a result of the scientific advances stemming from the Human Genome Initiative, which aims at unlocking the secrets of DNA, and would be the ultimate genocidal weapon for race war.

Alvin and Heidi Toffler in their thought provoking book *War and Anti-War*, published by Little, Brown, point out that in 1992 Bo Rybeck, director of the Swedish National Defense Research Institute, stated that, as we become able to identify the DNA variations of different racial and ethnic groups, "we will be able to determine the difference between blacks and whites and Orientals and Jews and Swedes and Finns and develop an agent that will kill only (a particular) group."

That this is being taken seriously was revealed in a report from Israel published by the *Sunday Times*, November 15, 1998:

"Israel is working on a biological weapon that would harm Arabs but not Jews, according to Israeli military and western intelligence sources. The weapon, targeting victims by ethnic origin, is seen as Israel's response to Iraq's threat of chemical and biological attacks."

"In developing their 'ethno-bomb', Israeli scientists are trying to exploit medical advances by identifying genes carried by some Arabs, then create a genetically modified bacterium or virus.

"The intention is to use the ability of viruses and certain bacteria to alter the DNA inside their host's living cells. The scientists are trying to engineer deadly micro-organisms that attack only those bearing the distinctive genes."

Before I am quoted out of context, I do not suggest that this projected horror of ethnic cleansing should be Britain's answer to the immigration problem.

As I have spent virtually the whole of my adult life advocating the importance of race in the world's past, present and future, it is fitting that I have given it most attention in these 'reflections'. It is, after all, the leitmotiv of this autobiography. To comment at length, therefore, on other important socio-political factors is probably out of place in this book. Perhaps the future (and it will have to be fairly immediate!) will give me an opportunity to give my views on education, music, art, the triumphalism of homosexuality, the exploitation of 'feminism', and animal rights and the cult of anthropomorphism amongst the youth.

However, like any good nationalist, I cannot resist making passing comment on the recent exposure of the fundamental weaknesses of global capitalism, now stoking the fire of what will be a global financial disaster. A principal weakness is that the international capitalist system cannot work unless there is inflation, that is the only way the finance houses can make their money. When that inflation is kept below two or three per cent, then the system can be made to work reasonably satisfactorily. The trouble is that every so often it then bursts, rather than creeps, above that figure, with resultant economic mayhem.

The latest financial crisis started in the Far East. Firstly, by mid-1997, two-thirds of Western finance houses and multinational companies who had invested in China over the previous decade found that they had *lost* money. All they achieved by modernising China's industry was to undercut the West. Ignoring the requirements of national political units, the global capitalists actions then spread to Indonesia, Malaysia, Brazil, and Japan to some extent. Apart from the world-wide monetary crisis all this has caused, the global capitalists saw it as another opportunity to acquire control of companies' assets cheaply and transfer manufacturing from the West to these more 'cost effective' areas.

Perhaps the old BNP and the early National Front had something when they said:

"It regards the uncontrolled flow of money and credit into the economy, exercised by private financial interests, as the greatest single cause of inflation. It proposes state control of all credit, which will prohibit banks from issuing loans in excess of money on deposit, and grant to the Bank of England - under firm government supervision - sole right to create new credit for the economy, which will take into account yearly increases in actual national wealth measured in goods and services."

* * * * *

In 1997 I read the two most enthralling books I had come across for at least a decade.

The first was Edward Rutherfurd's *Sarum*, the historical novel that traces the interweaving strands of several families in the Salisbury area over 10,000 years from the end of the last ice age. With detailed historical accuracy he describes the life of the original prehistoric Pictish people. Then the coming of the Beaker Folk, the Celts, the Romans, Saxons, Vikings, Normans and Huguenot refugees: an admixture of kindred tribes of a common European stock that led to a peculiarly English culture.

The second book was Gitta Sereny's remarkable study: *Albert Speer: His Battle With Truth*, in which she intricately details the cultured and intelligent Speer's tortuous struggle with his own soul and the collective German guilt for Hitler's legacy. As the overlord for the entire German war economy, he was a ruthless user of others, including many in the Nazi hierarchy. Until early 1945 he had been fascinated by Hitler. According to Gitta Sereny this fascination was to the point of love. During his twenty years imprisonment after the Nuremberg Trials he continually asked himself whether he really knew what terrible fate was being handed out to the Jews. Originally he had said: "I sensed ... that dreadful things were happening with the Jews."

By 1977 he had written: "... I still consider my main guilt to be my tacit acceptance of the persecution and the murder of millions of Jews."

According to Speer his mental conflict on whether he really knew the truth would give him recurrent nightmares of Auschwitz during the long nights of imprisonment.

Reading Speer's tortured thoughts, again brought up my own feeling of shame, and which at one time had even given me nightmares, that nearly forty years ago I drove a Landrover through the streets of London emblazoned with posters demanding the release of Eichmann, then on trial in Israel. And *Combat*, the paper which I had founded and then still edited, was full of articles either nit-picking over the numbers of Jews who had been killed or presenting selected evidence to show that gas chambers never existed. At least such articles were not under my name, but mainly that of Colin Jordan.

Unlike Speer, my attempts to use people had disastrously backfired.

There was some excuse for supporters at that time such as John Tyndall, who was only in his early twenties (and also slow to learn), but I was thirty-three. I had allowed the emotion of a sickening, bad taste, sixth form prank, designed to shock the public, to dominate the intellect.It was the turning point that led to my break with Jordan and his fellow Nazi sympathisers, but the lasting damage had been done.

Looking back at those years of strident action I can see that the analytical logic required by the true politician, of whatever hue, was for me never in contention against the all smothering power of idealistic romanticism. I suppose blood will out, and as I am talking of the Celtic blood of Scotland and Ireland it is, of course, fashionably permissable. Now if it was my English blood, derived from Saxon peasants, then that would be politically incorrect.

On the other hand it was the archetypal Englishman Enoch Powell,renowned for his analytical logic, who revealed the romanticism in his soul by not only requesting that he be buried in his brigadier's uniform but declaring that there were occasions when he wished he had been killed during the war. There are times when I feel that sad at what the politicians have allowed to happen to my dear Britain, and particularly poor England, that I wish I had been born twelve months earlier and died in aerial combat to keep out 'the invader'.

But is this just another mournful posturing of the Celt? Scots and Irish so often look to the past for their heroes and for their ideals. To deal with the present there is no better escape than a good 'craic', where the words must flow as readily as the drink and to the accompaniment, if only background, of one's own folk music with its whispers of folk memories.

My mistake was to listen to the siren voices of those who blamed our once proud nation's predicament on a 'conspiracy', in the manner of the Scots, the Irish and even the Welsh, who will mistakenly blame the English for their 'conspiracy' to hold them back and suppress their cultures. There was no conspiracy by Jewish international finance to destroy our power and to open the floodgates to Afro-Asian immigration. In the 1930s there were *individual* Jewish bankers who could see that Hitler was out to destroy the Jewish people and understandably used their power to oppose him. In the main this was the evidence that otherwise intelligent men, such as A.K.Chesterton, and Mosley for a time in the thirties, used to build up their plot theory. It's a theory that leaks like a sieve.

Was it not Benjamin Disraeli, Britain's great Victorian Jewish Prime Minister, who reminded us of the importance of race? He wrote:

"No-one may treat the principle of race, the racial question, with indifference, for it is the key to world history. History is often confusing for the sole reason that it is written by people who know neither the racial issue nor the moments connected therewith.

"Neither language nor religion make a race. Only one thing makes a race and that is blood. The peoples retain their strength, their morality and their capacity for great things only so long as they keep their blood free from any mixture. If they absorb alien blood, their virtues will quickly dwindle, as will their strength.

"All is race, there is no other truth."

251

The destruction of Britain's and Europe's, and in fact the world's individual cultures and ancient peoples - the culture bearers - is being brought about by the international bankers and the multinational companies in their drive for the global village. They are not really bothering with plots and conspiracies. Their actions are quite clear and speak volumes. They want to see all barriers come down in order to maximise their markets, their sales and their profits. They will utilise their power, which includes control of nearly all the world's mass media, to aid all means, directly or indirectly, that will achieve this objective. For them a one world, one people (perhaps United Nations dark buff?) would be an ideal marketing situation.

Although Jews are still well represented in Hollywood's film industry, which now determines much of what the world's cinemas and even TV companies will show, it is far from being a Jewish closed shop. Leading propagandists for the 'global village', such as Rupert Murdoch of News Corporation, Ted Turner of CNN (Cable News Network) or Bill Gates of Microsoft, are not Jewish, nor are the overwhelming number of directors of such multinationals as General Motors, Ford, Shell, BP, Mitsubishi, Glaxo, etc, etc. Nor are Benetton, the fashion house that promotes multiracialism purely for profit.

Perhaps my instincts were right, but certainly not my reasoning, all those years ago, when I sensed there was something wrong with the capitalist system and supported the school Communist candidate.

Marx may have diagnosed the sickness correctly, but he prescribed the wrong medicine.

Index

255